Doing Gender Justice

HEALTH COMMUNICATION

The Health Communication series features rhetorical, critical, and qualitative studies projects exploring the discourses that constitute major health issues of today and the past. Books in the series provide a comprehensive illustration of how health and medicine are communicated to, with, and through diverse individuals and populations.

Robin Jensen, Editor

Editorial Board

Jeffrey A. Bennett	John A. Lynch
Karma R. Chávez	Aimee Roundtree
Tasha N. Dubriwny	Shaunak Sastry
Elaine Hsieh	J. Blake Scott
Jordynn Jack	Priscilla Song
Jenell Johnson	LaTonya Trotter
Lisa B. Keränen	Guobin Yang

DOING GENDER JUSTICE

Queering Reproduction, Kin, and Care

SHUI-YIN SHARON YAM AND
NATALIE FIXMER-ORAIZ

JOHNS HOPKINS UNIVERSITY PRESS | *Baltimore*

© 2025 Shui-yin Sharon Yam and Natalie Fixmer-Oraiz
All rights reserved. Published 2025
Printed in the United States of America on acid-free paper

2   4   6   8   9   7   5   3   1

Johns Hopkins University Press
2715 North Charles Street
Baltimore, Maryland 21218
www.press.jhu.edu

Library of Congress Cataloging-in-Publication Data

Names: Yam, Shui-yin Sharon, author. | Fixmer-Oraiz, Natalie, author.
Title: Doing gender justice : queering reproduction, kin, and care /
Shui-yin Sharon Yam and Natalie Fixmer-Oraiz.
Description: Baltimore : Johns Hopkins University Press, 2025. | Series:
Health communication | Includes bibliographical references and index.
Identifiers: LCCN 2024025707 | ISBN 9781421451138 (paperback) | ISBN
9781421451145 (ebook)
Subjects: LCSH: Reproductive rights—Social aspects. | Sexual
minorities—Legal status, laws, etc. | Sexual minorities—Civil rights.
Classification: LCC HQ766 .F548 2024 | DDC 304.6/3—dc23/eng/20240724
LC record available at https://lccn.loc.gov/2024025707

A catalog record for this book is available from the British Library.

Special discounts are available for bulk purchases of this book.
For more information, please contact Special Sales at specialsales@jh.edu.

CONTENTS

Preface　*vii*
Acknowledgments　*xiii*
Glossary and Abbreviations　*xxi*

Introduction.　Reproductive Justice and Queer(ing)
Family Reproduction　1

1.　Networking Arguments: Gender and Reproduction
in Public Discourse　35

2.　Against Gender Essentialism: Reproductive Justice
Doulas and Gender Inclusivity in Pregnancy
and Birth Discourse　78

3.　Reimagining Family and Kin: Queer and Trans
Reproductive Storytelling　116

Conclusion.　Deepening Intersectional and Coalitional
Reproductive Justice　164

Notes　*177*
Index　*211*

PREFACE

Reproduction is both personal and political. Even as we arrive at this collaboration with professional expertise—including scholarly training and involvement with community organizing and advocacy—our relationship to the work itself is deeply informed by our lives. It is shaped by our experiences with family, relationships, reproductive health, and community struggle and is influenced by a cultural climate that is increasingly inhospitable—if not outwardly hostile—to social justice. We want to begin, then, with a reflection on the paths that brought each of us here.

Sharon (she/they)

Like many feminist scholars, I arrived at my research on reproductive justice, birth, and pregnancy through intimate personal experiences and reflections. I met my partner of seven years in my late twenties, just a few months after I moved to Lexington to begin my first tenure-track position. After six years of graduate school, I was ready to chart the course of my professional and personal life, in part by following normative social scripts on romantic relationships and family-building. Hence, like many couples in a monogamous cishet relationship, we discussed our respective views on children and family. My partner at the time subscribed strongly to a normative vision of family, one that entails having and parenting biological children. Meanwhile, I had always been ambivalent about, if not outright resistive to, having children, in part due to my mother's pregnancy and birth trauma and my memory of how she was entrapped by oppressive gender and familial norms throughout my childhood. Unwilling to foreclose what seemed to be a promising relationship with my then partner, I began interrogating my resistance toward pregnancy, birth, and parenting, attempting to reconcile our diverging desires and views on family-making.

While I ultimately decided against having children, that personal inquiry became the focus of my academic research. On the one hand, as a justice-oriented critical rhetorician, I was driven to unpack how normative discourse and practice about reproduction, bodies, sex, race, and gender had inflicted immense harm and trauma on so many—especially those who occupy multiply marginalized positionalities. On the other hand, I was—and still am—drawn to the transformative potential of doulas and birthworkers who enact radical ethics of care amid oppressive and punishing institutional contexts and material conditions.

When Natalie and I connected, I had been conducting ethnographic research on doulas and birthworker organizations, focusing primarily on obstetric violence against BIPOC women and the ways in which marginalized full-spectrum doulas enact community care. As our research, collaboration, and friendship deepened, I felt the persistent urge to reexamine my own attachments (or lack thereof), conflicting desires, and resistance toward normative gender constructions, kin ties, and family structures—questioning whether and how I could embrace a radical queer praxis not just in my scholarship but also in the intimacies of my personal life.

This praxis has not only informed my scholarship but also slowly and dramatically transformed how I imagine, embody, and enact care in relationships with others. Working on this project has deepened my commitment to dismantling a hierarchical view of relationships that places monogamous romantic relationships and biological nuclear families at the apex, and instead seeing our connections with each other as a web woven through mutual support and expansive forms of love and care.

As my friend and reproductive justice artist-activist Borealis poignantly states, "Our resistance is strongest through collaboration, mutual aid, imaginative reconfigurations of kinship, [and] remembering our habits of reciprocity."[1] I strive to always embody this praxis in my scholarship and life.

viii   *Preface*

Natalie (she/her)

This project draws my scholarship closer to my intimate life than any other project has to date. I arrived at this project as a longtime advocate for reproductive justice (RJ), with two decades of involvement in RJ organizing, advocacy, writing, and teaching. I arrived as a queer cis femme woman, joyfully parenting two small humans with my partner of nineteen years.

Well over a decade ago, when my spouse and I first discussed having children, we both imagined the possibility of carrying a pregnancy. We dreamed together of what that might look like—in one version of this journey together, perhaps they would carry our first child and I would carry a second.

My spouse identifies as transmasculine nonbinary. As we got closer to being ready to become parents, it became clear to both of us, but especially to my partner, that there were very few resources and places that felt safe for and affirming of transmasculine pregnancy care. And so, they made a really good decision for themself—and, by extension, for us—that they would not carry a pregnancy. I, on the other hand, was excited to try.

There is a lot of uncertainty—and a lack of guarantee—in this process for queer people. The road to becoming parents is not straightforward, if you will. Trying to conceive outside of systems of capitalist accumulation and repro-technological infrastructure (e.g., sperm banks, "infertility" clinics) is difficult, although we made a go of it. Our early attempts included a fair amount of heartbreak, due in no small part to our desire to honor my partner's Filipinx heritage and our experiences with how racial minoritization shapes access. There were many stops and starts, but in the end, I was fortunate to carry two pregnancies for our family.

As my partner and I journeyed into queer parenthood, conversations were beginning to emerge within RJ circles about trans inclusion. I was alarmed and dismayed by the hostility that I witnessed unfolding, even as that hostility was often rightly met with fierce challenge and critique. To me, the power of reproductive justice was—and remains—its deeply rooted and unshakable commitment to justice for all of us. I had a personal connection to just how profoundly desired it is and yet how impossible it feels for some people to carry a pregnancy to term because of their gender. Even as a cis woman, I myself had experienced numerous moments of intense, even suffocating, cishet gendering during pregnancy. I wanted to imagine alternatives. I wanted to understand how we might narrate pregnancy differently. Where, how, and with whom were we creating spaces for more trans-inclusive and gender-affirming reproductive care? Where, how, and with whom could we do more?

Sharon and Natalie

Our meeting felt like kismet! Sharon reached out to Natalie after reading her monograph *Homeland Maternity* at the airport. Prior to that, we had met only briefly at the Midwest Winter Workshop at the University of Illinois Urbana-Champaign, when Natalie was a junior professor and Sharon was still a graduate student.

We bonded quickly over shared intellectual and political investments, which broadened into a deep and enduring friendship beyond the writing of this book. Since we began writing in 2019, a conversation that was happening in activist enclaves migrated into mainstream dominant discourse. The political struggle over binary sex and gender is now everywhere. Anti-trans policies are the new darling of right-wing ethnonationalist movements in the United States, which aim to eviscerate gender-affirming care, police the usage of bathrooms, and dictate the participation of trans people in athletics. We are writing at a time of unfolding and intensifying trans antagonisms, and we do so from a space of heartbreaking familiarity.

Seeing our research participants and the queer archive we have compiled as interlocutors, we have aimed to write a book that is accessible to a wide range of audiences beyond scholars of communication, gender studies, and reproductive justice. We write to, with, and for the queer people and parents whose reproductive experiences are often erased, eclipsed, or undermined in dominant discourse; the reproductive justice activists and birthworkers who fiercely advocate and tenderly care for marginalized birthing and pregnant people; and the health care professionals who seek to provide more inclusive and gender-affirming care amid deeply oppressive institutional structures.

We close with a gesture of care to you, our reader. It is our hope that this book will reach numerous audiences—from health care providers and scholars in various disciplines to RJ activists and queer and trans parents. For some, the issues discussed in the following pages may feel familiar and perhaps also particularly acute and painful at certain points; for others, this is simply less true. We have content notices within chapters to signal what may be difficult content for queer, trans, nonbinary, and gender-nonconforming readers, with an invitation to skim those spaces that feel all too familiar, even harmful. We dwell in a moment of profound complexity—one of heightened visibility, antagonisms, state-sanctioned violence, and fierce gender-justice struggle all at once. We offer this book in the spirit of that struggle, with the hope that it may prove useful in the dreaming of a better, more just, and inhabitable world.

ACKNOWLEDGMENTS

This book unfolded in layers of community support—through institutions, professional organizations and networks, activist circles, and intimate communities of care.

We are grateful for the support of our institutions—the University of Iowa and the University of Kentucky—for supporting our collaboration through grant funding and part-time summer research assistantships for students. The Interdisciplinary Research Grant from the Obermann Center for Advanced Studies at the University of Iowa allowed us to host a writing retreat in Urbana-Champaign, where the two of us dedicated time and space in the earliest stages of this project. A special shout-out to Obermann Center staff—and especially to Erin Hackathorn, Teresa Mangum, and Jennifer New—for their early enthusiasm and support for our work. The University of Iowa's Arts and Humanities Initiative Standard Grant funded interview transcription, another writing retreat, and a rendezvous in Iowa City to finalize the manuscript, meet with students, and share our work with local reproductive justice coconspirators. The Department of Communication Studies at the University of Iowa made it possible for us to hire stellar research assistants. The University of Kentucky provided funding to support research and transcriptions as well.

The generosity of our interlocutors cannot be overstated. Our deepest gratitude to the queer parents, radical doulas, birthworkers, midwives, and birth educators who lent us their time and perspective, even at the height of a global pandemic. We are immensely grateful for the trust they placed in us and for the work they do in this world. We are also grateful for the words and activism of queer and/or BIPOC birthworkers, educators, podcasters, and writers: Monica Basile, Grover

xiii

Wehman-Brown, Jenna Brown, Stevie Merino, Gwendolyn Neumeister, Miriam Zoila Pérez, Khye Tyson, Sabia Wade, Chaney Williams, king yaa, Trystan Reese, and Josie Rodriguez-Bouchier. We would also like to thank Dr. Miles Feroli for his stellar dissertation research on trans parents and for his help transcribing some of our interview data.

Many thanks to the professional organizations and academic journals that have helped us to circulate early pieces of this project. Thanks to the anonymous reviewers at *Women's Studies in Communication* (*WSIC*) and the editors that supported our work, Marissa Doshi and Lore/tta LeMaster. An earlier version of chapter 2 appears as a full essay in *WSIC*; Lore/tta LeMaster solicited and published portions of our introduction in a *WSIC* forum. We are also grateful to the two organizations that recognized our article with awards—namely, the National Communication Association's Feminist and Gender Studies Division and the Organization for Feminist Research on Gender and Communication.

Several students offered critical research support in the early stages of this project. Thank you to Micki Burdick and Meghana Palagiri for sharing your research acumen and thoughtful critiques with us. Your expertise enhanced our work immensely.

Many thanks also to Robin Jensen, Matthew McAdam, and the editorial board for the Health Communication series at the Johns Hopkins University Press. To Robin in particular, we are grateful for your infectious enthusiasm, keen editorial insights, and deep care for this project.

Sharon

I often joke that I am motivated to write books so that I can publicly sing the praises of all the brilliant people and nonhuman beings in my life—and there is more than an ounce of truth in that joke. This book is about queer kin and care, and fittingly, I would not have been able to complete it without an immensely supportive, smart, and thoughtful constellation of friends, colleagues, and coconspirators who have inspired and nourished me and kept me buoyant.

Thank you, Natalie, for writing this book with me and for being a truly wonderful friend. Our friendship and coauthorship have weathered not only a pandemic but also a series of challenging events in our personal lives. Thank you for always finding and seeing the best in me and for modeling how to be a critical yet compassionate scholar-teacher, a courageous and thoughtful activist, and a kind and loving human who cares deeply. You and your beautiful family (V, Emmons, and Celso) are so special to me.

I am forever grateful to Elizabeth W. Williams and K. Lindsey Chambers (a.k.a. the "Privy Council") for stimulating and supporting my growth as a scholar-teacher across disciplinary bounds and for providing well-timed humor (and memes and spicy commentaries on reality TV), earnest advice, and unwavering love and support even during the most challenging times. They have shown me time and again the profound power of friendship and care beyond the confines of a biological or nuclear family. I love them both so, so much. Elizabeth and Lindsey, thank you for being in my life.

While I was writing this book, Lindsey was pregnant. We shared many intimate conversations about pregnancy, kinship, parenting, and relationships at the dog park, while our dogs ran with abandon. Benji "BenjiBeau" Chambers Price was born on June 24, 2023. Thank you for making me Auntie Squish, BenjiBeau—I take this role very seriously. I love watching you grow, and I can't wait to see you read this one day.

Laure Cagle, where and how do I even begin? I feel so immensely lucky to be hired at the same time as Cagle. We are not only departmental colleagues but also coconspirators in union organizing and partners in acro and climbing. We also share a deep love for knitting and dogs. I am inspired every day by Cagle's thoughtfulness, open-heartedness, intellectual acuity, and integrity. Cagle has always been one of my most enthusiastic cheerleaders—for that I am eternally grateful.

I am thankful for the Kenwick Brunch crew (Elizabeth, Asher Finkel, Jess Santollo, and Nari Senanayake), whose wit and commitment to Scattergories are unparalleled. Special thanks to Asher, who was my significant other for seven years and bore witness to the entire research and writing process of this book. I am grateful for our enduring friendship and love for each other beyond the confines of a romantic relationship.

While this book was written long after I graduated from the University of Wisconsin–Madison, I think of my graduate school mentors often. I remain grateful to Michael Bernard-Donals, Christa Olson, and Morris Young for being exemplary models of astute and ethical scholars, teachers, mentors, and administrators.

I would like to thank my colleagues in the Department of Writing, Rhetoric, and Digital Studies and the Department of Gender and Women's Studies at the University of Kentucky, who have cultivated an intellectually stimulating and supporting environment for researching, teaching, and learning. I am especially grateful for the friendship and mentorship extended to me by Srimati Basu, Kishonna Gray, and Carol Mason—I have learned a lot about how to be a kind and acute scholar-teacher from you all. I also thank Julia Bursten, Brandon Erby, Karrieann Soto Vega, Anastasia Todd, JWells, and Charlie Zhang for their friendship and Karrieann and Anastasia for the writing feedback they provided.

In 2021, I co-taught an interdisciplinary graduate seminar with Carol (gender and women's studies), Lindsey (philosophy), and Lydia Pelott-Hobbs (geography). That experience deepened my thinking on the relationship between gender and reproductive justice. I am grateful for my coteachers and students who expanded my perspectives beyond typical disciplinary confines.

Outside of my home institution, I am grateful for the many brilliant critical rhetoricians whose research, teaching, and activism on gender, race, and reproductive justice have made great impact on me, the field, and beyond, many of whom are dear friends: V. Jo Hsu, Stephanie Larson, Lore LeMaster, Jennifer LeMesurier, Lydia McDermott, Maria Novotny, Ersula Ore, Michelle Smith, and Emily Winderman. I am especially thankful for Emily. I am always in awe of her intellectual acuity, kindness, generosity, and deep concern for others. Emily has the unique ability to see the best in me, even when I am ridden with self-doubt. Thank you for being my friend, Emily. Shout-out to my Hong Kong academic friends—Kai Heng Cheang, Siufung Law, Carissa Ma, and Alvy Wong. Y'all make conferences infinitely more fun, and your comradeship keeps me afloat even when the political climate in Hong Kong feels despairing. I am also thankful for Chris Barcelos and Harlan Weaver—their work on gender, sex, and kin has deeply informed my thinking. I also thank Harlan for always sending me high-quality astrology, dating, and animal memes and for inspiring me to pursue a new research project on dog training.

That said, I would be remiss if I didn't mention the two great non-human loves of my life: Pita and Chips (especially Pita, my heart dog). Caring for these two gremlin dogs and watching them enjoy life have brought me immense joy (sometimes headache and heartache, but mostly joy). Pita reminds me of the pleasure of being aimlessly and exuberantly playful and unabashedly loud, while Chips nudges me to rest more, ideally under a soft pile of blankets. Pita especially has taught me how to be soft and tender, which I have come to see as the key ingredient of love. I am also grateful for the many other beloved nonhuman beings in my life: Annabelle, Beau, Bizu, Ellie Cat, Kylo, Rubin, and all the kitties wandering around the Kenwick neighborhood.

Natalie

So many brilliant beings made this work possible! Sharon, thank you for deciding to reach out for a Zoom chat. Little did I know how our connection would become a portal, not only to a new project but also to an incredible friendship. Thank you for believing in this project and in me, for offering up your sharp intellect, fierce activist commitments, and delightful way of knowing where to dwell and when to leap. I am forever, for the better, changed by our friendship and the richness it has brought to my life.

I am grateful to all of my reproductive justice (RJ) networks. The Obermann RJ Working Group has been a wellspring of solidarity and support—many thanks to my brilliant codirector, Lina-Maria Murillo, and to Andrés Restrepo Sanchez, Abigail Escatel, Berkley Conner,

Micki Burdick, Elissa Faro, and Danielle Sigler. On a local level, so much gratitude to Mandi Remington, Mica Doolan, Sikowis Nobiss, Francine Thompson, Gabriela Fuentes, Kate Reveaux, Mei-Ling Shaw, Abby Michael, and others on the threads. To my ReproSoc crew—Edmée Ballif, Julieta Chaparro Buitrago, Marcin Smietana, and Anika König—for online solidarity throughout the pandemic, and to Sarah Franklin, R. Sánchez-Rivera, and Aideen O'Shaughnessy for hosting me at the University of Cambridge and offering academic solidarity and friendship. To Asha Bhandary for sharing her sage advice and searing intellect. Others who have continued to inspire and buoy me over the years include Paige Johnson and Gwendolyn Neumeister. And to the luminous souls and gleeful coconspirators I hold close as beloved kin: Lina-Maria Murillo for unmatched enthusiasm, grit, and solidarity forever, and Jamie Brooks Robertson for dreaming bigger and better than I ever could alone.

A big shout-out to my intellectual communities, particularly those who make the University of Iowa home: all of my colleagues in communication studies and in gender, women's, and sexuality studies, and with particular thanks to Ari Ariel, Asha Bhandary, Emerson Cram, Naomi Greyser, Ashley Hall, Ashley Howard, Jiyeon Kang, Rachel McLaren, Lina-Maria Murillo, Yasmine Ramadan, Liz Rodriguez-Fielder, David Supp-Montgomerie, Jenna Supp-Montgomerie, and Eric Vázquez. My students, past and present, stretch my thinking and enrich my life: Micki Burdick, Michelle Colpean, Abigail Escatel, Michelle Flood, Ang Malenda, Meghana Palagiri, Heather Roy, Meg Tully, Andrew Boge, and Berkley Connor in particular. In the field of communication studies, many others have sustained me over the years: Leslie Baxter, Jeff Bennett, Peter Campbell, Karma Chávez, Robbie Cox, Bonnie Dow, Andy High, Phaedra Pezzullo, Vince Pham, Alyssa Samek, Isaac West, Emily Winderman, and Julia T. Wood.

To those who create belonging in my corner of the universe: Talia Meidlinger and MJ Meidlinger for magic, queer fandom, and big love. To Jenna Supp-Montgomerie and David Supp-Montgomerie, for game nights, podlucks, and mishpocha; for making life (even joy!) possible as we survived a global pandemic; to Jenna in particular for deep and enduring friendship. To the band—Ari Ariel, John Boller, Guillermo Morales, and Lina-Maria Murillo—so many thanks for sharing music, made ever more joyful by the hilarity that ensues when we gather our families. Grateful for this motley crew, which also includes Yasmine Ramadan, Ashley Howard, Chris Sang, and V Fixmer-Oraiz. To those who codelight in traveling karaoke, texting irreverence, shared meals, kid time, and walks in the woods: Rachel McLaren, Jesse Stone, Emerson Cram, Jiyeon Kang, Asha Bhandary, and Kumar Narayanan. And to our people across the pond—Jordan Robertson and Jamie Brooks Robertson—for being and believing in the dream.

To my parents, Tim Fixmer and Carson Fixmer: for believing in me, for leading by example, for modeling how the meaning of family itself—no matter its configuration—is big and steadfast love. I am so thankful for their steady presence and warm embrace. To Lindsay Fixmer, Dylan Off-Fixmer, Michele Bowman, Sarah Off-Fixmer, Jason Bowman, and Gavin Porter: with wild appreciation for the lifetimes of shared music, movie quotes, ridiculous games, and side-splitting laughter. I love you all so much.

There are truly no words that adequately capture my deep love and gratitude for my beautiful, boisterous crew. You have inspired my best impulses and greatest growth edges, and I feel so fortunate to reside in your eternal orbit. For V, Emmons, and Celso: thank you for gifting me your love and our family. In this, all things are possible.

GLOSSARY AND ABBREVIATIONS

BADT: Birthing Advocacy Doula Trainings—a reproductive justice–informed, Black-owned, and queer-run doula training organization founded by Sabia Wade.

BIPOC: Black, Indigenous, and people of color

DCT: Formerly Doula of Color Training, now Birthworkers of Color Collective—a reproductive justice–informed collective cofounded by Stevie Merino that provides accessible full-spectrum doula service, birthwork training, and advocacy.

DONA: Doulas of North America, now DONA International, is one of the most well-known doula training and certifying organizations.

DTI: Doula Training International—a reproductive justice–informed full-spectrum doula training organization founded by Tara Brooke and Gina Giordano.

full-spectrum doulas: Nonmedical careworkers who provide information and physical and emotional support to people through the full spectrum of reproductive experiences, including pregnancy, birth, miscarriage, stillbirth, abortion, and postpartum care.

LGBTQ+: lesbian, gay, bisexual, trans, queer, and others

MANA: Midwives Alliance of North America

QUEER: Following Cathy Cohen and other queer theorists of color, we use *queer* to refer to non- and anti-normative gender, sexual, political, and kinship practices that take into account the intersections of marginalizations and identities.

RJ: reproductive justice

TGNC: trans and gender nonconforming

Doing Gender Justice

INTRODUCTION

Reproductive Justice and Queer(ing) Family Reproduction

GENDER FUNDAMENTALLY SHAPES the cultural terrain of reproductive politics and family formation, from the discourse surrounding birth to the rhetoric of motherhood and reproductive rights. Investments in gendered and feminized language are varied—often affective, political, and/or historically grounded in the lived experience of cisgender women specifically, as those typically rendered responsible for conceiving, gestating, birthing, and rearing children. Those who argue against the usage of gender-neutral language in birth and reproductive justice (RJ) work note why gender specificity matters—that the broader discourse of parenting strips the politics from reproductive history and obscures how cissexism and misogyny are central to reproductive violence.[1] And yet, the narrowness of gendered language in reproductive politics fails to capture gestational birth and parenting beyond the gender binary, as well as the social justice concerns specific to queer and trans family formation, particularly beyond the normative white nuclear family model.[2] These conversations, unfolding in enclave circles of reproductive health care advocates and providers for over a decade, have recently migrated to mainstream public discourse as bodily sovereignty—from abortion to gender-affirming care—is increasingly and relentlessly attacked by the conservative right.

Examples of these struggles over gender and language abound. In 2015, the Midwives Alliance of North America (MANA) came under fire after releasing a position statement endorsing gender-inclusive language; it recommended, for example, referring to "pregnant people" in lieu of "pregnant women" or "parents" in lieu of "mothers." A large group of birthworkers, including those of national repute, co-signed an open letter denouncing MANA's decision and insisting on language that centered cisgender women's primary role in reproduction.[3] This incident within birthworker circles is increasingly visible in mainstream cultural contexts. It is echoed, for instance, in the refusal of several GOP senators to support the historic nomination of Ketanji Brown Jackson to the US Supreme Court because of their concerns that she would not define *woman* in biological terms. It is echoed again in the conservative backlash against Representative Cori Bush in 2021, after Bush used the phrase "pregnant people" when discussing racial disparities in pregnancy and birth outcomes. In recent years, feminist activists have passionately disagreed on whether it is more ethical and politically efficacious for reproductive rights organizations to use woman-centered or gender-neutral language when challenging restrictive abortion laws.[4]

Written at a time when anti-trans discourse and policies have become increasingly popular in the public sphere, this book complicates the dominant framing of this tension as, fundamentally, a choice between gender specificity and gender neutrality. Rather, drawing on the confluence of reproductive justice and trans* of color critique, we argue that anti-trans discourse that polices the boundaries of gender, reproduction, and family formation is a form of reproductive injustice. Deep attachment to gendered language reflects colonial and white supremacist histories and investments in the gender binary. Thus, struggles over gender and language are not merely a matter of semantics, nor are they of exclusive concern to trans, gender-nonconforming, and nonbinary (TGNC) people. *Doing Gender Justice: Queering Reproduction, Kin, and Care* intervenes in this conversation by interrogating gender and its relationship to reproductive justice through the lens of trans* of color critique. Fundamentally, we explore how RJ advocates, birthworkers, and TGNC parents craft spaces of radical affirmation and dignity for queer family formation.

Our introductory chapter historicizes and contextualizes this struggle over gender and reproduction, articulating the connections among nation-building, white supremacy, and cisheteronormative family norms. The rest of the book unfolds across multiple registers—through an interrogation of public discourse (chapter 1), within reproductive health care settings (chapter 2), and among the everyday experiences of TGNC parents (chapter 3)—to consider the complexity of gender in contemporary contexts of pregnancy, birth, and parenting. We center the struggle to craft radically inclusive spaces for queering and creating kin as a project most critical for reproductive justice, radical self-determination, and a more just future. We extend existing RJ scholarship by calling for a more robust and critical interrogation of the gender binary system, focusing specifically on how gender normativities are always intimately connected with the racial project of the white supremacist cis-tem.[5]

Significantly, this is not simply a matter of inclusion. The inclusion of LGBTQ+ people is not enough to challenge the interconnected system of cisness and whiteness and the myth of sex/gender dimorphism. The history of the binary gender system deserves our continual attention, particularly at a time when the dignity and humanity of Black, Indigenous, and people of color (BIPOC) and TGNC people are under attack. Weaponized by white colonizers to dehumanize colonized subjects of color, the gender binary has long been yoked to racialization and the subjugation of gender-variant individuals.[6] The interconnected forces of racism, settler colonialism, transphobia, and homophobia had led to the gendercide of Indigenous people who did not conform to the gender binary system.[7] Indigenous people and scholars have recounted the long history of violence committed by European white settlers against Indigenous people whose gender identity and performance fell outside the binary framework.[8] Spanish colonizers, for instance, actively exterminated third-gender Indigenous

Introduction   3

people in what is now known as California.[9] Since genderqueer Indigenous people traditionally were often the undertakers of their communities, responsible for liminal death and burial rituals, colonial gendercide had significant cultural, spiritual, and holistic health ramifications for Indigenous communities.[10] Such histories of violence continue to inform the contemporary terrain of reproductive health and politics, rendering the reproductive and familial lives of queer people of color particularly precarious. Only by dismantling oppressive systems and narratives about gender and race can we promote reproductive justice and self-determination beyond the confines of normativities.

Since the dominant binary gender system undergirds colonialism, white supremacy, and anti-Blackness without interrogating how gender is constructed, naturalized, and maintained, merely inserting TGNC people into the RJ framework will not accomplish the transformation we hope to see: namely, "a political agenda that seeks to change values, definitions, and laws which make these institutions and relationships oppressive."[11] By engaging with decolonial and trans* of color scholarship on sex/gender, this book intervenes in a particular (and ongoing) challenge within reproductive justice on the reproductive freedom of TGNC people. We posit that by complicating the dominant myths of sexual dimorphism and gender binarism within the RJ framework, we can achieve a transformational politics that allows all marginalized people and nonnormative bodies to exist and thrive on their own terms, rather than seeking to be assimilated into normative sociopolitical and reproductive relationships.[12]

This book, thus, exhorts readers to consider how we might think through and beyond vocabularies that bind gender to reproduction in narrow ways and, in turn, diminish the project of gender liberation for all. This chapter begins by contextualizing reproductive justice as an organizing tool, theoretical framework, and movement. Specifically, we focus on how existing scholarship and activism have taken up the charge of queer(ing) reproductive justice. To demonstrate the importance of critically interrogating the white supremacist and co-

4   *Doing Gender Justice*

lonial undercurrent of gender, we then offer a critique of the gender binary system, drawing from Indigenous studies, trans* of color theory, and decolonial feminism. Critiques of gender come to bear on the discursive and political decisions RJ activists and feminists make. Hence, we next examine the tensions among feminists stemming from their different conceptions of gender and the role gender should and should not play in RJ organizing. Before reviewing the focus of each of the following chapters, we articulate how queer studies, women's studies, and trans* studies converge and diverge in their conceptions of gender and sex. By doing so, we seek to harness the coalitional and liberatory potential among these fields of studies to illuminate how a critical examination of gender can expand the transformational potential of reproductive justice, specifically in the contexts of health communication.

It is worth noting that the language surrounding gender and reproduction in general has shifted rapidly in the last few decades; this is particularly true in the years since we began writing this book in 2019. We anticipate this shift may well continue, rendering some of the debates and concerns explored here dated. Still, the significant contributions of this book remain many. This book was written at a time when reproductive justice and rights advocates are combating cruel bans on abortion care in the aftermath of *Roe v. Wade*'s demise, anti-trans bills governing athletics and the use of bathrooms, and state interference in access to trans health care and antiracist, LGBTQ+ positive educational curricula. By illuminating the intersection between reproductive justice advocacy and queer family-making, this book offers a nuanced analysis of recent gender politics and debates in the United States. More importantly, *Doing Gender Justice* highlights how trans and nonbinary parents, reproductive justice advocates, and birthworkers are imagining and engaging in praxis toward a radically inclusive world that disrupts normative assumptions about gender and reproduction and renders the queering of kin possible. Ultimately, we write toward a world in which racialized binary gender does not fundamentally shape the conditions and possibilities of one's life.

Reproductive Justice: A Brief Introduction

The analysis and overarching orientation of this book is based on the framework of reproductive justice. A concept created by Black women and embraced by women of color and queer people, RJ centers the experiences and embodied knowledge of those who are multiply marginalized. Using reproductive justice as our analytical framework allows us to pay attention to how queer people, especially queer people who also occupy other marginalized positionalities, experience reproductive politics. In addition, RJ is a framework that emphasizes the importance of storytelling from the margins.[13] As Shui-yin Sharon Yam points out, "Contrary to individualistic stories that advocate a neoliberal market-based approach to reproduction, acts of storytelling championed by the RJ framework require the rhetor and audience to grapple with the structural causes of their lived experiences and narratives."[14] Reproductive justice, hence, informs not only the overarching focus of this book but also our methodologies and attunement toward uplifting the experiences and tactics of marginalized queer people as they navigate the tension in reproductive politics.

RJ History, Framework, and Movement

Reproductive justice is a revolutionary concept conceived and nurtured in circles of Black feminist organizing around the turn of the twenty-first century. The term itself was coined by a group of twelve Black women convened at a conference in Chicago in 1994; reproductive justice includes the right to have a child, the right to not have a child, and the right to parent our child(ren) in safe, clean environments.[15] More recently, LGBTQ+ activists added a fourth tenet: the right to bodily autonomy, gender identity, and sexual pleasure.[16] RJ significantly broadens the dominant approach to reproductive rights, which have been historically situated as private, as individual, and as a choice. In lieu of an emphasis on individual choices, reproductive justice is oriented toward the structural transformations necessary for families and communities to thrive—this would include, of course, access to birth control and abortion care, but it also necessitates freedom from poverty, environmental degradation, policing, and state violence. While the RJ framework is relatively new, it is inspired by the activism of feminists in the Global South and, simultaneously, is deeply rooted in generations of intersectional organizing led by radical women of color in the United States.[17]

Research and advocacy grounded in the reproductive justice framework is flourishing. This includes the thriving and proliferation of grassroots organizations such as Forward Together, SPARK Reproductive Justice NOW, and Bold Futures (formerly known as Young Women United)—organizations that are transforming conversations and policies around young parenthood, comprehensive sex education, and reproduction by nonnormative bodies. Public intellectuals such as Imani Gandy, Alexis Pauline Gumbs, Miriam Zoila Pérez, and Grover Wehman-Brown have brought RJ principles into broader public conversations surrounding pregnancy, childbirth, parenting, and health care.[18] Research across the humanities, social sciences, law, and medicine is drawing on RJ to consider how we might build a more just future—take, for instance, the work of Khiara Bridges, Dána-Ain Davis, and Patricia Zavella as recent exemplars building on the foundational work of Loretta Ross, Dorothy Roberts, and Rickie Solinger.[19]

Reproductive violence is a common tool of oppressive regimes. In the United States, reproductive violence has long been leveraged as a weapon of white supremacist patriarchy. Rape, sexual assault, and murder of Indigenous women and children specifically were a key component of colonizing the Americas.[20] In the early years of the US republic, control over enslaved Black women's reproduction was forcibly asserted, not only through sexual violence perpetrated by white slave owners but also through a web of laws that denied enslaved Black women the right to mother and create a family.[21] In concert with anti-miscegenation laws, racist immigration restrictions such as the Page Act of 1875—which closed the US border by barring entry of Chinese women—were designed to sabotage racialized immigrants' thriving through deprivation of family formation.

State-sanctioned population control strategies targeted low-wealth communities and communities of color throughout the twentieth

Introduction   7

century; these strategies persist today in the egregious sterilization abuse of incarcerated people, including asylum-seeking migrants detained by US Immigration and Customs Enforcement (ICE). In September 2020, a whistleblower complaint revealed that ICE had been performing hysterectomies at an alarmingly high rate among immigrant women under their custody—many of which had not consented to sterilization.[22] These violations are extensions of long-standing racist and eugenic state policies that violate the reproductive self-determination of poor Indigenous women and other women of color. For example, since the 1890s, the federal government has been enacting coercive tactics to sterilize Indigenous women and remove Indigenous children from their communities.[23] While straight white women of means are far less likely to encounter state-sanctioned medical abuses of reproductive autonomy, attempts to assert control over their reproduction are also commonplace and fundamentally driven by white supremacist patriarchy. Fears over the declining white demographic fueled the establishment of antiabortion laws in the nineteenth century and continue to shape the landscape of reproductive rights to this day. This fear has been evidenced more recently in the frightening uptick in laws restricting access to birth control and abortion care, and it has been reinvigorated by the egregious Supreme Court decision to overturn *Roe*, the primacy placed on so-called sexual purity and abstinence before marriage, and the social stigmas and punishments attached to young parenting, to name a few examples.

Reproductive justice is a powerful critical framework and organizing tool that has fundamentally altered the terrain of reproductive rights advocacy in the United States and internationally in the last twenty-five years.[24] Even as reproductive rights have faced unprecedented assaults by the state, RJ has provided a flexible and deeply intersectional model for challenging these assaults through broad-based coalition strategizing and collaboration. It has proved exceptionally adept at taking into account how race, class, age, and marital status matter in the struggles for reproductive, sexual, and familial dignity—and as RJ continues to deepen and expand as a kind of "open-source code," it is increasingly tasked with integrating issues such as migration, incarceration, and queerness.[25] Existing RJ scholarship and activism committed to queering reproductive justice is driven primarily by a logic of inclusions. We, on the other hand, seek and engage in a more vigorous interrogation of the dominant binary gender system. Without understanding how gender binary and normativities have undergirded reproductive injustice against BIPOC and colonized subjects, inclusion of LGBTQ+ people alone will not dismantle the intersecting systems of coercion. In short, without challenging the dominant sex/gender binary, we will leave intact a system that is at the core of reproductive injustice and violence.

For health practitioners, it is important to note that the RJ framework is intimately connected to reproductive health. Based on the International Conference on Population and Development (ICPD) in 1994 and the ICPD+5 Forum in 1999, the World Health Organization (WHO) defines reproductive health as a "human condition" that ranges from "healthy sexual development, comfort and closeness and the joys of childbearing, to abuse, disease and death."[26] Specifically, the WHO notes that social, psychological, and physiological factors are all interconnected with reproductive health. In this holistic framework to reproductive health, the WHO encourages practitioners to consider not only health needs but also "rights, equity, dignity, empowerment, self-determination and responsibility in relationships," as reproductive health is "also about transforming the status quo, away from the unfairnesses and indignities of the present."[27] In addition to considering how diverse societal and relational factors affect individuals' overall health and well-being, the WHO's comprehensive account of reproductive health also urges health practitioners and policymakers to implement "equity-oriented policies and strategies that emphasize solidarity."[28] This normative definition of reproductive health clearly articulates a networked and justice-oriented approach that coheres with the RJ framework, both recognizing the need to attend to sociopolitical factors in order to promote individual and communal well-being.

Queering Reproductive Justice

Crafting inclusive and culturally competent spaces within which to create and nourish LGBTQ+ individuals and families is a cornerstone of the third pillar of reproductive justice. It is also integral to a holistic model of reproductive health that accounts for the impact of social stigma and sanctions on individuals and communities.[29] Individuals who identify outside of the dominant gender binary have long been targets of discrimination and systemic marginalization that negatively impact their reproductive health. For example, research shows that 33% of trans people and 48% of trans men have delayed or avoided seeking preventive reproductive health care out of fear of discrimination and dehumanizing treatment.[30] Further, TGNC parents have repeatedly reminded us of the transphobia and cissexism they experience in reproductive care and family formation.[31] The concrete challenges of creating a more inclusive space for TGNC people and their families are both structural and quotidian; they are legal and infrastructural as much as embedded in clinical practices and everyday beliefs (see chapter 3). There are deep ideological alliances between reproductive rights and LGBTQ+ struggles—for example, in the right to pleasure, bodily autonomy, and non-procreative sex. Still, these alliances have not been widely recognized or embraced until more recently. Historical fractures between movements reflect at least two dynamics: First, these fractures reflect the disparate origins and trajectories of each struggle, rooted in distinct communities investing energy and attention in a narrow set of issues. Second, just as mainstream reproductive rights advocacy has long centered the needs of middle-class, straight white women, so too have fledgling movements for LGBTQ+ rights often reflected the experiences of gay white men—and, to a lesser extent, lesbians—thus fueling advocacy efforts that remained singular in focus. These histories are not the focal point of this book; indeed, they are told with great depth, nuance, and acuity elsewhere by historians and critics on lesbian feminist activism and trans women activisms.[32] For our purposes, we simply wish to note that these trends echo broader patterns of inclusion and exclusion in the histories of social movements writ large—that the entanglements of feminist and LGBTQ+ struggle are as troubling as they are often generative.

Of particular significance to this project is the fact that LGBTQ+ people are just as central to as they are invisible within the histories of feminist struggle itself.[33] The examples are many. They include what we might now refer to as lesbians, queer women, and/or transmasculine folx in the leadership of the mainstream women's rights movement. These include prominent suffragists in intimate "Boston marriages" in the early twentieth century, the gender queerness of notable figures in feminist history such as Frances Willard and Pauli Murray, and the infamous "lavender menace" proudly reclaimed by lesbians such as Rita Mae Brown in the National Organization for Women.[34] In addition to mainstream feminist advocacy, other movement activists were interrogating oppression at the nexus of gender and sexuality (and, for some, race and class as well) in collectives such as the Combahee River Collective, the Radicalesbians, the Furies Collective, the Street Transvestite Action Revolutionaries, Olivia Records, and Kitchen Table: Women of Color Press. This is not to deny the homophobia and transphobia persistently and devastatingly present within feminist struggles, nor is it to ignore the cis/sexism and trans/misogyny embedded within LGBTQ+ movements. Those histories, too, are richly detailed and elaborated elsewhere.[35] For now, however, suffice it to say that feminist and LGBTQ+ movements have a deep, complicated, and long-standing history—one that reveals the presence of queer people (lesbians, bisexuals, nonbinary, and trans-identified folx alike) within feminist struggles at every turn and that also underscores a consistent pattern of alliance between issues, concerns, and organizing.

This alliance is increasingly explicit in mainstream feminist organizing and advocacy, due in no small part to the increasing primacy of intersectionality in feminism. Much like reproductive justice, intersectionality is indebted to US Black feminism; Kimberlé Crenshaw coined the term in a landmark essay in 1989 to offer "a lens through which you can see where power comes and collides, where it interlocks and intersects."[36] Crenshaw's theory of intersectionality draws

Introduction 11

on the centuries-long legacy of Black feminist thought, from Sojourner Truth to Angela Davis and Patricia Hill Collins, which finds enduring expression in recent scholarship and activisms that are increasingly mainstream. At the same time, how intersectionality is commonly deployed has also been critiqued by scholars such as Jasbir Puar, Marquis Bey, and Jennifer Nash.[37] For instance, Puar argues that by assuming intersecting identities are steady nodes of reference, intersectional feminism has not taken into account the broader systems, conditions, and "perpetual motion of assemblages" but rather is trying "to capture and reduce them, to harness their threatening mobility."[38] For Bey, an unfixed mobility is exactly at the core of Black trans feminism.[39] By insisting on the mobility and unsteadiness of gender, Black trans feminism urges us to deconstruct sex/gender as political categories that are invented to police and regulate Black bodies and bodies of color.

Intersectionality maintains deep currency in feminist activism and scholarship. Reproductive justice has long been grounded in intersectionality, and thus it is not surprising to find RJ work expanding to include LGBTQ+ concerns. In 2006, SisterSong collaborated with the National LGBTQ Task Force and Ipas—an international organization on safe abortion rights and contraception—to put together an interactive online database that ranks different US states based on their laws concerning reproductive and LGBTQ+ rights.[40] More recently, in June 2019, the National LGBTQ Task Force published a toolkit entitled *Queering Reproductive Justice*. In it, the task force outlines the intimacies between RJ and LGBTQ+ liberation, specifying barriers queer people frequently face in accessing health care, for example, and noting the shared legal histories and oppressions among reproductive rights and justice movements and LGBTQ+ rights. A recent feature in *Out* magazine introduces readers to the "queer folks revolutionizing the reproductive justice movement," noting how grassroots RJ organizations are increasingly led by young queer, BIPOC leaders. In short, these deep alliances are increasingly nurtured and expressed in reproductive justice. As Monica Simpson, the current executive director of SisterSong, explains: "In doing LGBTQ+ work, it couldn't hold my Blackness. In doing work around the prison industrial complex, you couldn't talk about queerness. [With RJ,] you didn't have to check off the boxes at the door. . . . The Reproductive Justice Movement felt like my political homecoming."[41] Simpson's reflection highlights the capaciousness of RJ that coheres with the overarching coalitional aim of Black trans feminism: "It is less about joining groups based on who one is, it is about coming together by way of how work is put in" to subvert hegemonic structures.[42] The importance of the confluence between RJ and trans justice came to the fore in the United States after the overturning of *Roe v. Wade* in June 2022. As the RJ legal scholar Khiara Bridges and trans lawyer-activist Chase Strangio argue, we must include trans and nonbinary people in our advocacy for abortion rights in order to cultivate a truly transformative political change that does not sideline or exclude anyone.[43] Strangio emphasizes that many activists traverse both RJ and trans justice movements, sharing intersecting embodied experiences and insights to cultivate reproductive freedom for all.[44]

In addition to activism, interdisciplinary scholarship is also thriving at the intersection of queer politics and reproductive justice.[45] This interdisciplinary work explores how LGBTQ+ rights activists build political coalitions with other social movements and advocacy groups through the intersectional framework of RJ; how and whether we can leverage RJ to analyze and dismantle the legal, material, and sociocultural barriers queer people face in reproduction and family formation; and how researchers and activists can productively draw on the confluences of stratified reproduction, reproductive justice, and queer reproduction as three key theoretical frameworks with distinctive lineages. Scholars hold different perspectives on the queering of reproductive justice. While some advocate for an intersectional cultivation of coalition between RJ and the LGBTQ+ movements, others argue that not all queer reproduction and family-making fit within the RJ framework and critique the homonormative impulse entailed therein.[46]

Doing Gender Justice proffers another vision of queering RJ—one that extends beyond inclusion to critique the sex/gender binary itself as a form of reproductive injustice. We hold that while *queer* is not synonymous with *radical*—nor need it necessarily be—the potential of queering kin is real. As LGBTQ+ people create family, both within and beyond biogenetic or otherwise legible configurations, the concept of family itself is productively reimagined and remade. Moreover, as Loretta Ross often notes, reproductive justice may be rooted in Black women's experiences in the United States, but reproductive justice is for everyone.[47] Reproductive justice meets a critical edge in its consideration of LGBTQ+ lives: without considering how the binary sex/gender categories and structures have been used to police bodies and reproductive choices, we cannot make the promise of RJ real.

Queer, Feminist, and Trans Understandings of Gender and Sex

As transphobic and misogynist public policies and discourse have become increasingly popular in the early 2020s, women's rights and trans justice are often pitched against each other: trans-inclusive language is misconstrued as an attack against women's rights by both right-wing politicians and gender-critical feminists who abide by a sex/gender alignment and biological gender essentialism.[48] This tension has led to murkiness and slippage surrounding the language and conceptual frameworks we use to interrogate gender, sex, and trans-inclusive intersectional feminism, and it necessitates that we articulate how we understand these concepts in relation to each other. As we consider trans-embodied experiences and epistemologies that challenge the stability of binary gender and sex categories, we do not see sex and gender identities as stable categories that exists a priori. As Judith Butler indicates with the term "sex/gender," gender and sex are mutually constructed by dominant institutions and discourse.[49] Butler and other postmodern gender theorists rightly point out that in public discourse, sex and gender norms are frequently conflated with one another.[50] The mainstream discourse we analyze frequently discusses sex/gender according to this reductive and transphobic framework that assumes the immutability of sex and gender. We seek to problematize the collapse of gender, sex, and the body in language

14   *Doing Gender Justice*

use, but when discussing primary texts in their original contexts, we will use language that reflects the dominant sex/gender framework these texts abide by.

As Heath Fogg Davis helpfully reminds us, more often than not, in mainstream public discourse, women are assumed to be female, and the dominant sex classification uses the binary sex identities "male" and "female" as "a proxy for particular body parts."[51] According to this formulation, women are females who possess reproductive organs that allow them to gestate and give birth. Davis and the trans author-activist Julia Serano understand traditional sexism as the belief and practice that sees femaleness and femininity as inherently inferior to maleness and masculinity; they also respectively argue that while trans women and cis women both experience sexism, only the former are targets of both transphobia *and* "trans misogyny," as trans women are commonly portrayed as sexual predators against cis women and as deceivers of heterosexual men.[52]

In addition to problematizing the dominant belief that sex/gender are durable categories that are natural, trans* studies and trans bodies also complicate undergirding theoretical assumptions in some forms of women's studies and queer studies. Elucidating the gaps between these frameworks is necessary for us to acknowledge trans bodies and experiences on their own terms. As Cáel Keegan points out, "subordination feminisms" tend to "fix gender in order to link it to the binary power relations that undergird their foundational critiques of patriarchy (M > F) and heteronormativity."[53] Thinking in terms of trans* studies thus necessitates that we think intersectionally and contextually about oppression instead of considering *all* women or *all* gays and lesbians as inherently oppressed as a class.

Trans bodies and trans* studies also pose complications for feminist queer studies that seek to dismantle gender norms and gender normativity. While both share the common ground of challenging the binary model of gender and demonstrating the performativity of gender, feminist queer studies may discipline trans bodies and deny their embodied experiences.[54] Janet Halley and Jay Prosser have demonstrated the epistemological gap between the two fields, as trans*

Introduction   15

studies "contain[s] strains of theorization and praxis that understand gender to be innately sensed and actual—in other words, constative rather than performative."[55] By focusing on gender anti-normativity, feminist queer studies may fail to take seriously the desire many trans people have to live as "real and normal" men and women and "pass as 'real-ly gendered' in the world without trouble."[56] Serano observes that the queer/trans communities she was in often celebrated gender-nonconforming people while criticizing gender-conforming trans people as reinforcing the sex/gender binary.[57] Trans people's desire to experience gender as "real" has been weaponized by the prominent lesbian-feminist Sheila Jeffreys and other gender-critical feminists to accuse trans people of reifying and reproducing gender essential-ism and stereotypes.[58] As Bey poignantly articulates, while "transness has a history that rejects feminism (Virginia Prince, Caitlyn Jenner)," feminism also "has a strain of its history that is transantagonistic (Janice Raymond, Michele Wallace, Sheila Jeffreys)."[59] By articulating the overlaps and epistemological gaps between feminist queer studies and trans* studies to refute these strains of oppression, we are better positioned to advance a radical agenda of trans feminist resistance and coalition. Keegan cogently summarizes the tension among trans* studies, women's studies, and feminist queer studies as follows:

> To the extent that women's studies seeks the liberation of women and others (gay men, lesbians) who are oppressed by sex "like women," trans* studies must perform a *but* that insists against the founda-tional schema of sexual subordination (M > F), saying but gender is not real like that. However, in response to queer studies' investment in deconstructing the gender binary (M/F) to unravel heteronorma-tivity, trans* studies must turn inside out, articulating a constative *but* that asserts but gender is real like this.[60]

Since trans* studies and trans experiences cannot and should not be subsumed under women's studies and feminist queer theories, we need a decolonial trans feminist reproductive justice framework that considers the different experiences of gender identity and trans em-bodiment. Despite the fissures among trans*studies, women studies, and feminist queer studies, when taken together, these frameworks are useful in interrogating how different forms of sexism, transphobia, and misogyny intersect. Intricately connected and sustained by the harmful myth of a stable sex/gender binary, these forces are mobilized to police people's bodies and their sex and gender identities. As Bey argues, "Feminism and transness need one another" so that we can more comprehensively create a coalitional politics that is radically inclusive.[61] Without the autonomy to fully explore and express one's sex and gender identity and embodied reproductive experiences and desires, there can be no reproductive justice. By articulating the intersections and fissures among these ideological forces, we are able to be more pointed and precise in our language and critique.

Sex/Gender Binary as Racist Colonial Control

Gender and sex, like race, were both political categories constructed by white colonizers and settlers to delineate and justify the hierarchy between white colonizers and Black and brown colonized subjects.[62] Until quite recently, "sex," "gender," and "sexuality" were not understood as concepts that could be separated, so we use "sex/gender" to denote this historical conflation and to acknowledge that the colonial construction of sex/gender harmed a wide range of LGBTQ+, genderqueer, and gender-nonconforming people.[63] As María Lugones argues, the "colonial/modern gender system . . . understood race as gendered and gender as raced in particularly differential ways for Europeans/'whites' and colonized/'non-white' peoples."[64] Historians of colonialism have cogently demonstrated that by inventing sex and gender, which were understood as durable categories that were always aligned, white colonizers were able to argue that they were superior to their colonized subjects because only white people possessed binary gender and sex differences.[65] Black, brown, and Indigenous people, meanwhile, were portrayed as animalistic and primitive for their lack of differentiation between the sexes.[66] We posit that understanding the particular history of sex/gender construction is crucial to reproductive justice: to achieve a truly intersectional and transformative politics, we must investigate how the construction of sex/gender

Introduction   *17*

and racialization have historically both been deployed in conjunction to oppress people of color.

Reproductive justice has made intersectional politics requisite to rigorous and thoughtful engagement with reproductive politics. This commitment has led to a deep interrogation of how white patriarchy has exploited sex differences through rape and forced birth and how the denial of Black motherhood and womanhood has separated families.[67] A more thorough and historical critique of the dominant sex/gender binary, however, remains necessary, as it has long been used to uphold racism, colonialism, and reproductive violence. As Alyosxa Tudor pointedly articulates, "The sex/gender system must be understood as a race/gender system."[68] For example, Black and Indigenous people—defined by colonizers as sexually ambiguous or indistinguishable—were marked as savages who must be governed and controlled.[69] Sexologists in the 1880s continued to believe that only the "civilized" white race would demonstrate marked physical differences between the sexes.[70] Examining the colonial history of the Americas, Scott Morgensen argues that "the queering of Native peoples defined not only settler sexuality, broadly, but also the definition of queer subjects among white settlers: as a primitive, racialized sexual margin akin to what white settlers attempted to conquer among Natives."[71]

More insidiously, conformity to the white heteronormative gender system was weaponized by colonizers to cultivate a hierarchy among colonized, indentured, and enslaved people of color. For instance, Lisa Lowe observes that in the late eighteenth to early nineteenth century, Chinese women were repeatedly used by British colonizers to highlight "the capacity of the colonized to develop into a reproductive, family community," while suggesting that Chinese—and later Indian—people were superior to Africans.[72] The white colonial gender system, in V. Jo Hsu's words, divided people of color based on their perceived "ability to approximate (but never fully inhabit) white, heteronormative" performances of gender, sexuality, and family formations.[73] With anti-Blackness, anti-Indigeneity, and trans antagonism at play, Black and Indigenous people of color were never seen as possessing the ability to approximate whiteness. Binary biological sex and gender, hence, cannot be separated from racial subjugation. The normativity of sex/gender does not exist a priori but is rather constructed through the queering and othering of Native peoples and people of color. Thus, homophobia and transphobia have always been key components of settler colonialism, bolstered by the naturalization of a binary gender/sex system.

Settler colonial violence against Indigenous people was intricately connected to trans violence supported by the binary gender/sex systems. Bethany Schneider argues that "Indian hating" and "queer hating" have served as "a powerful pair of pistons in the history of white colonization of the Americas."[74] Scholars in Native studies have further demonstrated that the destruction of Native communities, specifically those community members who did not fit neatly into Western colonialist gender binaries, was accomplished in part by "reinvent[ing] and assimilat[ing] them as straight, private property-owning, married citizens."[75] Indigenous people who did not identify as either male or female and did not perform gender the way settlers expected were brutally persecuted; some were even targeted for extermination.[76] Gregory Smithers argues that as settler colonial writers and social scientists classified gender-fluid Native people into "homogenizing categories" invented by the West—such as "berdache," "homosexual," "transvestite," and other derogatory terms applied exclusively to Two Spirit Indigenous people—they inadvertently applied white supremacist and colonizing cultural assumptions onto Native Americans in ways that reinforced settler imperialism.[77] Native boarding schools, run by settler colonizers to assimilate and destroy Indigenous families and communities, enforced a strict sex/gender binary among Native children. In addition to RJ scholars who note this deliberate destruction of kin ties as a form of reproductive violence, queer Indigenous scholars have argued that colonial violence dispossessed Native people of their home, their land, and their bodies.[78] The dominant binary gender/sex structure—and, importantly, its tethering to reproductive regimes—has been instrumental in securing the settler colonial state and in maintaining the power hierarchy between white settlers and Indigenous communities.

Introduction 19

The relationship between the colonial gender system and anti-Indigeneity demands that we turn to decolonial critiques of gender. As the Cherokee Two Spirit scholar Qwo-Li Driskill elucidates, the term *Two Spirit* is an intertribal designation for gender-variant Native Americans that is intended to be political and decolonial. Driskill, and later Smithers, points out that the Two Spirit framework is necessarily an anti-assimilation one because it refuses to pathologize those who do not fit into the gender binary.[79] As Hsu articulates, "Two Spirit is then an assertion of self-determination and coalition in response to colonial knowledge systems."[80] Without romanticizing and mythologizing Indigenous cultures, a critical interrogation and refusal of the dominant gender system is thus critical to challenging colonial logics.

In addition to coloniality, the relationship between the construction of race and gender/sex is also deeply connected to chattel slavery and anti-Black racism. Hortense Spillers's canonical work examined how the emergence of the gender binary was intimately connected to processes of racialization: in the colonial framework, if an individual does not possess one of two genders, they are not considered human.[81] Elaborating on Sylvia Wynter's work, Greg Thomas argues that Black people were historically excluded from gender and sex categories because those categories were race-specific.[82] Hence, as Eva Hayward and Che Gossett opine, "Blackness is trans/gender trouble."[83] The normative gender/sex binary, in other words, cannot be separated from anti-Blackness.

Tracing public discourse on gender and race from the mid-nineteenth century to present times, the queer Black scholar C. Riley Snorton points out that Blackness and transness have always intersected. Snorton shows how the genders of enslaved Black people were manipulated to justify "racial slavery's political and visual economy."[84] In his case study of James Marion Sims's publicized vesicovaginal fistula operation on enslaved Black people, Snorton demonstrates the incommensurability between Blackness and womanhood, or gender more broadly. While the surgery was performed to develop "the key to restoring a woman's health," the enslaved people on the public operation table were not recognized as women, as (white) womanhood is "conferred in relation to an unwillingness to view white female genitalia."[85] Echoing earlier critical gender theorists like Jack Halberstam and Judith Butler, and through his historical analysis of how gender has always been racialized, Snorton demonstrates not only that gender is mutable but also that it has been repeatedly mobilized to bolster anti-Black and anti-trans legislation and violence.[86] Snorton is not alone in articulating the intimate connection between Blackness and transness. Marquis Bey, similarly, argues that Blackness and trans*ness are both always "on the outskirts of order" and are "perpetually disruptive" to the logics of white supremacy and cissexism.[87] A reproductive justice politics that takes seriously anti-Black racism, hence, must also entail a critical analysis of the binary sex/gender construction.

Reproduction and the Maintenance of the White Supremacist Nation

An interrogation of the co-construction of gender and race is necessary not only because we need to historicize how the gender/race matrix has been weaponized against BIPOC communities, but also because it has continual ramifications on reproductive politics and the maintenance of a white supremacist nation. The phenomenon of stratified reproduction, which describes "the power relations by which some categories of people are empowered to nurture and reproduce, while others are disempowered," has always been shaped by systems of oppression and hierarchies that mark certain bodies as unfit citizens— and hence, as unfit parents to produce the next generation.[88] The tight scrutiny placed on pregnancy and reproduction cannot be separated from the celebration of cishet white nuclear-family structures as the ideal. The nation is often figured via familial metaphors that signal its exclusivity and fragility: the nation-family accepts only those who adhere to a white supremacist, neoliberal construction of citizenship (white, middle-upper class, able-bodied, cishet), while treating non-normative bodies as threatening contaminants.[89] In right-wing public discourse, any threat to this familial ideal is constructed as a threat to the nation-state itself.[90] Through this imaginary co-construction of

Introduction   21

family and citizenship, the reproductive desires of BIPOC, trans and queer people, poor people, and disabled people are all marked as dangerous to the futurity of the nation.

The connection between the regulation of reproduction and family and the maintenance of a white supremacist nation is maintained through mainstream culture and public policies. For example, educated middle-upper-class cis white women, especially those who are married, are encouraged to reproduce or to preserve their fertility through egg freezing.[91] In addition, as we explore further in the next chapter, anti-trans commentators and policymakers frequently argue that the fertility of trans youths—especially white trans boys, whose gender identity is vehemently denied by right-wing actors—is in danger.[92] In both of these examples, a pronatalist agenda is intricately connected to the preservation of a patriarchal definition of womanhood, family, and gender.

While middle-class cishet white women are encouraged to reproduce, poor BIPOC communities are disempowered from having and parenting their own children. The Black legal scholar Dorothy Roberts has traced the many ways in which Black women are systematically disempowered from reproducing and parenting their children.[93] As mentioned earlier, since Black women have historically been denied womanhood, their ability to mother and parent is frequently called into question by the state and by dominant white culture. Not only have poor Black women been targets of forced sterilization and been discouraged from having children, they also face frequent criminalization as parents because of poverty.[94] Due to the biased nature of social-welfare algorithms and the neoliberal regime that expects individuals to be self-sufficient and self-enterprising, parenting while poor is equated with poor parenting.[95] Given systemic and historical racism, BIPOC are more likely to face poverty, which in turn places them in government systems of surveillance. Under the regime of stratified reproduction and white supremacy, social-welfare systems that are meant to protect children and families become, as Roberts points out, a tool to police, surveil, and demolish Black families.[96] By disempowering Black women from being parents and by forcibly separating Black children from their parents, the state actively upholds a middle-upper-class nuclear-family structure as the ideal.

The policing of regulation extends beyond Black families. Immigrants also face intense scrutiny by the US state because of gendered and racist assumptions about their fertility and family structures. Anti-immigration discourse represents poor immigrant women of color as overly fertile. Their fertility, in turn, poses a threat to the nation because they will be reproducing so-called anchor babies that drain public resources and, worst of all, contaminate the quality of the citizenry.[97] Racialized and gendered as baby-making machines that threaten the future of the nation, immigrant women of color face state-sanctioned reproductive violence. In 2020, a whistleblower revealed that US Immigration and Customs Enforcement had been sterilizing woman detainees without their consent.[98] Earlier, in the 1970s, Chicana feminists brought a class-action lawsuit against physicians at the Los Angeles County + University of Southern California Medical Center for the coerced sterilization of Mexican-origin women during, or immediately following, birth.[99] These horrific examples illustrate that state control of reproduction is motivated by the interconnected web of racism, sexism, xenophobia, and white nationalism.

In addition to experiencing reproductive violence that occurs at the intersection of race, gender, class, and citizenship status, immigrants also bear the burden of proving how their family structure and kin ties uphold the American ideal of the white cishet nuclear family. For example, US immigration law prioritizes the reunification of families based on the cishet nuclear-family ideal and a biological definition of kinship.[100] Familial and care relationships that do not fit this model, such as single-parent households, LGBTQ+ families, multigenerational families, and cohabiting-parent families, are not accepted under family reunification provisions. In many non-white and/or non-Western contexts, *family* is defined and practiced in more expansive ways that are not limited to a cisheteronormative nuclear structure.

Introduction   23

The narrow definition of family in US immigration law connects Eurocentrism and white supremacy with the policing of the nation-family. This policy has important ramifications: by accepting only heterosexual biological parents, the US government separates many immigrant children from their primary caregivers, denying their right to family as defined by the United Nations Convention on the Rights of the Child.[101]

While some immigrants are barred from entering the United States because their race, gender, sexuality, and kinship practice fail to uphold the ideal of the US nation-state, others are admitted because their filial ties to a heterosexual nuclear family render them intelligible to the state. Examining the Illegal Immigration Reform and Immigrant Responsibility Act (IIRIRA) and public discourse surrounding immigration, Jennifer Wingard argues that public narratives from across the political spectrum position the nuclear family as central to the immigrant's right to enter or remain in the United States. Immigrants who have already formed a heteronormative nuclear family with US citizens are deemed more worthy of inclusion because their filial relationship mirrors the US family ideal and because they are already attached to the US through a legally recognized relationship (marriage or biological parentage).[102] In a subsection titled "Exception for Certain Battered Women and Children," the IIRIRA makes clear that it recognizes intimate partner violence against women only in a traditional family setting, where filial relationships are recognized by law. By accepting only immigrants that meet the white supremacist familial ideal of the US, the immigration system perpetuates stratified reproduction and reproductive injustice.

In sum, at both the local and transnational levels, reproductive control is enacted by the state and by dominant actors—such as mainstream media outlets and corporations—to promote a vision of the middle-class white hetero- (and through pinkwashing, sometimes homo-) normative nuclear-family structure. Understanding reproductive surveillance and regulation in relation to nation-making allows us to interrogate how the colonial and white supremacist root of gender and the nuclear family continues to bolster reproductive injustice.

Gender and Language: A Tension in the RJ Movement

Naming the gendered dynamics of reproductive violence and oppression has long been a critical component of organizing against it. For instance, woman-centered language has historically aided in these efforts in dominant US settings, from the naming of sexism in Western medical contexts to the critique of patriarchal institutions that have denied cisgender women bodily autonomy and reproductive self-determination. Thus, for some, shedding gender-specific language in reproductive contexts signals a profound loss—the loss of the capacity to name the (cis) misogyny that undergirds reproductive violence by specifically referencing (cis) women. Given the intersectional ethos of the reproductive justice movements, most major reproductive justice organizations, such as SisterSong and Pregnancy Justice (formerly National Advocates for Pregnant Women), include TGNC people in their organizing and advocacy. However, gender remains a site of struggle that continues to animate debate in reproductive health and rights advocacy circles.

As we illuminate in the next chapter, this tension is due in part to the misguided belief that the use of gender-neutral language is totalizing, a replacement of woman-centered language. The use of gender-neutral language, in turn, is interpreted by some feminists and women as yet another erasure of their humanity and gendered experiences. For women of color, especially Black and Indigenous women, whose womanhood and gender has always been racialized and systematically denied, this is a particularly bitter pill to swallow. As Corrine Sanchez from the Tewa Women United notes, "We've experienced what we've experienced as Native women *because* we're Native women, and to erase that and put a gender-neutral frame on that is erasing our experiences again."[103] Rather than policing gender based on biological essentialism, feminists of color who resist using gender-neutral language do so through an intersectional lens that seeks to highlight the lived experiences of those who are multiply marginalized by patriarchy and racism. Women-of-color feminists who are reluctant to adopt gender-neutral language also argue that by using gender-neutral language, women will be silenced as political subjects who organize under their shared gender identity. Troubling the trend of using the gender-neutral *Latinx* to replace *Latina/o*, Nicole Trujillo-Pagán states that when used as a "totalizing" concept, *Latinx* "decenters conceptual, analytic and political attention to patriarchy and embodied experiences of race/ethnicity that are always gendered."[104] Trujillo-Pagán argues that the gender-neutral term is often deployed in a way that "subordinates a gender identity that is profoundly meaningful and marginalized by demographic imbalances."[105] Gender-neutral language, in other words, could function in a similar fashion as colorblind discourse, erasing the systemic marginalization (cis/trans) women face.

Motivated by the overarching goal to challenge existing patterns of injustice, the concerns raised by feminists of color in defense of woman-centered language are deeply important: they rightly insist on specificity as we name the interconnected forms of oppression that shape the politics of reproduction. Black trans feminist scholarship offers a critical direction for reproductive justice scholars and advocates to foster a radical transformational agenda. Black trans feminism reminds us that to interrogate and dismantle structures such as gendered hierarchies and heteropatriarchy, we must also destroy the validity and stronghold of gender itself.[106] Marquis Bey argues for "gender abolition," as "Blackness's antagonism toward cisgender and cisgender's normativity, its antiblackness, calls into question the very apparatus of gender itself as an organizing frame . . . it is a matter of disposing of the frame."[107] For Bey, the binary sex/gender framework has always been intricately connected with racism and anti-Blackness and hence must be deeply interrogated, if not fully abolished. Similarly, in her work on decolonial feminism, Lugones argues that "woman" must be bracketed and interrogated critically rather than normalized.[108] Echoing Lugones's argument, Xhercis Méndez points out that "rather than destabilize its colonial logic, incorporation [of gender binaries] instead obscures the profound dehumanizing and racializing work that gender performed."[109] Only by constantly interrogating the constructedness and history of gender can we resist its coloniality. Hence, we need better—more robust, thorough, and expansive—

theorizing of how gender shapes reproductive violence through, as opposed to within, binary modes of thought.

Decolonial and Black trans* feminist critiques align with reproductive justice if we see RJ as a critical framework and organizing tool imagined as "open-source code" and designed to evolve toward a future that we can only begin to imagine. In interviews we have conducted with queer RJ advocates of color, several argued that rather than holding on to dominant binary gender categories and taking them for granted, it is more important to challenge or dismantle them entirely. As Khye Tyson, a nonbinary Black RJ activist, poignantly stated, "Gender is a racist concept."[110] Similarly, the Indigenous queer birthworker and educator Stevie Merino pointed out that by degendering birth and pregnancy, her program is not erasing (cis) women, but rather reasserting an Indigenous understanding of gender and family formations to challenge Eurocentric assumptions.[111]

Trans* of color feminism's interrogation of womanhood is particularly useful in resisting the systemic erasure and dehumanization of Black women through race and gender. Bey reminds us that during the Jim Crow era, bathrooms were segregated into "Men's," "Women's," and "Colored."[112] Since gender distinction is reserved only for white people, Black women are often not seen as women, as they cannot perform white femininity. Demanding recognition through sex/gender dimorphism, however, does not promise liberation. Analyzing Sojourner Truth's famous speech "Ain't I a Woman?," Méndez argues that if Truth were to be recognized as a "woman" according to the white supremacist understanding of gender and femininity, she might gain the benefit of being recognized as human and be freed from slavery.[113] However, that would also necessarily entail that Truth be incorporated into an oppressive mode of gender/sex relation that cast women as weak and their bodies as tools for the reproduction of racial capital. As Emi Koyama points out while interrogating the genealogy and continuation of white feminism, in many historical examples, women's rights were extended only to white/Western women.[114] Méndez sees gender respectability politics among people of color as both a response and continuation to the violences of the white su-

Introduction   27

premacist race/gender system. Tyson agrees. For Tyson, subscribing to a white supremacist gender label is "a reach for respectability politics" that reinscribes Black people and people of color into the white homo/heteronormative society.[115] Maintaining gender respectability by observing the white colonial framework of gender binary especially harms disabled, trans, and gender-nonconforming Black people and people of color. As Tudor poignantly asks:

> If Black women . . . are already excluded from the category "woman" ("ungendered" in Spillers' term), how can we make sure that within this theoretical claim, Black intersex, non-binary and trans people are not rendered abject—the impossible positions in an understanding of racialised gendering as always already excluded from normative (white) gendering?[116]

The twin forces of the gender binary and racism, in other words, dehumanize those who are not white and cisheteronormative. That loss of humanity, in turn, threatens their reproductive health and overall well-being.

Doing Gender Justice draws on trans* of color critiques and Black trans feminism that argue for a radical interrogation—if not the abolition—of gender.[117] Grounding our analysis in primary data that illustrate the lived experience of TGNC people, we call on RJ and reproductive health practitioners and scholars to engage deeply with critiques of the dominant gender system, as it is intricately bound up with other forms of oppressive power relations and reproductive injustice. As Brooklyn Leo pointedly argues, the colonial binary gender system "could not maintain its supremacy without the abjection of Trans, Two-spirit, and Gender-Nonconforming peoples of color."[118] While queer people of color bear the brunt of the violence wreaked by the dominant gender system, the sex/gender binary ensnares all. Hence, for reproductive justice to be transformational for *all* people— and not just those who are cis and gender conforming—it must include a strong critique of gender through the lens of trans* feminism of color. In the same vein, the reproductive health of BIPOC and TGNC individuals will remain precarious if health practitioners and policymakers do not account for the oppressive history and deployment of the gender binary.

Methodology and Preview of Chapters

Our methodology is informed by the RJ framework, which centers the stories and experiences of multiply marginalized people and communities. As RJ practitioners and theorists put it, personal narratives and acts of storytelling are "a vehicle for personal and social transformation."[119] The narratives and experiences of those in the margins are a valuable source of knowledge because they possess epistemic privilege: as the feminist scholar Uma Narayan notes, "Members of an oppressed group have a more immediate, subtle and critical knowledge about the nature of their oppression than people who are nonmembers of the oppressed group."[120] Such intimate embodied knowledge and lived experiences, however, are often eclipsed in mainstream political discourse dominated by powerful actors, such as policymakers, social media influencers, and prominent cultural critics. In the context of this study, we understand the narratives and experiences of trans and nonbinary parents as "counterstories" that disrupt dominant conservative discourse on gender, reproduction, and family-making.[121] We analyze a wide range of public texts to illuminate how conservative discourse on gender binaries and its insistence on upholding a cisheteronormative nuclear-family structure dehumanize trans and nonbinary people, threatening their right to parent and create families. Through interviews and by analyzing podcasts, personal narratives, and memoirs created by queer and nonbinary parents and birthworkers, we highlight the tactics and counterstories they deploy to create more inclusive reproductive spaces.

In addition to the RJ framework, our methodological approach draws on "participatory critical rhetoric."[122] Critical rhetoric, as Raymie McKerrow points out, "seeks to unmask or demystify the discourse of power."[123] In the context of reproductive health and gender justice, a critical rhetorical approach entails deep interrogation into how dominant institutions and stakeholders use health communication practices to uphold and maintain power at the expense of marginalized bodies. On the flip side, critical rhetoric also prompts us to examine how marginalized communities and individuals have, through embodied, discursive, and multimodal means, invented rhetorical practices that not only resist dehumanization and exclusion but also actively cultivate an alternative praxis of care, survival, and relating to one another. Participatory research methods center the experiences, voices, and knowledge productions of marginalized people who are most impacted by systemic injustice and hence possess the epistemic privilege necessary to critique and dismantle existing exclusionary systems.

As critical rhetoricians who deploy qualitative methods—including participant observations and semistructured interviews—we understand that we are coproducing knowledge with our research participants. A participatory approach necessitates that we see research participants as interlocutors in a dialogic knowledge-making process. In our analytic processes, we focus on "how discourse advances or stymies the interest of marginalized communities."[124] In order to reveal and examine the interconnectedness among the narratives of our research participants, the histories of reproductive (in)justice, and other systems of power and oppression (e.g., racism, misogynoir, transphobia), we contextualize and triangulate the interview data with analysis of other primary data, such as field notes from participant observations and multimodal artifacts produced by various stakeholders. Doing so allows us to highlight how stakeholders simultaneously influence and are influenced by the existing systems of power and dominant discourse on gender, race, sexuality, and reproduction.

Our selection of artifacts and analysis is guided by a participatory critical approach. It calls for an expansive archive of communicative acts and artifacts so that our critique and analysis are situated intimately with the shifting contexts, rhetors, and audiences, as well as with the relationships and dynamics among them. Reproduction, family-making, and gender are simultaneously deeply personal and intimate and provocatively public and political. The organization of our chapters reflects this complex interplay between contentious public discourse and politics and personal intimacies, situating the intimate and political rhetorical acts of health care providers and TGNC people amid dominant trans-antagonistic discourse about pregnancy, birth, and reproduction.

Our first chapter, "Networking Arguments: Gender and Reproduction in Public Discourse," examines mainstream public discourse on gender, reproduction, and family-making through an RJ framework. In the early 2020s, the proliferation of right-wing bills that threatened the rights of trans people—especially children and youth—was accompanied by the rise of transphobic discourse outside of the policy and political sphere. Such public discourse on the gender binary bolsters a conservative cisheteronormative nuclear-family structure that erases the reproductive experiences of trans and nonbinary people. In this chapter, we first situate the controversy surrounding gender-neutral language amid the transnational anti–gender ideology movement, a big-tent movement comprising right-wing populists, Christian fundamentalists, and trans-exclusive feminists. Drawing on scholarship on the rhetoric of science—particularly scientific discourse on race and gender—we analyze how biological-essentialist and anti-trans ideologies have informed discursive practices in reproductive health settings. Attacks against the use of gender-neutral terms to discuss pregnancy and birth, we demonstrate, are networked in a way that supports racist and misogynistic colonial ideologies. Anti-trans discourse, hence, not only threatens genderqueer people but also actively undermines the humanity of other marginalized people, specifically their rights to bodily autonomy, reproduction, and family-making. Contextualizing and interrogating dominant anti-trans arguments and their circulation in mainstream rhetorical ecologies, chapter 1 helps situate the rhetorical responses, inventions, and resistance of gender-inclusive birthworkers and TGNC parents.

Birthworkers such as doulas and midwives straddle the intimate, private realm of pregnancy and birth and the public sphere that is hostile and dehumanizing to TGNC parents. Hence, after foregrounding dominant anti-trans arguments in the context of reproduction, our second chapter, "Against Gender Essentialism: Reproductive Justice Doulas and Gender Inclusivity in Pregnancy and Birth Discourse,"

Introduction   31

turns to an emerging group of birthworkers whose praxis is informed by principles of reproductive justice. Specifically, we examine how RJ birthworkers navigate the simultaneously personal and political arenas of gender-inclusive birth practices. This chapter centers the voices of reproductive justice birthworkers and educators who seek to dismantle gender essentialism and other exclusionary practices in reproductive care. This chapter explores how RJ doulas support trans and nonbinary birthing people, while advancing more inclusive practices within the birth world. Drawing on rhetorical analysis of educational materials by foundational birthworkers, we begin by tracing historical changes in mainstream birth and pregnancy care to highlight how biological naturalism and woman-centered discourse became ingrained. We then draw on participant observations at two doula trainings, fifteen semistructured interviews with reproductive justice doulas, interviews with four queer birthworkers featured on the podcast *Evidence Based Birth*, seven workshops and conference panels, and educational materials on queer and trans birth created by queer-affirming birthworkers and educators. In our analysis, we illuminate how RJ doulas and educators mobilize reproductive justice principles to provide gender-affirming advocacy and inclusive care to pregnant and birthing people of all genders. We identify the key rhetorical strategies that reproductive justice doulas deploy, namely advocacy, radical inclusion, and self-reflexivity. Taken together, chapter 2 amplifies the experiences of birthworkers whose praxis challenges heteronormative assumptions about reproduction and family-making.

After examining political and health discourse on trans reproduction, as well as the interventions in birth culture made possible by reproductive justice birthworkers, we turn to the ways in which TGNC parents practice community care and resistance through public storytelling. In our third chapter, "Reimagining Family and Kin: Queer and Trans Reproductive Storytelling," we assemble and analyze a vast archive of primary materials created by TGNC parents for diverse public audiences, including cis people and other TGNC people and parents. These artifacts highlight the radical reimaginings of family and kinship that TGNC people engage in outside of exclusionary gen-

32   *Doing Gender Justice*

der norms. Continuing to navigate the simultaneously public, political, and intimate nature of gender and birth, we focus on artifacts that communicate TGNC reproductive experiences to the public, countering mainstream trans-antagonistic discourse while cultivating communal care among TGNC people. The texts we analyze range from Thomas Beatie's memoir, *Labor of Love*, to more recent publications such as A. K. Summers's graphic novel *Pregnant Butch*, Trevor MacDonald's *Where's the Mother?*, and Krys Malcom Belc's *The Natural Mother of the Child*. In addition, we also examine documentaries on TGNC birth experiences that target a public audience, such as the critically acclaimed *Seahorse* and *A Womb of Their Own*. While these works represent a recent expansion of narratives about queer and trans pregnancy and parenting, most are authored by white people, which reflects the multiple marginalization that queer people of color experience in mainstream contexts. We thus supplement our analysis of texts and films published in more mainstream outlets with podcasts created by and for TGNC parents and with other public narratives by queer people of color to uplift their experiences and inventions. Drawing upon Shui-yin Sharon Yam's concept of deliberative empathy and Aja Martinez's work on counterstory, we explore how TGNC storytellers utilize distinct rhetorical strategies to address specific audiences and exigencies. In addition to narrative strategies that normalize TGNC reproduction to claim social and political inclusion, TGNC storytellers also adopt strategies of deliberative empathy to prompt the possibility of political solidarity with mainstream audiences and embrace counterstory to challenge and rewrite dominant configurations of kin. Our analysis amplifies the myriad practices embraced by gender-expansive families to queer reproduction, family-making, and kinship in ways that offer new modes of gender, belonging, and community care.

The conclusion is exploratory by nature. In it, we consider the stakes of this study for scholars of communication, health care providers, TGNC birthing people and parents, and the movement for reproductive justice writ large. We identify creative rhetorical strategies of inclusion and redress that have emerged across chapters 2 and 3, considering how each strategy might begin to address significant reproductive health care disparities between cis and trans communities. We query: How are reproductive justice and queer-positive providers shaping better health-care practices for TGNC parents and queer families? How do these strategies offer expansive enactments of the rich possibilities—both interpersonal and political—of queer kin? What might scholars and activists learn from TGNC storytellers about rhetorical strategies that foster coalition and the possibility of shifting dominant narratives? In this concluding chapter, we identify the most promising trajectories that allow us as scholars and activists to speak of a reproductive justice that accurately reflects our histories of struggle while articulating a vision for a future that is both just and gender expansive.

CHAPTER ONE

Networking Arguments

Gender and Reproduction in Public Discourse

———————

IN 2023, TRANS antagonism reached a boiling point when a record number of anti-LGBTQ+ bills were introduced across the United States, targeting primarily trans youths. At the time of this writing, there are 467 anti-LGBTQ+ bills, many of which prohibit trans people from accessing gender-affirming health care, using bathrooms that match their gender identity, and participating in sports and other school activities.[1] While these bills, introduced right on the heels of the *Dobbs v. Jackson Women's Health Organization* decision, signaled a heightened moment of intense vitriol and surveillance against trans and gender-nonconforming (TGNC) people and women, state-sponsored attacks on reproduction, gender, and bodily autonomy had been brewing for several years. In 2021, Representative Cori Bush came under fire for "smearing bio-women and virtue signaling trans women" when she used the term "Black birthing people"—along with gendered terms like "Black mothers" and "Black women"—to highlight the racial disparities in pregnancy and birth outcomes.[2] In early 2022, several GOP senators refused to support the historic nomination of Ketanji Brown Jackson to the US Supreme Court over concerns that she would not define *woman* in biological terms.[3] Later that year, testifying on the racial injury the *Dobbs v. Jackson* decision had inflicted,

Khiara Bridges, a law professor and reproductive justice (RJ) activist at the University of California, Berkeley, challenged Senator Josh Hawley for insisting that only women could be pregnant, calling his line of questioning "transphobic." She was described by right-wing outlets as hysterical and nonsensical.[4]

While abortion access and trans justice are intricately connected on the basis of bodily autonomy and reproductive freedom, not all abortion rights advocates support the use of gender-neutral language. Over the past few years, feminist activists have passionately disagreed on whether it is more ethical and politically efficacious for reproductive rights organizations to use woman-centered or gender-neutral language when discussing abortion care or when challenging restrictive abortion laws.[5] Editorials in mainstream media outlets outline the contour of this debate. For example, the *New York Times* published an article referring to *women* as a "vanishing word in [the] abortion debate" and declaring that "today, 'pregnant people' and 'birthing people' have elbowed aside 'pregnant women.'"[6] Amid broader public discourse on reproduction, including on birth and pregnancy, similar arguments have appeared in *The Atlantic*, *The Economist*, *New Statesman*, and *The Times*.[7] The consistent claim here is that gender-neutral language in reproductive health unfairly marginalizes, or worse, erases cis women.

Outrage against gender-neutral language, hence, betrays people's rigid adherence to biological essentialism and their expectation that biological sex and gender are natural and should always align with the binary model. These beliefs are common among what researchers call the "anti-gender movement," which we will discuss in greater detail later in this chapter.[8] We argue that anti-gender and anti-trans logics are networked with nonintersectional white feminism,[9] which sees sex-based oppression against cis women as the most extreme form of oppression, regardless of other social factors and privileges. As such, anti-trans and anti-gender arguments perpetuate both gender and racial violence against marginalized bodies.

This chapter traces public discourse and arguments against the use of gender-neutral language in reproductive politics. In addition to analyzing the tension in using gender-neutral language in health care settings, we also analyze popular anti-trans texts such as Abigail Shrier's *Irreversible Damage* and discuss her appearance on Joe Rogan's podcast—which at the time of writing, boasts 14.9 million subscribers—to demonstrate that this discursive tension is intimately connected to ideological struggles over gender in the broader public sphere, such as the demonization of critical gender studies in schools and the passage of anti-trans policies that specifically harm trans children and youths. An intersectional approach demands that we interrogate the current and historical forces and ideologies that sustain such a fervent commitment to biological essentialism and dimorphic sex/gender alignment. To do so, we read current anti-trans and anti-gender discourse through the lens of critical feminist and gender studies, which highlights how the binary gender/sex system was constructed by white colonizers to dehumanize colonized subjects and people of color.[10] In this framework, white women were touted as the moralizing and civilizing agents of the nation to correct against sexually deviant colonized subjects.[11] This dynamic, as we will demonstrate in this chapter, continues to echo in more contemporary contexts on gender.

The goal of this chapter is twofold: first, to contextualize and critique the ways in which trans-antagonistic ideologies circulate in reproductive health and public discourse so that activists and health care providers and communicators will be better equipped to identify and strategize against insidious anti-trans arguments; and second, to amplify the discursive practices of gender-inclusive reproductive health care providers and activists. The second point makes clear that providing trans-inclusive reproductive care *does not* come at the expense of cis women's rights and welfare but is rather concomitant with it. To do so, we interrogate the common rhetorical strategies anti-gender actors deploy to undermine and dehumanize trans people—some of these strategies tarnish the coalitional potential between cis women and TGNC people by falsely pitting their interests against one another's. While mainstream media outlets—outlets that reflect and are compatible with dominant social imaginaries and ideologies—tend to focus on the bombastic narratives of anti-trans lawmakers and com-

Networking Arguments   37

mentators, we amplify and analyze the languaging strategies proffered by trans-inclusive reproductive health providers and activists who see trans justice as inseparable from reproductive justice. By doing so, we showcase how seemingly disparate public arguments against the use of gender-neutral language in pregnancy and birth care do in fact cohere around anti-gender logics.

After elucidating our critical methodology, we will examine the broader rhetorical context before zooming in to analyze specific primary artifacts in the debates on gender-neutral and woman-centered language in pregnancy and birth discourse. Since debates surrounding language use and gender are intricately connected to the transnational anti-gender movement, we will catalog the rhetorical strategies and narratives commonly deployed by anti-gender actors to undermine the existence of trans and nonbinary people. We argue that anti-gender discourse and ideologies not only harm trans, nonbinary, and genderqueer people but are also often networked with racist, ableist, sexist, and right-wing praxes that uphold a white supremacist patriarchal structure.

After reviewing the common tactics deployed by anti-gender actors, we examine the controversy and approaches surrounding the use of gendered language in reproductive health, focusing especially on birth and pregnancy since they hinge upon the conservative ideal of upholding the cisheteronormative nuclear family. We analyze how anti-genderists repurposed debates about the use of gender-neutral language in reproductive health care to support a deeply essentialist understanding of womanhood as one that must involve reproduction and mothering. We argue that while anti-trans activists frequently describe themselves as "protecting the children" by refuting gender-affirming care and education for youths, their objects of protection were in fact the white, cisheteronormative framework of the nuclear family and the gender norms that relegate girls and women only to reproductive labor. Hence, we argue that criticisms against the use of gender-neutral language function more as a Trojan horse that popularizes anti-gender and anti-trans logics that harms not only TGNC people but also BIPOC, cis women, and other nonnormative bodies. Most insidiously, this controversy undermines the coalitional networks between trans justice and reproductive justice, hindering an advocacy framework that is truly inclusive and transformative.

In the final section, we examine gender-inclusive approaches to language enacted by health care providers, researchers, and birthworkers who are on the forefront of reproductive care. Specifically, we highlight the *additive approach to language* they adopt to acknowledge the wide range of bodies, experiences, and identities pregnant and birthing people possess. Their efforts, however, are commonly misconstrued in public discourse as an attempt to erase women from reproductive discourse. As this discussion enters the broader public sphere, it becomes a flash point, generating outrage, confusion, and anxiety about gender and reproduction. We argue that these public emotions not only highlight the ideological stronghold of the gender binary and biological essentialism but also signal a rupture in the status quo—an opening for activists and researchers to imagine and enact a trans-inclusive language model of reproductive justice.

We organize this chapter in this way—first foregrounding the anti-gender movement and common trans-antagonistic arguments before spotlighting gender-inclusive approaches to reproductive language—to contextualize the networked anti-trans forces TGNC parents and gender-inclusive health care providers and activists are up against. By first analyzing and challenging transphobic arguments that circulate both in mainstream public discourse and in reproductive medical discourse, we highlight the affective stronghold such texts and arguments have created to reinforce existing ideologies and sentiments at the confluence of gender essentialism, cisnormativity, and reproduction. Hence, the additive approach to language alone is necessary but insufficient for combatting anti-trans arguments and ideologies that have been networked with anti-Blackness and white supremacy. As we will demonstrate in the chapters that follow, TGNC parents and RJ health care workers and activists engage in complementary forms of queer care, narrativization, and relationality to make life more liv-

Networking Arguments   39

able and joyous for TGNC parents. By doing so, they resist dominant logics and institutional practices that render their desires and families illegitimate and as somehow unworthy of recognition or care.

Critical Methodology and Rhetorical Analysis

Our methodology and analytical process are deeply informed by the praxis of critical rhetoric, as a rich tradition of inquiry committed to "naming and meditating on the rhetorical mechanisms through which power itself is produced."[12] Coined by Raymie McKerrow to illuminate the discursive dimensions of power alongside available modes of challenge and critique, critical rhetoric is a remarkably elastic and useful praxis in justice-oriented scholarship on race and gender.[13] Scholars such as Karma Chávez, Lisa Flores, Darrel Enck-Wanzer, V. Jo Hsu, Tamika Carey, GPat Patterson, and Leland Spencer—to name a few—have deployed critical rhetoric to interrogate the ways in which non-white queer bodies are racialized, gendered, and disciplined by dominant discourse and ideologies. At the same time, their research has also demonstrated how marginalized rhetors engage in meaning-making practices and forms of relations that directly or obliquely undermine the dominant discursive structure.[14] As we illustrate in the introductory chapter, the co-construction of gender and race has historically been a discursive and political project used to uphold structures of white supremacy, coloniality, patriarchy, and hetero- and cisnormativity. Insidiously, race and gender have often been naturalized as if they were indisputable biological facts in public and medical discourse in ways that conceal the oppressive ideological forces that animate such constructions.

Adopting a critical approach to rhetorical analysis, we seek to critique and make explicit the ways popular and seemingly credible texts perpetuate and intensify racist and transphobic ideologies in the public sphere. We analyze texts that have been widely circulated across media to a high number of audiences because, penned and/or endorsed by public figures and media outlets that possess a great deal of political and cultural capital, these artifacts are immensely powerful in influencing public views, institutional practices, and legislation on gender and reproduction. It is, hence, important for communication scholars to interrogate and challenge how these actors and artifacts mobilize language with material consequences. Informed by critical rhetoric's activist orientation, our analytical goal is to provide diverse audiences—reproductive and trans justice activists, marginalized birthing and pregnant people, health care providers, for instance—with deep contextual knowledge on how transphobic ideologies permeate and circulate in mainstream reproductive discourse. We also aim to provide discursive tactics to effect change and promote what Walter Mignolo calls "an other thinking" that delinks birth and pregnancy care from oppressive constructions of gender.[15]

The Anti-gender Ideology Movement

The anti-gender ideology movement represents a recent flashpoint in what are often referred to as the "culture wars"—public struggles that animate long-standing moral panics over race, gender, sex, and sexuality. James Davison Hunter, who coined the term "culture wars" in 1991, notes that for most of US history, religious differences informed the deepest chasms in American society. The 1960s was a turning point: "As America became more culturally diverse, the Protestant consensus gave way to a Christian consensus, and later a 'Judeo-Christian' one."[16] In the wake of mid-twentieth-century movements like civil rights and feminism, issues such as abortion, prayer in school, sex education, and the teaching of America's colonial and white supremacist history captured public attention and upended traditional political divides. In lieu of divisions between religious communities, Evangelicals aligned with conservative Catholics and Jewish communities on the right as progressive secular and faith-based communities consolidated on the left.[17] The concept of the culture wars entered mainstream vernacular during the Republican National Convention in 1992, where Pat Buchanan famously declared, "There is a religious war going on in this country. It is a cultural war, as critical to the kind of nation we shall be as the Cold War itself, for this war is for the soul of America."[18] At that time, the Cold War was officially over. National security efforts—such as military weapons and surveillance—were re-

Networking Arguments   41

directed internally to control minority communities.[19] The Culture War itself, hence, is deeply rooted in white nationalism and needs to be understood as such.

The anti-gender movement is broadly acknowledged as the most recent instantiation of mainstream US culture wars. The points of conflict have shifted over time, but they tend to coalesce around matters that are perceived as threatening to the status quo and that reanimate moral panics over gender, race, sex, and sexuality.[20] In the early 2000s, for example, the popularity of father-daughter purity balls and abstinence pledges surged in conservative communities across the United States as sex education, the availability of emergency contraception, young motherhood, and the HPV vaccine prompted rancorous political debate.[21] These panics over sexual "purity" were compounded by cultural anxieties over queer sexualities and "threats" to the traditional family, expressed overtly in the state constitutional bans on gay marriage that swept the nation in the 2004 election cycle. In the late 2010s to early 2020s, right-wing Christian organizations such as Alliance Defending Freedom, Family Research Council, the American Center for Law and Justice, the Heritage Foundation, and the Council for National Policy orchestrated concerted legal, political, and cultural efforts to promote anti-trans legislation and campaigns that demonize trans and gender-nonconforming people as contaminants and threats to children.[22] More recently, as conservative politicians attempt to ban books from public school curricula and bar educators from teaching a fuller account of US history, the rights of trans people—from using public bathrooms to participating in girls' sports— have come under fire, assembling an unlikely coalition of conservative lawmakers and self-professed "gender-critical" feminists along the way.[23]

As scholars of reproductive politics, we understand these culture wars as rooted in a much longer lineage of struggle—one preoccupied with exerting control over pregnancy and reproduction to determine the future of the nation (see the introduction). Motherhood endures in dominant US imaginaries as a vehicle for the nation writ large. While the particularities of idealized motherhood tend to shift in ac-

42   *Doing Gender Justice*

cordance with dominant cultural values and norms—see, for example, the nineteenth-century cult of domesticity or the postwar suburban housewife—they remain consistently tethered to biological essentialism, a rigid sex/gender binary, compulsory heterosexuality, and white middle-class identity. In this way, the mythic maternal ideal has long shaped reproduction according to a narrow vision of a white Christian nation—hemming in the aspirations of cisgender white women while, at the same time, fueling reproductive violence against those who occupy its constitutive outside. Powerful tropes such as the "teen mom" and the "welfare queen" have pathologized those who parent outside of whiteness, marriage, and/or wealth, justifying the destruction of marginalized families through stigma, deprivation of resources, child removal, eugenic sterilization, and population control. Significantly, the most recent wave of anti-trans legislative violence coincides with widespread assaults on reproductive autonomy and education censorship against critical race theory (CRT) and LGBTQ+ issues, each pivoting on hackneyed arguments about white purity and virtue, the sanctity of the heteronuclear family, and the need to protect the innocence of white (and ostensibly gender-conforming and heterosexual) children. Chris Barcelos refers to this set of interconnected legislations as a "gendered racial project . . . that uphold[s] white supremacy, normative gender, and heterosexuality."[24] Antiabortion, anti-trans, anti-LGBTQ+, and anti-CRT legislations share the same ideological and political root: while anti-CRT legislations are overtly racist and anti-Black, the proponents of anti-trans and antiabortion policies both evoke the white supremacist "great replacement theory" to justify their stance.[25] For white supremacists, controlling the reproductive autonomy of white girls, cisgender women, and trans and nonbinary people is imperative to replenishing a white nation.[26] In short, the undercurrent of this particular moment in the so-called culture wars is deeply indebted to long-standing efforts to police motherhood in service of a white supremacist vision of nation.

Contextualizing and historicizing the transnational anti-gender movement in this way is necessary to understanding how anti-trans arguments are networked with other dehumanizing ideologies. As

Graeme Reid from Human Rights Watch opined, "The anti-gender movement has successfully consolidated disparate constituencies around a flimsy but effective moral panic over gender and sexuality" to attack comprehensive reproductive care, LGBTQ+ rights, and gender justice.[27] Since anti-gender activists often deploy similar rhetorical strategies and narratives to undermine the existence and humanity of trans and nonbinary people,[28] an understanding of the anti-gender movement is also crucial in unpacking the "depravity narratives" and "God terms" commonly deployed by anti-trans activists.[29]

The anti-gender movement consists of various right-wing actors, loosely configured against LGBTQ+ rights, feminism, and reproductive rights (to name a few) but largely united in opposition to what they refer to as *gender ideology*. The concept of gender ideology was originally developed by the Vatican, Catholic scholars, and conservative activists in the 1990s and then later deployed in mainstream public discourse that continues to garner the support of activists from a wide range of ideological positions.[30] The term is used to refer to "a set of notions revolving around the idea of radical 'gender feminists' and the homosexual [*sic*] agenda advancing an idea that dismisses the *natural* order of things (i.e. the natural hierarchy of men and women, for instance), which in pushing for individual identity over social expectations undermines the anthropological basis of the family, and, therefore, society."[31] As Judith Butler points out, in the context of transnational anti-gender movements, "gender is understood as a single 'ideology' that refutes the reality of sexual difference and that seeks to appropriate the divine power of creation for those who wish to create their own genders."[32] Under the guise of protecting the sanctity of the nuclear family and the "natural order," the anti-gender movement constructed *gender* as a unifying threat that brings together religious conservatives, right-wing think tanks, white supremacists, and anti-Muslim and anti-immigrant groups.[33]

As a floating signifier, *gender ideology* functions as a "symbolic glue" that has mobilized people from different positionalities and from different nation-states to challenge progressive social causes and protest against the perceived decline of cishet white patriarchy and nationalism.[34] The sociologists Roman Kuhar and David Paternotte observe that as an umbrella term, *gender ideology* unites actors across their differences by positing gender / gender ideology as an attack on "at least one of the three Ns" they want to defend: "nature, the nation, or normality."[35] In this framework, racial, gender, sexual, and economic hierarchies are seen not only as natural but also as the cornerstone of a white supremacist and patriarchal nation-state. The anti-gender movement, hence, must be understood as a transnational coalitional movement that networks together racist, ableist, misogynist, anti-immigrant, and trans- and homophobic ideologies. For example, Mark Gevisser explains that in the anti-gender movements in Russia, Poland, and Hungary, homophobia in public is seen as a performance of national identity against migrants and open-border policies.[36] As the researchers Damjan Denkovski, Nina Bernarding, and Kristina Lunz point out, the anti-gender movement may be less about opposing *gender* per se and more about "advanc(ing) alternative value systems to maintain existing power dynamics" so that those who are already marginalized will continue to be so, perhaps to an even greater extent.[37] In the US context, the anti-gender movement is funded largely by right-wing Christian fundamentalist groups that seek to promote a patriarchal white nation.[38]

While anti-gender campaigns are not new, researchers theorize that the rise of transnational anti-gender movements, most visible in Europe, Latin America, and increasingly the United States, is connected to the general shrinkage of civil societies, the decline in academic freedom, the passage of repressive laws, and the erosion of state protection over civil liberties.[39] As repressive laws are copied and deployed across borders to threaten the freedom of women, LGBTQ+ people, people of color, immigrants, and other minoritized communities, researchers have observed a proliferation of actors, including state governments, that are forming an increasingly organized transnational network.[40] While *Doing Gender Justice* examines popular anti-gender discourse only in the United States, this context is important because it reminds us that what we observe and analyze domestically is a transnational phenomenon influenced by forces and organizations

Networking Arguments   45

that are not immediately visible. Further, the transnational nature of the anti-gender movement highlights the potential ripple effects US anti-trans discourse and policies could have in other nation-states.

As a decentralized movement organized under an umbrella term, the anti-gender movement is made up of different actors. Researchers have identified close connections and "opportunistic synergy" between the anti-gender movement and right-wing populists.[41] While they may form coalitions, the two groups do not overlap entirely and are not subsumed by one another. For instance, right-wing populists in Europe have eschewed anti-gender discourse in favor of homonationalist language and what Sara R. Farris terms "femonationalist" language to mainstream white women and white gay men while violently racializing and excluding immigrants.[42] In addition to powerful long-established actors such as the Catholic Church, right-wing think tanks, and public interest law firms (e.g., the Heritage Foundation and the Alliance Defending Freedom in the United States), the anti-gender movement is also supported by allies that include political commentators, academics, policymakers, journalists, and media outlets.[43]

Not all allies and actors associated with the anti-gender movement identify as right wing. Nevertheless, by platforming and supporting anti-gender discourse and ideologies, those allies form an important part of the rhetorical ecology that sustains oppressive notions of gender, sex, race, and reproduction. Identifying allies of the anti-gender movement—especially those who are not immediately apparent—is key because anti-gender campaigns frequently form coalitions with medical providers and self-proclaimed feminist activists and scholars who are trans-exclusionary.[44] For example, in 2019, the Heritage Foundation hosted two panel discussions that, respectively, featured trans-exclusionary feminists and medical providers to oppose trans rights and gender-affirming care for trans youths.[45] Under the guise of being "pro-woman," trans-exclusionary lesbian activists have also networked with the anti-trans American College of Pediatricians (ACP) and right-wing think tank Family Research Council to promote pseudoscientific claims about biological sex and the gender binary.[46]

In addition, attacks on gender-affirming health care for trans youths have been fueled by 4thWaveNow, an online community started by Denise Caignon, "a left-leaning parent who is critical of the dominant paradigm regarding transgender politics and treatment."[47] The group has played a pivotal role in promoting the pseudoscientific claim that transgender youths are victims of social contagion; this erroneous belief, in turn, delegitimizes gender-affirming support and health care for trans youths.[48] As the trans activist and journalist Imara Jones has found, this group has attracted liberal parents who are uncomfortable with their children's trans identity and who subsequently delay or deny gender-affirming care for their children.[49] Despite the harm pseudoscience and mis/disinformation has caused to trans youths, liberal journalists and media outlets such as the *New York Times* and *The Atlantic* have amplified anti-trans beliefs and medical practices that go against the recommendations of major medical associations, global health authorities, gender-affirming health care providers, and the lived experiences of trans people themselves.[50] These articles, in turn, are cited by right-wing media and lawmakers to justify the need for anti-trans legislation.[51] These connections illustrate the insidiousness of transphobia, specifically how it has been networked across different institutions and actors, even as it is met with strong opposition rooted in medical expertise.

Common Anti-gender Arguments

Anti-gender campaigns and their allied actors often deploy similar narratives and rhetorical strategies to undermine not only LGBTQ+ rights but also assisted comprehensive sex education, the right to abortion, and the use of reproductive technologies.[52] Anti-gender ideologies, hence, threaten reproductive justice on multiple fronts. Given the decentralized and coalitional nature of the anti-gender movement, recognizing such discursive patterns is useful in detecting how, when, and where anti-gender rhetorics are deployed across contexts.

Pseudoscientific and Naturalistic Claims. Researchers have identified a set of narratives that anti-gender actors commonly mobilize transnationally,[53] several of which are particularly pertinent to our analysis of public discourse and policies in the United States. First, anti-gender actors frequently appeal to naturalistic claims about gender, family, and reproduction. In this narrative, dimorphic biological sex is seen as natural and the sole determinant of one's gender; men and women are, by nature and by biology, irrevocably different, and women are defined by their reproductive capacity and their inherent connections to motherhood.[54] Though not always, naturalistic arguments are often linked to religious narratives about protecting a "natural and traditional social order" in which legitimate families must consist of a father, mother, and children.[55] Gender and feminism, on the other hand, are represented as going against the natural order designed by God.

In more secular circles, the naturalistic narrative is supported not by evoking God and religion but by appealing to science.[56] To support anti-trans ideologies, trans-exclusionary activists often reference dimorphic biological sexes as a scientific fact to add legitimacy to their belief. The wave of anti-trans policies and discourse in the United States, for instance, is supported by the argument that dimorphic biological sex is a *scientific fact* and gender is not; hence, a trans or genderqueer person's gender identity should not be recognized.[57] This narrative was mobilized by the Trump administration in an attempt to revise the definition of gender and sex under Title IX. The draft memo notes that gender should be determined "on a biological basis that is clear, grounded in science, objective and administrable."[58] The memo further defines sex as either male or female, "based on immutable biological traits identifiable by or before birth."[59] In a position statement, the ACP, a right-wing pseudoscientific advocacy group of pediatricians and health care professionals, similarly dismisses the gender identity of trans youths as grounded in "unscientific gender ideology."[60] Despite a wealth of scientific research and general consensus among scientists that challenges the assumption of biological sex as dimorphic, unchanging, and easily determined by one's chromosomes or genitals, anti-gender actors continue to mobilize the authority of science to give legitimacy to their anti-trans ideologies and policy proposals.[61]

Contrary to scientific findings that biological sex is a spectrum, anti-gender activists have also repeatedly argued that binary biological sex is a scientific fact to deny the existence of trans people and ridicule their allies.[62] This argument is effective because most people are taught in school a simplistic version of biological sex: that sex is determined by either XX or XY chromosomes and made evident by dimorphic and unambiguous genitalia. Other biological, environmental, and social factors that influence one's sex hormones and sex development—which is to say nothing of the variety of chromosomal structures—are often not taught in school.[63] Hence, by appealing to what appears to be common sense, anti-gender actors are able to invalidate the existence of trans people with an air of authority. The evocation of science to support the sex/gender binary echoes the waves of widely criticized racial science that purport to have found a biological basis for race, a decidedly political category.[64] Given the colonial history behind the constructions of gender and racial categories, the insistence that race and gender both have a stable biological basis serves to uphold a cis white patriarchal system and epistemology that dehumanizes genderqueer people and people of color.

In addition to peddling the sex/gender binary as if it were a biological fact, anti-trans actors also deploy pseudoscience to discredit and limit the access of gender-affirming care to trans youths. In 2018, Lisa Littman, a physician-researcher, published an article on what she coins "rapid onset gender dysphoria" (ROGD). Using survey data from parents who are distraught about their teens' trans identity, Littman posits that trans identity among youths is a social contagion spread through social media and internet use.[65] Researchers and trans activists have criticized Littman for her faulty research method: rather than surveying or interviewing trans youths, Littman distributed surveys to parents of trans children through three anti-trans online communities (4thWaveNow, Transgender Trend, and the now defunct Youth Trans Critical Professionals).[66] This narrow and biased sampling, along with other statistical and analytical errors identified by Arjee Javellana Restar and other researchers, renders Littman's findings specious at best.[67] Despite these criticisms, anti-trans parents, lawmakers, and

Networking Arguments   49

political commentators have repeatedly invoked the concept of ROGD as a scientific argument against gender-affirming care for trans youths.[68] Other researchers have criticized Littman for citing flawed desistance research to prove that 60% to 90% of gender-dysphoric children will grow up to be cis.[69] The outsized focus on pseudoscientific desistance research, queer trans activists point out, echoes earlier claims made to support conversion therapy for gay people, which has caused a great deal of lasting harm.[70]

Mobilization of Public Fear and Anger. Anti-gender arguments frequently evoke the innocent child figure to generate public fear. Right-wing politicians and other anti-gender actors have long used "protect/save the children" as a rallying call to mobilize the public against comprehensive gender, sex, and sexuality education.[71] In this narrative, LGBTQ+ people and their allies are vilified as sexually depraved and predatory toward impressionable children.[72] The rise of the Twitter account Libs of TikTok in early 2022 is a key example. With more than 1.3 million followers as of June 2022, the account reposts and denigrates TikTok videos and other social media posts from LGBTQ+ people and allies to generate anger and fear among viewers. LGBTQ+ people and educators who talk about gender identities and sexualities are called "predators" and are accused of "grooming" unsuspecting children into "gender identity radicals."[73] Circulated and amplified by popular right-wing media, such as Joe Rogan's podcast and Tucker Carlson's TV show, the argument that children are in danger from the teaching of gender has gained a lot of valence, influencing the public to fear gender as a concept. The mobilization of public outrage and fear is networked with the final strategy anti-gender actors commonly deploy: the invocation of competing rights.

Invocation of Competing Rights. This narrative suggests that since other inalienable rights are currently under threat by promoters of gender ideology, anti-gender policies and ideologies are necessary to protect such rights. For example, in Florida, parental rights are invoked to legally prohibit classroom teaching on sexuality and gender identity. Anti-gender actors argue that without the law, parents would lose the right to decide what, how, and when their children learn about gender.

The invocation of parental rights is made powerful because collective outrage and fear toward gender education has already been stoked in the public's affective economy.[74] The invocation of parental rights and the mobilization of fear and moral panic are not unique to gender. Parental rights bills and conservative advocacy surrounding parental rights prohibit teachers from teaching not only about gender and sexuality but also about race and racism—or what the right broadly refers to as "critical race theory."[75] Anti-gender ideology and advocacy, in other words, are intricately connected with racism and the protection of a cishet white supremacist structure. The trans scholar V. Jo Hsu uses *affective drift* to identify "how rhetoric can channel affect associated with one topic or ground toward another. Relying on affective associations rather than explicit reasoning, affective drift can recruit allies through a felt—even if imagined—shared enemy."[76] In this context, anti-gender and anti-CRT activists are both mobilized by "a pervasive sense of persecution" because teachings about gender and racial justice unsettle existing systems of power, structural privilege, and conservative ideology.

In addition to parental rights, anti-gender actors also invoke freedom of speech and freedom from censorship when they are criticized by feminist and queer scholars, activists, and commentators. Abigail Shrier, a well-known journalist who promotes the anti-trans concept of ROGD through her popular book *Irreversible Damage: The Transgender Craze Seducing Our Daughters*, argues that she is being canceled, suppressed, and censored by mainstream media and big tech.[77] Other famous libertarian and right-wing anti-gender actors support Shrier's claim that criticisms against her book signal "the ongoing death of free speech."[78] Such claims about censorship and suppression are misleading, as *Irreversible Damage* was named by *The Economist* as one of the best books of 2020, and it topped Amazon's sales list, ranking number one in the categories Transgender Studies and LGBTQ+ Political Issues, "despite (or perhaps because of) its actively transantagonistic stance."[79] Whether it is parental rights or the freedom of

Networking Arguments   51

speech, at the core of the invocation of competing rights is the belief that the rights and comfort of anti-gender actors trump the rights of trans and nonbinary people to exist and be respected on their own terms.

The invocation of competing rights is insidious because it tarnishes the coalitional potential among different actors—for example, trans-inclusive reproductive justice activists and women's rights activists. Trans-exclusionary feminists frequently argue that trans and nonbinary inclusivity infringes on women's rights. For example, in an op-ed published by the *New York Times* soon after the overturning of *Roe v. Wade*, the columnist Pamela Paul cites activism by progressive reproductive justice and trans activists as causing "moral harm" to the women's rights movement, in part by erasing "women as a biological category."[80] In a stunning false equivalency, and in lieu of focusing on far-right ideologies that propel the antiabortion movement, Paul argues that by insisting on gender-neutral language, progressive activists are just as responsible as the right for marginalizing women. Paul's argument echoes claims made by other trans-exclusionary scholars, such as Janice Raymond and Kathleen Stock, who network the binary naturalistic view about sex/gender with the narrative that trans inclusion is not only incompatible with but also a direct threat to women's rights and freedom of speech.[81] By framing women's rights and trans inclusivity as mutually exclusive, anti-gender actors—including those who identify as politically liberal—create division rather than coalition. Intersectional feminists and women-of-color activists have rightly criticized this narrative as prioritizing white cis women over the experiences and humanity of others.[82] As Khiara Bridges and Chase Strangio poignantly argue, those who refuse to overcome the narrowness of gendered language betray their proximity to power and their self-interest in upholding the current system of power.[83] The RJ framework of organizing has shown that to accomplish reproductive freedom for all, we need a radically intersectional and coalitional model, not one that centers only a specific group of people.

As demonstrated above, anti-gender arguments rarely function on their own. Rather, they are often mobilized simultaneously and networked with one another to generate public outrage, fear, and resentment against LGBTQ+ people and people of color—especially trans and Black people. As Hsu poignantly articulates, "Trans liberation is inseparable from futures where BIPOC (Black, Indigenous, and People of Color), queer folks, and disabled people can live more freely."[84] In the context of reproduction, people from marginalized communities are all marked as unfit parents or as active threats against the cishet ideal of the white Christian nuclear family. Hence, when anti-gender arguments are mobilized in the context of reproductive care, they harm not only trans and nonbinary people but also anyone who is deemed to be outside the dominant national imaginary.

Anti-gender Logics in Pregnancy, Birth, and Postpartum Care

While debates over gender-neutral language have only recently migrated to mainstream public discourse, these conversations have been unfolding in reproductive health care and politics for well over a decade. Health care providers, movement leaders, activists, and community birthworkers have engaged in deep internal discussions, at times heated, on the increased use of gender-neutral language to capture the diversity of those seeking reproductive care. Overlapping controversies surrounding language use revolve around pregnancy and birth and around abortion care and advocacy. Certain reproductive clinics and birthworkers advocating for an additive approach—using both gender-neutral and woman-centered language to accommodate a wider range of experiences. This, however, has not stopped critics from calling the move toward gender inclusivity impractical, misogynistic, and demeaning to women. By analyzing the arguments about gender-neutral language in reproductive health care settings, we can see how anti-gender ideologies and assumptions about what constitutes "natural" come to bear in determining whether pregnancy, birth, and abortion care will be gender inclusive and affirming to all. In this section, we analyze how opponents of gender-inclusive practices deploy anti-gender rhetorical tactics to attack gender-neutral language as censorship and a violation of (cis) women's rights. We demonstrate

Networking Arguments   53

that by insisting on the cis white framework of the gender/sex binary, anti-gender actors are not only threatening trans and nonbinary people's right to self-determination but also actively traversing in logics of anti-Blackness and racism.

In both the US and the UK, the usage of gender-neutral language in public discourse and health care settings—even when it is supplemented with woman-centered language—has drawn the ire of anti-trans actors and people who subscribe strongly to biological essentialism. For example, when discussing the Ministerial and Other Maternity Allowances Bill, Baroness Hayman, a member of the House of Lords of the United Kingdom, criticized gender-neutral terms as "an awkward and ugly distortion of the English language and an affront to *common sense.*"[85] In the same debate, Lord Hunt called the introduction of gender-neutral terms in health care settings "inelegant" and "absolute nonsense" and said they "do not seem to add to what we understand as good English."[86] In the United States, Representative Cori Bush was attacked and mocked by conservative lawmakers and political commentators for using both gendered and gender-neutral language to discuss racial disparities in pregnancy-related deaths.[87] While the criticisms traverse two different countries, the arguments made against gender-neutral terms are similar: the language demeans or erases women—especially mothers—in the realm of reproduction. Implicit in these arguments is a set of anti-gender assumptions which we will analyze below. Health researchers and medical providers from different countries have also deployed similar anti-gender arguments to disprove the use of gender-neutral language in birth and pregnancy care. Their research has gained traction among mainstream news media transnationally. The anti-gender stance among health researchers and medical providers has detrimental effects on trans and nonbinary parents, especially when the US right wing is gaining traction in passing bills that, in Louise Melling's words, attempt to "obliterate transgender people."[88]

Given the harm such marginalizing health communication could inflict on all pregnant and birthing people, we now analyze a representative anecdote to interrogate how anti-gender arguments are deployed in health contexts and offer critiques that would lead to a more inclusive reproductive health environment. In February 2022, a group of ten health researchers from Australia, the US, the UK, India, Vietnam, and Sweden coauthored a peer-reviewed article that asserted "the importance of sexed language" and claimed that using gender-neutral language—including the additive approach—is dehumanizing, exclusionary, confusing, and detrimental to mothers.[89] We analyze this article closely because it has been circulated widely and discussed in a positive light by news media such as the conservative US outlet *The Hill*, Australia's *Sydney Morning Herald*, and the UK's *The Guardian* and BBC *Woman's Hour*. In an op-ed published in the *New York Times*, the article is cited as evidence that gender-neutral language undermines women's rights, especially in the wake of the overturning of *Roe v. Wade*.[90] Although this article is published in the Opinion section of a health science journal, news outlets report it as research findings by health experts, further giving anti-gender arguments the valence of scientific authority. In addition to the article's transnational reach in the rhetorical ecology on gender, language, and reproductive care, its arguments are very similar to those made elsewhere by anti-gender cultural and political commentators. By unpacking this set of arguments and viewing them through a rhetorical lens, we reveal how scientific and public health discourse can be made complicit in promoting anti-gender ideologies.

Rhetoricians of science have long argued that science writing is rhetorical in the sense that its assertions are *not* stable, objective facts but rather are attempts to persuade the audience.[91] Philip Wander thus argues that scientific and rhetorical discourses "cannot be distinguished structurally."[92] Scientific discourse has always been intimately connected to the existing dominant cultural concepts and ideologies.[93] In Thomas Kuhn's paradigmatic framework, dominant narratives of reality and epistemologies are often used to suppress alternative methodologies, interpretations, and findings that challenge the current status quo.[94] Since scientists are also influenced by dominant social norms and ideologies, science writing inevitably reflects normalized cultural assumptions.

In the context of gender and sex, researchers have found that it is not uncommon for scientists to design experiments with the a priori goal of finding a biological explanation for the differences between cis men and cis women.[95] Such experiments are based on the assumption that "sex is naturally dichotomous and can be operationalized based solely on the appearance of external genitalia."[96] Further, in mainstream science reporting and public discourse, sex and gender are frequently conflated or represented as interchangeable. This narrative assumes that sex and gender always align and that there is a strong biological basis for both.[97] Media reports on science also tend to naturalize gender and sex differences even when the research findings in question have been disproven.[98] While popular in science writing, these assumptions about dichotomous sex and sex/gender alignment are not scientific facts. Scientists have found abundant evidence demonstrating that, like gender, biological sex is not binary—rather, sex and gender both exist on a spectrum that defies the dimorphic framework.[99] That biological sex is not binary poses a huge challenge to the anti-gender and biologically essentialist claim that all people must identify as either man or woman based on the two binary sexes of male and female. As we will demonstrate next in our analysis of a published article and other similar artifacts, the arguments made by opponents of gender-neutral language are based exactly on biological essentialism about womanhood and the conflation of sex and gender.

Conflation of Sex and Gender. One's identification as a woman or man reflects one's gender identity, rather than sex. However, in the article "Effective Communication about Pregnancy, Birth, Lactation, Breastfeeding and Newborn Care: The Importance of Sexed Language," published in *Frontiers in Global Women's Health*, Karleen D. Gribble et al. refer to "women" and "mothers" as "sexed terms" rather than as gendered language.[100] The promotion of gender-neutral terminologies, according to the authors, is an effort to "desex" language when describing female reproduction.[101] To justify this conflation, the authors argue that "woman" and "mother" have "long-established sexed meanings"—meanings that the authors subscribe to. Based on this understanding, they posit, "Everyone who gives birth is indeed a woman."[102] This argument is similar to the one made by the group of "woman-centered" midwives who oppose the adoption of gender-neutral language by the Midwives Alliance of North America (MANA), as they believe that only women can give birth (see chapter 2).[103] In both instances, opponents of gender-neutral language see birth and pregnancy as inherently tied to womanhood, which in turn is determined by the female sex.

This conception is problematic on multiple fronts. First, it is based on the debunked assumption that biological sex is a binary. Gribble et al. deny that sex is a spectrum by misconstruing a research article by Morgan Carpenter about intersex people.[104] Carpenter's article argues that the creation of a third sex as a legal category for intersex people will paradoxically reinforce a narrow normative gender binary.[105] Gribble et al., on the other hand, cite Carpenter's research as proof that there are in fact just two biological sexes. The basis of Gribble et al.'s argument against gender-neutral language, hence, is built on willful misconstruction and ignorance of current research. It is also built upon the anti-gender assumption that the dyad of gender/sex constitutes a natural order that should not be challenged.

What the authors have omitted, however, is the history behind binary biological sex and gender. Historians and gender scholars have repeatedly reminded us that binary sex and gender was created by white colonizers to justify the colonization and subordination of Indigenous people and people of color.[106] Scholars from Indigenous studies have further demonstrated that colonizers systemically committed "gendercide" against trans and nonbinary Indigenous people while mobilizing "new sexual sciences" to pathologize the gender and sexual performances of Native people.[107] These historical findings highlight that binary sex and gender has never been natural. Instead, this binary system is constructed to subjugate queer people of color in order to uphold a white supremacist settler colonial system.

The conflation of biological sex and gender leads anti-gender health researchers to argue that any use of gender-neutral language in reproductive care would make "biological sex conceptually less visible and much more difficult to clearly explain in health care and medical education."[108] For example, Sara Dahlen argues that "woman's health" signifies the field of medicine that focuses on "issues affecting the female biological sex (in a similar way as the root of the word 'gynaecology' comes from the Greek word for woman)."[109] Hence, Dahlen and Gribble et al. argue that gender-neutral language risks "confusing the broader population."[110] Put differently, Dahlen and Gribble et al. are saying that because language use in pregnancy and birth care has traditionally assumed a binary gender/sex alignment, the audience will not be able to make sense of gender-neutral terms in the context of reproductive health. This argument is based on the assumption that gendered and sexed terms are unchangeable and stable signifiers. Linguists and historians remind us, however, that language is constantly in flux as it influences and is influenced by dominant worldviews and cultural assumptions.[111] Language reform, on the other hand, has the power to challenge or alter the existing status quo. For example, LGBTQ+ activists and linguists around the world have created or reinvented gender-neutral and nonbinary terms in grammatically gendered languages such as English, Spanish, Arabic, German, French, and Hebrew.[112] Such efforts are not without pushback, but contrary to Dhalen and Gribble et al.'s concern that gender-neutral language would create public confusion, LGBTQ+ activists and linguists have shown that the reinvention of language is absolutely possible, and with education and grassroots activism, gender-neutral language can prompt people to reconsider the narrowness of the gender binary.[113]

Repurposing Social Justice Discourse. In addition to conflating sex and gender, Gribble et al. also repurpose social justice discourse to argue against the use of gender-neutral language. This set of arguments refutes the claim made by LGBTQ+ activists and health care providers that adding gender-neutral language promotes reproductive justice because it renders birth and pregnancy care more inclusive for trans and nonbinary people. Instead, Gribble et al. argue that gender-neutral terminologies that use human anatomies (e.g., "individuals with a cervix") is exclusionary: specifically, it excludes women—especially those from marginalized communities—who do not have the knowledge of anatomy and reproductive physiology to know that those terms refer to them. In other words, they evoke the trope of competing rights to argue that the use of gender-neutral language "decreases overall inclusivity."[114]

This argument scapegoats gender-neutral language as the cause of medical exclusion while committing the straw person fallacy by distorting the approaches recommended by gender-inclusive birthworkers and health promoters. First, Gribble et al. posit that "even women with high levels of education may not be familiar with female reproductive processes and terms of female anatomy and physiology," not to mention women who have low education or literacy levels.[115] The problem they point to is a serious one that warrants attention. However, they are misguided about the main cause of concern. Gender-neutral language, especially when used in conjunction with woman-gendered language, is not the key exclusionary force that prevents women from seeking and receiving appropriate reproductive care; the lack of comprehensive sex education and public health promotion is. Rather than blaming gender-neutral terms for excluding women, we can instead consider *why* even women with high levels of education remain unfamiliar with important anatomical terms and reproductive processes.

Further, Brighton and Sussex University Hospitals NHS Trust (BSUH) in the United Kingdom published guidelines positing that medical providers should use language and terminologies that are clear and relevant to their patients in one-on-one settings.[116] In other words, contrary to what Gribble et al. are implying, proponents of using gender-neutral language in reproductive care *have not* advised a wholesale approach to language use. One interviewee who works as a nurse midwife told us that she used gender-neutral language as a default in clinical settings before she found out her patients' gender identity and language preferences, at which point she adjusted her language accordingly to reflect her patients' needs. When treating Somali and Oromo women who relied on an interpreter, she used gender-

specific pronouns to avoid confusion in translation and to accommodate her patients' cultural contexts. In these interactions, she knew
that her patients all identified as women and were all married to men.
The addition of gender-neutral language in clinical settings, hence,
does not necessarily infringe upon the plain language principles of
health communication, nor does it exclude people. Rather, it allows
health care providers to tailor their care for patients accordingly.[117]

Outside of clinical settings, Gribble et al. mobilize another common
anti-gender narrative to argue that the addition of gender-neutral language is oppressive to health care providers outside the United States.
They state that "the concept of gender identity originated in the 1960s
in the United States of America" and was refined in the 1990s "through
a postmodern philosophy called Queer Theory" to promote the idea
that sex and gender are both socially constructed and that gender is
more important than sex.[118] The accusation that gender is manufactured by Western feminist and gender studies scholars is a common
trope deployed transnationally by anti-gender actors.[119] Representing
researchers from both Western and non-Western countries, Gribble
et al. argue that birthworkers and breastfeeding counselors may experience the increasing encouragement to use gender-neutral language as "colonialist" and "oppressive" and as a "cultural and linguistic imperialism" imposed by the United States and the West.[120] This
argument, ironically, reverses cause and effect. In lieu of understanding the sex/gender binary as a weapon of colonial violence and racial
subjugation, anti-gender actors claim that it is, rather, the *critique* of
colonial binary sex/gender that functions as oppressive: the root of
Western cultural imperialism and totalitarianism.[121] In short, anti-
gender actors like Gribble et al. turn the feminist decolonial argument
on its head by representing themselves as victims who are forced to
recognize gender identities beyond the binary.

In addition, by falsely accusing queer theory of inventing gender
identity, anti-gender actors undermine the lived experiences of trans
people. Gribble et al. further allege that queer theory has caused a
dramatic rise in the number of trans people and the problematic idea
that "not everyone who gives birth is a woman."[122] This argument not

60   *Doing Gender Justice*

only misconstrues the historical origin of the binary gender/sex framework but also echoes the widely criticized anti-trans argument made by Shrier and Lisa Littman, that youths become trans because of "social contagion [and] positive reinforcement by peers."[123] In addition, by representing the concerns of trans and nonbinary people as manufactured "Queer Theory–derived concerns," this line of argument casually dismisses the lived experiences and marginalization of trans and nonbinary people.

Gendered Biological Essentialism. In addition to blaming the use of gender-neutral language for being exclusionary and complicit in "cultural imperialism," Gribble et al. also argue that gender-neutral terms that refer to body parts or physiological processes are dehumanizing to women.[124] This anti-gender argument is also commonly deployed in public discourse whenever gender-neutral language is used. For instance, Timothy Carney, a conservative columnist, accused Cori Bush of dehumanizing mothers for referring to them as "birthing people."[125] He further complained that the use of gender-neutral terms in the context of pregnancy and birth is an example of what "gender ideology" does: "Reduce us to atomized autonomous individuals without a role or connection."[126] Although they evoke the dehumanization of women to support their stance, Carney and other anti-gender commentators are in fact more concerned with the degendering of pregnancy and birth. Carney's insistence on reinscribing (Black) birthing bodies into the dominant binary gender system cannot be separated from the racist history of gender (see the introduction). The "role or connection" Carney seeks is a specific gender and racial hierarchy that grants Black people humanity only if they conform to the oppressive binary gender model. When Bush used both gender-neutral and woman-centered language in her speech, she not only included Black birthing people who did not identify as women, but she also resisted the racist colonial construction of the sex/gender binary that aims to discipline and displace Black bodies as nonhuman. But when Carney and other white anti-trans feminists and conservative commentators vehemently insist on the use of *only* gendered

Networking Arguments   61

language, they traffic in the anti-Black logic that forces Black people to conform to a white supremacist legacy that tethers Black bodies to the reproduction of chattel slavery.

In the colonial framework of binary gender, the only way to be human is to have a legible gender that aligns with a dimorphic understanding of sex.[127] All biologically assigned females are seen as women, in heteronormative patriarchy, and women's role is to reproduce and bolster the nuclear family structure and the nation.[128] The conservative construction of sex, gender, and reproduction sees giving birth and being a mother as the natural calling and responsibility of women. For example, the tradition of Republican motherhood emphasizes the importance of white women acting as "mothers of the Republic who educate their children to be virtuous citizens."[129] Biological essentialism, pronatalist white nationalism, and the gender binary, hence, are inextricably linked. As such, the detethering of pregnancy and birth from the domain of biological essentialism and the gendered conception of womanhood is extremely threatening to those who want to uphold the existing gender and racial status quo.

By decrying the use of gender-neutral language as dehumanizing to women, anti-gender actors are implying that women cannot be separated from the experience of reproduction and motherhood. Conservative congresswoman Nancy Mace's attack against Bush is a good example. Mace tweeted: "'Birthing people'—you mean women or moms? The left is so woke they're stripping from women the one thing that only we can do."[130] The anti-gender outrage against gender-neutral language, in other words, cannot be separated from the anti-gender actors' expectation for cis women—more specifically, white and able-bodied cis women—to reproduce and mother. Such biological essentialism and gendered expectations of reproduction extend beyond the contestation of gender-neutral language: they are also mobilized to generate fear among the public against gender-affirming care for trans youths and to promote a white nationalist reproductive future. Shrier, for example, argues that hormonal replacement and top surgery would render trans boys "angry, regretful, maimed, and sterile" because in her eyes, trans boys are "vulnerable girls" who would later regret missing out on the opportunity to have biological children and become mothers.[131] It's important to note that the trans youths Shrier and her ilk are most concerned with are, as Shrier puts it, "middle to upper middle class white girls."[132] As Hsu acutely observes, the fearmongering narrative about the sterility of white trans boys is inextricably tied to the white nationalist agenda that charges middle-upper-class cis white women to produce more white babies.[133] Anti-gender sentiments and affects, in other words, are networked together across rhetorical contexts to delegitimize the lives and concerns of trans people and to support a white Christian nationalist vision of the future.

The evocation of motherhood is affectively powerful because it taps into the gendered expectation and socialization for cis women to be unwaveringly nurturing. One concern Gribble et al. raise is that gender-neutral language in pregnancy and birth undermines "the significance of the word *mother*" by erasing the connotations *mother* holds: " 'nurturing,' 'nourishing,' 'love,' 'responsibility,' and 'child rearing.' "[134] While many trans women identify as mothers, Gribble et al. are not concerned about them, recognizing only cis women as mothers. Implicit in this argument, hence, is a form of gendered biological essentialism that places the burden of reproductive labor solely on the shoulders of cis women, while casting men, trans people, and non-binary people as inferior parents. Stevie Merino, a queer Indigenous birthworker and RJ activist, argues that the expectation of gender roles within a nuclear family is a colonial white supremacist construct imposed upon LGBTQ+ people and people of color.[135] The affective attachment and gendered political connotations of motherhood, hence, should be critically examined rather than naturalized.

The stakes behind maintaining woman-gendered language in birth and pregnancy is immense. The trans activist and birth parent Jude Doyle argues that gender-neutral language such as "birthing people" is threatening to right-wing ideologies because it disrupts the narrative that the "biologically ordained destiny" for cis women is to bear children with men and carry out most of the labor of rearing them.[136] By using gender-neutral terms to denaturalize the connection between womanhood, motherhood, and reproduction, Doyle argues, we make

Networking Arguments   63

room not only for trans and nonbinary people but also for cis women to consider whether they want to have children and become parents at all.[137] Gender-neutral terminologies in pregnancy and birth, in other words, carry the potential of fostering reproductive and family justice in myriad ways—both by recognizing queer family formations and by inviting cis women to exercise their right to not have children.

Division over Intersectional Alliances. Many reproductive justice activists and intersectional feminists assert that women's rights, trans rights, and racial justice are all interconnected.[138] However, in the debates surrounding gender-neutral language in reproductive care, women, trans people, and nonbinary people are pitted against each other, while racial injustice is either not mentioned or is dismissed. Gribble et al.'s overarching argument posits that cis women are marginalized and excluded by any use of gender-neutral language in birth and pregnancy care. As Strangio observes, this line of argument often assumes that womanhood is a zero-sum game that cannot simultaneously include trans and cis women.[139]

Gribble et al. are not alone in framing women's rights and trans' rights as mutually exclusive or incompatible with each other. An article published in the *New York Times* implicitly supports this argument by noting that in Australia, trans birthing people have been reported to constitute only about 0.1% of all births, while women constitute 50.8% of the population and are the majority of people who give birth and have abortions.[140] These statistics have not taken into account the underreporting of trans identities in birth contexts, as TGNC people may not feel safe or comfortable disclosing their gender to health care providers.[141] Further, even if these statistics are accurate, they need not imply that we ignore the needs and/or presence of trans and nonbinary people altogether. Doing so would suggest a tyranny of the majority, whereby trans and nonbinary birthing people are expected to either conform to cissexism or abnegate their needs. The article quotes a self-proclaimed radical feminist who argues that "battles over gender and language . . . [are] distant from the urgent needs of women."[142] The interviewee expounds, "This is about women and our rights; it's not a language game."[143] The article further quotes an editorial published in a British medical journal to suggest that the use of gender-neutral terms amounts to forcing women to "go along silently with language in which they do not exist" and "risk losing a larger audience."[144] In an op-ed published in the *Washington Post* after the leak of *Dobbs v. Jackson*, the columnist Megan McArdle similarly posits that gender-neutral language would dilute the power of the women's movement, questioning whether "'people who become pregnant' constitutes the same kind of effective political coalition that 'women' did."[145]

Taken together, this line of argument sees gender inclusivity in reproductive justice movement-building as a threat to cis women rather than a move toward stronger coalitions. The argument assumes that language cannot be used in ways that include women, trans people, and nonbinary people simultaneously; it assumes a substitution of language instead of an addition to it. By framing gender inclusivity as a direct assault on or erasure of cis women, this argument hierarchizes certain bodies as more worthy of protection, while undermining the significant coalitional potential between cis women and genderqueer people in the fight for reproductive justice.

This argument has been deployed beyond birth and pregnancy contexts and generated controversies among abortion rights activists. The feminist critic Katha Pollitt, for instance, echoes the *New York Times* article and argues that since women historically are the majority of people who have abortions, the use of woman-centered language in abortion advocacy is justified and does not infringe upon the rights of trans people.[146] She further argues that gender-neutral terms erase the specific oppression women face, as the target of abortion bans are women, not all people. Using gender-neutral language, she opines, would undermine women as a political identity for feminist and reproductive organizing.

Intersectional feminists informed by RJ principles disagree. Rather than seeing women and trans and nonbinary people as two separate communities with different concerns, intersectional feminists argue that the reproductive freedom of cis women and genderqueer people are both at stake.[147] As Strangio argues, abortion bans are a form of sex discrimination because they target people's reproductive capacities, regardless of their gender identity.[148] Sidelining TGNC people in the fight for abortion rights and reproductive justice, Bridges and Strangio posit, will only result in a narrow political vision that is not truly transformational and liberatory.[149] In addition, intersectional feminists acknowledge that trans and nonbinary people have always been involved in feminist organizing toward reproductive freedom.[150] Framing reproductive justice as a (cis)woman-only issue, hence, is misguided, narrow, and limiting. Moreover, the argument that gender-neutral language in reproduction cannot capture the unique marginalization of cis women is based on the assumption that language use is fixed rather than inventive. As Louise Melling from the American Civil Liberties Union posits in an interview with Emma Green, women's rights and trans inclusion are not an either/or situation. While Melling uses "pregnant people" to include trans and nonbinary people, she also talks about the ways in which abortion restrictions target women specifically to perpetuate gender stereotypes about reproduction.[151] She notes that one can simultaneously advocate for women as the main group targeted by antiabortion legislation *and* acknowledge that women aren't the only people who seek abortion care. The interviewer Emma Green repeatedly pushes Melling to discuss gender-neutral language as exclusionary to pregnant women and mothers, but Melling refuses to abide by the binary logic that pits women's rights against trans and nonbinary inclusion. When Green asks whether gender-neutral language is always exclusionary in some ways, Melling pushes back: "Not if you are doing it right. You can have more expansive language. . . . You can put emphasis in different places while still recognizing broader harm. You just have to be more intentional. You have to do more work."[152] Melling's answer draws attention to the inventiveness and intentionality behind language use. Her response suggests that rather than debating whether gender-neutral language excludes cis women, we ought to be reflecting on how and why we use language in the context of gender and reproduction.

Given the expansiveness and rhetoricity of language, we can—

through attunement to specific situations and audiences—invent, re-purpose, contextualize, and combine terms and phrases to acknowledge diverse gender identities without erasing anyone. Hence, the claim that gender-neutral language is exclusionary is a straw person argument. In addition to harming the coalitional potential between cis women and trans and nonbinary people, this argument also eclipses the connection between racial and reproductive justice. When anti-gender actors decry the erasure of women, they have in mind cis white women who meet the image of ideal mothers for the future of the nation.[153] Gribble et al. use the example of obstetric violence to argue that woman-centered language in the birth context is necessary in order to recognize the unique challenges cis women face. However, the authors never once discuss the significant racial disparities in pregnancy and birth-related health outcomes. White cis women, in other words, come to stand in for *all* women. Black women and other marginalized women of color are not under threat because of the additive use of gender-neutral language; they are under threat because of systemic and obstetric racism and the increasing number of legal restrictions, even forms of criminalization, placed on reproductive health care.[154] After being targeted by conservative lawmakers and commentators for using the phrase "birthing people," Cori Bush tweeted, "I testified in front of Congress about nearly losing both of my children during childbirth because doctors didn't believe my pain. Republicans got more upset about me using gender-inclusive language in my testimony than my babies nearly dying. Racism and transphobia in America."[155] Her response articulates that at the core of the anti-gender outrage against gender-neutral language lies the twin forces of racism and transphobia, which seek to uphold and maintain the existing system of oppression.

In the next section, we analyze what we believe to be a more generative site of possibility for reproductive justice—namely, gender-inclusive approaches to language in reproductive health. In addition to tailoring language use to affirm the gender identity of each individual, RJ-informed health care workers also adopt an additive approach to language. While there are limitations to these approaches, they

Networking Arguments   67

demonstrate the malleability of language and the possibility to accommodate different gender identities without erasure.

Trans-Inclusive Approaches to Language in Reproductive Discourse

Reproductive health practitioners and institutions have been moving toward using more gender-inclusive language to acknowledge the reproductive lives and experiences of trans and nonbinary people. In addition to MANA, which we discuss in chapter 2, the American College of Nurse-Midwives has also established in a statement their decision to endorse the World Professional Association for Transgender Health's (WPATH) standard of care by moving to gender-inclusive language.[156] In the latest set of guidelines, the WPATH recommends health care professionals to provide TGNC people with gender-affirming support and services on the full spectrum of reproductive experiences: fertility preservation, pregnancy and postpartum care, and pregnancy termination.[157] Outside of the United States, the Association of Ontario Midwives has likewise issued a statement on gender inclusivity and human rights, supporting MANA and the Canadian Association of Midwives' decision to use inclusive gender-neutral language.[158] More recently in mid-2024, a group of practicing midwives and perinatal care scholars published what they termed "a guide and argument for justice" in the journal *Birth: Issues in Perinatal Care*, articulating the need for midwives to uphold reproductive justice by using gender-neutral inclusive languages.[159] After MANA revised its core competency for midwives to include the use of gender-neutral language, Elephant Circle—a queer and people-of-color birth justice organization—issued a position statement in support of MANA's decision. The statement, published on MANA's website, challenges the anti-gender conception that dimorphic sex is an undisputed biological fact.[160] Rather, the statement argues that biological sex has never been a straightforward dichotomy; the use of woman-only language in pregnancy and birth settings is therefore misleading.

Echoing the teachings of feminists, queer scholars, and activists that gender and sex are not to be conflated, Elephant Circle makes clear that woman-centered language is inaccurate in describing people who are assigned female at birth but do not identify as women. Refusal to use gender-inclusive language, Elephant Circle argues, can negatively affect one's birth experience. Anticipating criticisms that gender-inclusive language erases women, the statement clarifies that for practitioners who serve primarily or only women, the use of woman-centered terminologies is appropriate. Instead, the organization promotes an additive approach: "Using gender-neutral language in no way forces people to eliminate woman from their vocabulary. ... Inclusive language can be added to current language without subtracting anyone. We have found that families respond positively to inclusive language, even when none of them identify as trans or gender-non-conforming."[161] In other words, rather than dictating that *all* woman-centered or gendered terminologies be replaced by gender-neutral language, they invite birthworkers to adopt more expansive vocabularies that would benefit a wider range of clients. This approach echoes the practice adopted by RJ doulas, who work often with women, trans, and nonbinary pregnant and birthing people. Rather than eschewing gendered terms and language altogether, these doulas adapt their language based on their clients' identities and preference to honor everyone's autonomy and dignity (see chapter 2).

Elephant Circle and RJ-informed birthworkers are not the only ones promoting additive language use in pregnancy and birth care. For example, Brighton and Sussex University Hospitals NHS Trust (BSUH) in the United Kingdom was the first hospital in the country to introduce "the additive use of gender-inclusive language in perinatal services" so that "all women and people see themselves reflected in the services they use."[162] In consultation with queer and trans birthworkers, the organization issued a twenty-page mission statement and set of guidelines—authored by two midwives who identify as gender inclusive—that provides detailed explanation and examples of their additive approach to language. At the time of writing, this document is the only guide to reproductive gender inclusivity written by a trust under the UK's National Health Service.[163] Helen Green, one of the coauthors, remarks that the document is guided by the intersecting

Networking Arguments 69

frameworks of health inequality, access, and human rights: the lack of gender-inclusive reproductive health care not only contributes to health inequality but also infringes upon the rights of TGNC people.[164]

Recognizing that women—especially women of color and migrant women—*and* trans and nonbinary people are both frequently marginalized, BSUH advocates for using woman-centered and gender-neutral language alongside each other.[165] Despite this additive approach to language, several news outlets published misleading articles about the document, wrongly suggesting that all gendered language would be erased under the new guidelines.[166] The mis/disinformation and vitriol against the document suggests that the introduction of gender-neutral language alone in the reproductive health context is seen as threatening to the status quo, which includes the erroneous assumption that people who need reproductive health care all identify as women. Similar to the approach adopted by Elephant Circle and RJ doulas in the United States, BSUH's guidelines encourage rhetorical attunement to context and audience. BSUH is clear in stating that when caring for individuals in a one-on-one capacity, health care providers should use language that reflects the individual's gender identity.

The guidelines encourage providers to use terms such as "woman," "mother," and "breastfeeding" if they are "meaningful and appropriate to the individual."[167] In documents and protocols that discuss pregnancy and birth at the population level, however, BSUH recommends using qualifiers to refer to women or people who are experiencing pregnancy, birth, and parenting—in other words, saying "*pregnant* women and people" instead of assuming that the term "women" on its own is sufficient.[168] Finally, in the table of language examples the BSUH document provides, woman-centered language remains present alongside gender-neutral terms.

Advocacy for an additive approach to gendered language extends beyond birth and pregnancy care and is now widely embraced by reproductive rights advocates. For these organizations, additive language recognizes the diversity of gender in the context of reproduction and demonstrates a commitment to inclusive movement-building.

SisterSong is explicit on this front. Not only do they deploy additive language across their website in describing their vision and work, they also open the origin story of the RJ movement as follows: "Indigenous women, women of color, and trans* people have always fought for Reproductive Justice."[169] Here and elsewhere, SisterSong take great care in how and when they deploy gender-inclusive and gender-specific terminology. This ethic is increasingly common. In advocating for "abortion access for all," the National Network of Abortion Funds use "people" instead of "women." Planned Parenthood Action Fund describe their advocacy efforts, from abortion access and birth control to health care equity and voting rights, using gender-inclusive terminology, including the statements "All people deserve access to the full range of birth control methods" and "Everyone should have equal access to sexual and reproductive health care." References to women are not absent; rather, language is tailored to context and pays attention to specific histories and impacted communities.

More recently, the evolving view of gendered language has even inspired name changes among high-profile RJ organizations. In 2022, the most prominent organization addressing the criminalization and punishment of pregnancy in the United States embraced a new moniker: Pregnancy Justice (formerly known as National Advocates for Pregnant Women). They describe this language choice in ways that include but also exceed the question of gender identity:

> Pregnancy Justice uses the terms "pregnant people" and "pregnant person" more frequently than "pregnant women." This is because in the face of the "fetal personhood" movement, it's important to recognize the personhood of people who are pregnant. This is also in recognition of the fact that not everyone who becomes pregnant identifies as a woman. At the same time, we must acknowledge that sexism based on the gender binary is a common link in pregnancy criminalization cases and the patriarchal desire to impose traditional gender roles on women. In recognition of all of these complexities, we use the terms "pregnant person/people" and "pregnant woman/ women" depending on the context and as appropriate.

Networking Arguments

Similarly, in 2023, when NARAL Pro-Choice America changed its name to Reproductive Freedom for All, they underscored a need to shift strategy dramatically in the post-*Roe* era. Mini Timmaraju, recently named president of this organization, explained in an interview with *Elle* magazine the need to expand NARAL's work beyond the traditional choice framework to build a more inclusive movement: "We have a majority white women membership. We can't win political wars with only white women." The shift in naming, and in particular the phrase "for all," signals a commitment to communities of color and young people specifically, Timmaraju noted.[170]

Shifting sensibilities and norms are reshaping public discourse on abortion as well. In the guide the Trans Journalists Association (TJA) recently released on best practices in media coverage of abortion care, TJA clarifies the necessity of recognizing the need for abortion care in trans and nonbinary communities. It provides language suggestions that include "abortion patients" and "reproductive health" but also recommends against a complete avoidance of the term "women" and substitutions such as "people with uteruses." These recommendations are accompanied by an emphasis on context and accuracy. As TJA writes in its best practices:

> It is sometimes important to use more limited and specific language. For instance, if discussing a study that only includes cisgender women, it would be most accurate to use gender-specific language (e.g. "pregnant women") to reference that study's findings. If the word *women* is preferable but transgender and nonbinary people *are also* referenced, phrasing like *women and other abortion patients* can provide an inclusive alternative.[171]

Indeed, the question of accuracy and specificity matters. As some trans activists and scholars have pointed out, embracing gender-inclusive language in a study that focuses exclusively on cisgender women is a kind of dual erasure—signaling inclusion while failing utterly to recognize or address the needs and experiences of trans and nonbinary people. In these contexts, thoughtful and explicit linguistic engagements of gender can offer clarity and nuance while also rendering the rich diversity of gender itself quite visible. In public discourse, the danger is that when we, as a culture, think of gendered language and gender-neutral language as an either/or, more nuanced claims about when gender-specific language might be useful could either be falsely accused of trans exclusion or be used as cover for those who actually are transphobic.

The additive approach aligns with the RJ framework on multiple fronts. First, it takes into account the different ways in which people experience gender and reproduction and acknowledges all of these experiences as valid and legitimate. Further, as the RJ activist and birth doula Miriam Zoila Pérez points out, it is untrue that only cis women prefer woman-centered language.[172] In their experience, gendered language can be very affirming for trans people when it reflects their identity. On the other hand, some cisgender pregnant and birthing women prefer gender-neutral terms and do not always identify as mothers. The additive approach acknowledges the diverse intersections of birth experiences and gender identities without dictating how one ought to experience pregnancy and birth. Without subsuming women's experience of marginalization—but rather being mindful of the structural violence women encounter in a patriarchal institution—this approach serves as a corrective to existing transphobia and exclusion in midwifery and in public discourse about pregnancy and birth.[173] As Trevor MacDonald, a trans activist who has given birth, argues, "We do not need to choose between celebrating women and including people of all genders. Why can't midwives serve 'women and people of all genders'?"[174]

Second, as an intersectional and coalitional framework, reproductive justice invites activists to build alliances across marginalized communities. The position statements penned by Elephant Circle and by Brighton and Sussex University Hospitals both recognize the systemic marginalization of genderqueer people and cis women. In his impassioned op-ed on transphobia in midwifery, MacDonald likewise acknowledges that cis women have experienced marginalization because of their gender identity. But that experience, he argues, should not be mobilized to dismiss the reproductive experiences and gender iden-

Networking Arguments   73

tities of genderqueer people. By acknowledging oppression as intersectional and by promoting the additive approach to language, trans activists and trans-inclusive birthworkers refuse to abide by the non-intersectional white feminist framework that sees sex-based oppression against cis women as the most extreme form of oppression.[175] Dismissing the oppression and dehumanization other marginalized communities face under the guise of honoring cis women is detrimental to reproductive justice—it not only oppresses trans and genderqueer people, as this analysis demonstrates, but also denigrates the marginalization of people of color, as Audre Lorde has argued.[176] As Elephant Circle cogently articulates, "We don't win the fight for women by erasing others who also lack a place/name/voice."[177]

Third, the additive approach to language refutes the anti-gender assumption that gender exists in binary and must always be aligned with a dimorphic understanding of biological sex. This view is often used to support the sexist and biological-essentialist idea that *all* women are destined to give birth and become mothers.[178] Without the addition of gender-neutral language, MacDonald argues, trans and non-binary birthing people are forced into the dominant sex/gender binary that denies their existence.[179] The denial of intersex, genderqueer, and trans birthing people is a form of reproductive injustice. In the organization's position statement, the BSUH clarifies that *women* refers to both cis and trans women and that the birthing person's co-parent(s) may have any gender identities. By inviting health care providers to use *both* woman-gendered and gender-neutral language in public communication and adapting their language use to specific clients, this document destabilizes dominant cisnormative assumptions in perinatal care, while also inviting health care practitioners to expand their view of what constitutes a family. Queer RJ activists and scholars have argued that the dominant cisheteronormative nuclear-family model is detrimental to reproductive and family justice because it vilifies trans and nonbinary people as unfit parents and threatens their right to have children and parent in a safe environment.[180]

In addition to the additive approach, reproductive health clinics can also deploy language that describes physiological processes without gender—such as prenatal, perinatal, and birthing care. While the additive approach is useful in contexts with wide audiences and where providers cannot ascertain the gender identities of everyone (e.g., in educational pamphlets and on signage in clinics and hospitals), RJ-informed reproductive health workers prefer a more tailored approach when working with individual clients. Driven by a client-centered, gender-inclusive, and nonjudgmental ethos, these health care workers invite input from their clients and use terminologies that are accessible and affirming to them. In the next chapter, we analyze in detail the rhetorical strategies deployed by RJ-informed birthworkers to attend to the diversity of gender identities in reproduction.

Conclusion

In this chapter, we connected anti-trans discourse in reproductive health care and the broader public sphere with the transnational anti-gender movement that upholds biological essentialism and the gender binary. It is important to recall the insidious history of the binary gender system (see the introduction) and the harm it continues to inflict on people of color and TGNC people. More alarmingly, as our analysis has demonstrated, health care providers who oppose the use of gender-neutral language in reproductive care often deploy similar arguments and rhetorical strategies as anti-trans actors. By doing so, they reinforce both the sexism and cissexism that see pregnancy, birth, and parenting as only a woman's responsibility. This framing eclipses the coalitional potential between cis women and TGNC parents, while also omitting the sordid reproductive injustice Black women and poor women of color continue to face. Anti-trans discourse, we reiterate, is grounded in racism, anti-Indigeneity, and anti-Blackness.

In addition to examining narratives and rhetorical tactics deployed by anti-trans actors, we have also outlined the additive approach to language proposed by queer parents, activists, and trans-inclusive reproductive health care providers. Their proposals and arguments make clear that the use of gender-neutral language in reproductive care is not meant to be totalizing, nor is it an attempt to deny or erase women's gender identity and embodied experiences. Their attempt to

Networking Arguments

render reproductive language more inclusive, however, continues to be misconstrued by anti-trans actors. This willful misinterpretation illustrates that the controversy surrounding gender-neutral language is less about the discursive practice itself and more about upholding a white supremacist construction of sex and gender. Debates surrounding gender-neutral language, hence, distract from the more pressing project of building intersectional and coalitional networks that would address overlapping reproductive injustices. And yet, mainstream news media, including liberal outlets, have added fuel to the fire, further fanning the sentiment that gender-neutral language in reproductive discourse is antithetical to the fight for reproductive freedom.

Given the stronghold of the gender binary and how it has informed people's worldview and identity formation, any challenges to, or invitations to change, the status quo are perceived as dire threats that would undo the current society. The introduction of gender-neutral language in reproductive health, then, becomes a canary in the coal mine for people who are already anxious and uncertain about the shifting conceptual terrain. Influential and powerful right-wing actors, meanwhile, have used gender-neutral language in reproductive discourse as a straw person to generate outsized public confusion, anxiety, and unease. To resolve this tension, on the surface, it may seem that we as communication scholars and reproductive justice activists ought to find a discursive model or template that could encompass diverse gender identities and reproductive experiences. The urge to find and promote a one-size-fits-all solution to gender and language, however, is counterproductive to the goal of decolonizing gender and promoting reproductive freedom for all. Our subjectivity, our relations to others, and the rhetorical contexts we find ourselves in are always in flux. Rather than seeking a definite solution that could be applied to all contexts, we could instead invent and practice different language use according to specific contingencies and audiences. Further, the urge to codify language to avoid the feeling of anxiety and unease echoes the colonial project to classify and thus to make certain and knowable those concepts, objects, and people that do not fit neatly into the existing dominant schema. As the Black feminist activist Aph

76   *Doing Gender Justice*

Ko argues, social change stems from finding oneself "in a new space of confusion" and probing at the confusion and uncertainty to "produce new blueprints for change."[181]

While the anti-gender movement has risen in popularity in recent years, along with right-wing populism and Christian fundamentalism, RJ activists and practitioners have been combating it through coalitional organizing, education, and everyday practices that uphold everyone's bodily autonomy and reproductive freedom. In the next chapter, we center the praxis of RJ-informed birthworkers to examine how they invent and deploy language and care practices that are trans inclusive. Their work makes clear that reproductive liberation for all must entail respect and care for the reproductive lives of TGNC people.

CHAPTER TWO

Against Gender Essentialism

Reproductive Justice Doulas and Gender Inclusivity in Pregnancy and Birth Discourse

Only when our whole selves are recognized and honored in the care we receive can we come closer to obtaining birth justice—for true reproductive freedom means celebrating the needs of every person at all stages of sexual and reproductive life, not subsuming all bodies within one paradigm of reproductive care. The task of activist birth work is to uphold and further a culture of support in which all people feel they can access appropriate care for the full spectrum of their reproductive needs.

—ALANA APFEL

QUEER FAMILIES FACE significant challenges in reproductive and birth settings, and this is particularly true for trans and nonbinary parents. As we will elaborate in this chapter, many challenges are structural in nature, including providers' poor understanding of trans and queer fertility care and the occurrence of homophobic and/or transphobic treatment—even violence—in health care settings.[1] Research demonstrates that medical macro- and microaggressions have detrimental effects on trans and nonbinary people, including deferral or avoidance of care.[2] Moreover, as we explored in the previous chapter, the dominant culture surrounding pregnancy and birth compounds these structural concerns through everyday discourses and material practices that center white, straight, cisgender women and heteronuclear family formation.[3] Fortunately, queer, trans, and nonbinary birthworkers—such as those of the Queer Doula Network—

are growing in number, claiming space in the world of birthwork and offering new models of inclusive care that center the needs of LGBTQ+ and often BIPOC communities. In this chapter, we explore the rhetorical practices of reproductive justice (RJ) doulas working with deep grit and determination to build more affirming spaces for LGBTQ+ families, and, more specifically, for transmasculine and nonbinary birth.

In the last chapter, we contextualized RJ advocacy amid increasing trans-antagonistic discourse; we also examined how trans-inclusive health care workers and birthworkers adopt the additive approach to language to demonstrate the expansiveness of language and gender experiences in reproduction. This chapter takes a more intimate look at how trans-inclusive doulas and birthworker organizations invent and enact similar rhetorical tactics to promote a safe and fulfilling reproductive experience for trans and gender-nonconforming (TGNC) pregnant and birthing people. Their tactics illustrate that the expansiveness of language allows for the coexistence of gender-specific language and gender-neutral language, as we need a variety of language practices to accommodate diverse gender. In addition, doulas provide physical and emotional support to birthing people during pregnancy and childbirth and in the postpartum period.

We focus specifically on doulas in this chapter because as educators, support companions, and mediators between patients and medical providers, doulas are uniquely positioned to intervene directly in a setting that affords primacy to whiteness, wealth, and heteronuclear family formation.[4] Previous studies have revealed how gender essentialism, white supremacy, and the technocratic model of childbirth are deeply ingrained in mainstream reproductive rhetoric.[5] Marika Seigel's work underscores how the intense medicalization of childbirth pairs with consumerism in ways that position the pregnant body as risky, dangerous, and in need of management, and Mary Lay Schuster has written extensively on the rhetoric of midwifery—its rhetorical reliance on naturalism as an embodied alternative to the mainstream medical establishment.[6] In addition, a growing body of scholarship in gender studies explores how RJ doulas are shifting the dominant ter-

Against Gender Essentialism   79

rain in which reproduction and childbirth unfold.[7] RJ birthworkers abide by the three pillars of reproductive justice: "the right not to have a child; the right to have a child; and the right to parent children in safe and healthy environments."[8] Drawing on this framework, doula care has evolved significantly in the last two decades and seen the rise of the "full-spectrum doula" who serves clients "during the full spectrum of pregnancy—from birth to abortion to miscarriage to adoption."[9] Many full-spectrum doulas embrace reproductive justice and strive to offer nonjudgmental and culturally competent care to underserved pregnant and birthing people, such as Black women, young parents, and queer and trans people.[10] In this way, many radical doulas see their birthwork as a form of activism.[11]

For many, pregnancy and birth care take place in dominant medical institutions that are part of the medical-industrial complex, which prioritizes efficiency, profit, and what the anthropologist Robbie Davis-Floyd calls a "technocratic model of medicine and birth."[12] In this institutional context, birthing people—especially those from marginalized communities—are treated as patients who should always defer to the authority of health care providers.[13] The pathologization of childbirth under the technocratic model leads to increased use of interventions, which in many cases conveniently expedite an otherwise uncertain and lengthy physiological process.[14] Scholars and activists such as Dána-Ain Davis, Khiara Bridges, Robbie Davis-Floyd, Cristen Pascucci, Chanel Porchia-Albert, and Miriam Zoila Pérez have revealed the ways in which dominant medical institutions alienize and dehumanize nonnormative pregnant and birthing people, leading to significant trauma and poor health outcomes.[15] Because they are not trained to provide medical care but are nevertheless more educated and experienced in birth contexts than the layperson, doulas occupy a liminal space in the medical-industrial birth complex that often perpetuates obstetric violence, racism, fatphobia, homophobia, and transphobia. While such liminality renders doulas precarious in hospital birth settings (for example, a doula might be asked to leave by a medical provider), it also affords RJ doulas a unique position in both witnessing and disrupting hegemonic structures, discourses, and prac-

80   Doing Gender Justice

tices in birth and pregnancy.[16] In this way, RJ doulas can create safer and more empowering reproductive experiences for marginalized birthing people. The birthworker and activist Alana Apfel notes that reproduction is political, and there is "subversive potential inherent in birthwork."[17] Radical doulas who serve marginalized people, hence, can serve as "potentially vital political mediators within intersectional struggles for freedom and dignity."[18]

This chapter proceeds in three movements. We begin with a brief elaboration of method: our study blends rhetorical analysis of curricular programs alongside qualitative interviews with doulas, many of whom identified as radical doulas of color. Next, we contextualize the doula's role in greater detail, while examining how the dominant language and practice in birth and pregnancy perpetuate gender essentialism and cissexism and exclude genderqueer, nonbinary, and trans birthing people. Finally, we explore how RJ doulas engage in education, advocacy, and carework to affirm expansive transmasculine and nonbinary birthing people and families. We identify three key dimensions of RJ doulas' world-making efforts that span both their educational efforts and the direct services they provide to clients. These strategies include (1) advocacy, (2) radical inclusion and nonjudgmental care for all, and (3) self-reflexivity. These rhetorical practices allow gender-affirming birthworkers to disrupt conventional exclusionary practices that do not take into account the reproductive experiences of queer and trans people. We conclude by contemplating the stakes of RJ doulas' interventions, not only for individual birthing people and queer families but also for their potentially broader impact on queer family justice and the bodily and reproductive autonomy of LGBTQ+ people.

Methods

We collected primary data from different sources: the data we analyze in this chapter stem from fifteen semistructured interviews we (Sharon and Natalie) conducted with RJ doulas, participant observations that Sharon conducted at two doula trainings, interviews with four queer birthworkers featured on the podcast *Evidenced Based Birth*, seven workshops and conference panels, and educational materials on queer and trans birth that were created by queer-affirming birthworkers and educators. Our method is informed by what Michael K. Middleton, Samantha Senda-Cook, and Danielle Endres call "rhetorical field methods," in which we simultaneously deploy "critical-rhetorical principles with a participatory epistemology to examine the lived experiences of individuals who are embedded within rhetorical social practices, particularly attuned to issues of power, marginalization, and resistance."[19] Hence, we deploy both field-based rhetorical criticism and textual analysis of printed texts. By doing so, we can more fully contextualize the barriers marginalized birthing people and RJ doulas face, and we can capture the different tactics and outlets RJ doulas use to advocate for their clients and educate their peers and medical providers on providing inclusive care. By juxtaposing our analysis of field-based data with that of conferences, panels, and printed texts, we are able to illustrate how birthworkers adapt their strategies of advocacy and education when speaking to different audiences across contexts.

Sharon conducted the two participant observations in 2018. The field notes collected during those trainings offered us a keen understanding of how gender is discussed in mainstream birth discourse, specifically in ways that are exclusionary. Interviews with RJ doulas were conducted by Natalie and Sharon in 2020 and 2021 to examine how queer doulas promote and practice gender-inclusive reproductive care. When conducting rhetorical analysis on the field notes taken during participant observations and on the interview transcripts, we focused on moments in which the instructors, interviewees, and authors discussed gender. While some of these discussions—especially in RJ-informed outlets—were explicit, some were not, because conventional birth discourse often assumes that only women give birth. As such, in our analysis, we paid close attention to moments of silence as well to identify unspoken assumptions about gender and reproduction. Since RJ is an intersectional framework, during our analysis, we were particularly attuned to moments when research participants connected gender with other identity markers, such as race and class.

We used a similar approach when analyzing training materials, conference panels, and other printed texts produced by mainstream doula-training organizations and RJ doulas. To contextualize the rhetorical ecology in which RJ doulas are currently situated, we examined the canonical texts and training materials that have dominated the birth industry until very recently.

Building on the foundation of reproductive justice, we deploy an "RJ model of rhetorical analysis" to amplify the rhetorical practices RJ doulas have invented to promote gender inclusivity, while also paying attention to the intersecting positionalities our research participants occupy.[20] To amplify the experiences of those who are most impacted by the cishet gender norms in pregnancy and birth, we were intentional about the data we analyzed for this chapter, focusing primarily on doulas from marginalized backgrounds and/or those who serve queer people of color. To do so, we subscribed to mailing lists, podcasts, and social media accounts created by RJ doulas and birthworkers of color. We attended educational workshops hosted by them and invited them to participate in semistructured interviews. Since both authors had already had contacts with RJ doulas prior to this research—Sharon previously conducted qualitative research on doulas and advocacy strategies, and Natalie worked with RJ doulas in reproductive rights organizing—we reached out to our existing networks to recruit participants as well.

Among the interviewees, four were doula trainers who designed their own curriculum. Our dataset includes interviewees with various racial, gender, and sexual identities. Eleven identified as cisgender, four identified as trans or nonbinary, and three used a range of pronouns and descriptors to indicate fluidity. Fourteen identified as queer or bisexual, and three as straight. Finally, eight interviewees identified as Black, eight as white, one as biracial (Black/white), and one as Pacific Islander and Latinx. Sharon participated in two birth doula trainings, one offered by the most established mainstream organization, Doulas of North America (DONA), and the other hosted by a community-based full-spectrum doula program that offered voluntary birth and abortion doula services.

Against Gender Essentialism   83

In the analysis that follows, we first discuss through analysis of field data and canonical texts in the birth industry how mainstream pregnancy and birth discourse has historically upheld—and continues to uphold—a ciswoman-centered approach to reproduction. After establishing the dominant rhetorical ecology, we then examine the ways in which RJ doulas challenge such exclusionary discourse and practices by providing care to queer, trans, and nonbinary pregnant people and by educating the public and other doulas on a more expansive view of gender and birth.

Gender in Mainstream Pregnancy and Birth Discourse

Dominant discourse on pregnancy and birth is promulgated by guidebooks, the media, and the everyday language used by medical providers and birthworkers. In this section, we contextualize the challenges faced by RJ doulas by analyzing mainstream doula-training materials. We note three matters upfront. First, the doula profession is ideologically and politically diverse, spanning a range of community enclaves from white evangelical mothers to RJ advocates. Compounded by mainstream doula trainings that center straight white women's experiences, many doulas do not subscribe to the same intersectional political commitments as their radical reproductive justice peers. Second, we use both gender-neutral and woman-centered language in this section to reflect the complex history of birth, because although medical authorities and past studies focused exclusively on pregnant and birthing women, TGNC people have long been giving birth. As such, we will use *women* when referring to particular contexts—specifically, historical research and advocacy efforts that have focused exclusively on cisgender women. Finally, at times, we use both *birthworker* and *doula* to describe people who provide nonmedical labor support. For some, *birthworker* includes direct-entry midwives who are not recognized by most US states as medical professionals. For others, *birthworker* and *doula* are interchangeable terms, with the former increasingly gaining traction among birth justice advocates who eschew the gendered and subservient connotation of *doula*.[21]

84   *Doing Gender Justice*

The History of Birthwork

The history of doula care and childbirth support in the United States has been widely studied.[22] In this section, we analyze canonical pregnancy and birth guides, such as those authored by the world-renowned, influential midwife Ina May Gaskin, and we analyze discourse commonly used by mainstream doulas who do not always subscribe to the same intersectional political commitments as their radical reproductive justice peers. We use both gender-neutral and woman-centered language in this section because trans and nonbinary people have given birth throughout history, but medical authorities and past studies focused exclusively on pregnant and birthing cis women and often assumed that all people capable of giving birth identified as women. As such, we use *women* when referring to historical research and advocacy efforts that have focused exclusively on cisgender women or abide by cissexism.

Historically, when home births were common, doula care and childbirth support were commonly provided by the birthing person's relatives and by women in their community. As pregnancy and childbirth became increasingly medicalized between the 1930s and 1960s, childbirth support provided by obstetrics nurses replaced community care at the homes of the birthing person. As Christine Morton points out, during this period, nursing care for birthing people transformed from a model of individualized care to a model of "one-on-many."[23] The medicalization of pregnancy and birth connects closely to what Robbie Davis-Floyd calls the "technocratic model of birth," in which the birthing body is seen as a machine and the patient is alienized from the medical provider, who is seen as the ultimate authority.[24] In the technocratic model, care is standardized rather than individualized. Aggressive medical interventions are often used to promote desired short-term effects. Care and treatment modalities that do not fall under the "technomedical hegemony," such as midwifery, are not tolerated by mainstream medical institutions and providers.[25] This development erased the contributions and immense knowledge of com-

Against Gender Essentialism   85

munity midwives and birth coaches of color. The hegemony of white-led medical institutions in pregnancy and birth worked in tandem with government policies that enforced binary gender and the nuclear family, thus targeting people of color who traditionally had a more fluid understanding of gender and family formation.[26]

Put differently, in addition to being more tightly managed and surveilled by medical authorities, pregnant and birthing people—especially people of color—were receiving less personal physical and emotional support. Obstetric care in the early twentieth century included problematic forms of treatment to manage labor, such as twilight sleep combined with sensory deprivation and physical restraints, in lieu of providing birthing people with sufficient physical and emotional support.[27] To combat the dehumanization of birthing people, advocates began to successfully challenge mainstream obstetrics, beginning with the "natural childbirth" movement in the 1940s and 1950s.[28] In 1956, the French physician Fernand Lamaze published his work on psychoprophylaxis in obstetric wards, which emphasized one-on-one education and emotional support for the birthing person, and soon after, childbirth educators and midwifery advocates began articulating the importance of empowering the birthing person and attuning to their emotional needs. Birth activists organized childbirth classes and advocated for husbands to be allowed at births.[29] Childbirth education at the time, however, continued to teach birthing people to follow through with all medical interventions suggested by the obstetrician, even when the intervention might be unnecessary.[30] Hence, the nursing historian Margarete Sandelowski reminds us that the movement at that time was "distinctively non-feminist . . . and pro-medical in control of the childbirth arena."[31] Rather than having doulas to provide nonmedical support, obstetric nurses at the time were tasked with caring for both the emotional and medical needs of the birthing person. As Morton points out, obstetric nurses in the United States differed significantly from the trained midwives in Europe.[32] Both were gendered as occupations only for women, but midwives in Europe could independently attend births, whereas obstetric nurses in the US must always defer to the male obstetrician's authority. Child-

86   *Doing Gender Justice*

birth support, in other words, has long been gendered and marginalized by a patriarchal and white medical institution.

It was not until the period from the 1960s to the 1980s that childbirth reformers began explicitly critiquing medicalized childbirth for failing to provide adequate agency and social and emotional support to birthing people. In the 1970s, the feminist women's health movement gained significant traction. Published in 1972, *Our Bodies, Ourselves* provided women the language and knowledge to understand their bodies away from the surveillance and authority of dominant medical institutions.[33] Of particular significance in the recent history of birthwork and labor support, Ina May Gaskin published *Spiritual Midwifery* in 1975, a germinal text that champions unmedicated vaginal home births. Drawing on her midwifery practice on The Farm community in Tennessee, Gaskin argues that as the "maternal" body undergoes "good pain" from unmedicated vaginal birth, the birthing woman will experience a euphoric and orgasmic experience.[34] But as Ashley Noel Mack points out, Gaskin and other advocates of unmedicated home birth often deploy gender-essentialist language for womanhood, thus tethering "moralistic and naturalistic" ideals to motherhood.[35]

This emphasis on motherhood, and the related essentialist claims of women's innate biological power and intuition, was widely embraced to challenge the patriarchal authority of obstetrics, which had long wielded sexist assumptions in its treatment of pregnancy and traditional forms of reproductive expertise. While essentialist claims may have proven politically expedient in particular contexts, reifying sex and gender binaries has its costs—not only for LGBTQ+-identified people but also for cisgender women who refuse motherhood altogether or who parent outside of heteronuclear, white, middle-class expectations. Gender essentialism as a vehicle for justifying reproductive autonomy retains an indelible imprint on contemporary birth culture. Like Gaskin's *Spiritual Midwifery*, most mainstream guidebooks on pregnancy and birth assume that pregnant and birthing people are exclusively cisgender women and are, by and large, straight. For instance, although Penny Simkin's *The Birth Partner* does not assume that all doulas and birth partners will be of a particular gender, the first four editions of the book refer to all birthing people as either "women" or "mothers."* These texts also are mostly written by middle-class cis white women for other cis white women. They bolster hegemonic familialism and fail to reflect the reproductive experiences of nonnormative birthing subjects, including queer, trans, and nonbinary people.

Mainstream doula practice and discourse in the United States have been heavily influenced by these texts and historical developments. In the late 1970s and early 1980s, around the time when Gaskin's teaching gained widespread attention, increased emphasis on patients' rights and women's health and the rise of the alternative medicine movement propelled a "humanistic" turn in childbirth.[36] Birthing people began experimenting with different forms of nonmedical labor support with the aim of having an unmedicated birth: they were often accompanied by either their spouse, a Lamaze-trained nurse who performed some clinical duties, or a childbirth assistant.[37] Medical researchers who studied relationship-centered birth care drew on the anthropologist Dana Raphael's concept of the doula to define the role of childbirth assistance.[38] Raphael understood doulas as experienced mothers who could provide support to new mothers.[39] While Raphael focused primarily on breastfeeding assistance, the term *doula* entered mainstream discourse and scientific literature as "a supportive lay woman" who provides general labor and postpartum support.[40] Studies in the 1990s found that the presence of a doula is effective in reducing overall the rate of cesarean sections, the length of labor, and the use of pain medication and epidural anesthesia.[41] More recent research finds evidence that doula support reduces serious birth complications among BIPOC women and people with disabilities.[42]

Given the increased attention on and demand for nonmedical childbirth support, doula as a profession was developed in the early 1990s by Polly Perez and Penny Simkin, who founded Childbirth and Family Education and Doulas of North America, respectively. Although an

---

*The fifth edition, published in 2018, includes a new preface that integrates gender-neutral terms ("birthing person" and "laboring person") alongside woman-centered language.

increasing number of doula organizations have offered training and certification in the last few years, DONA remains the leading and most recognized professional organization for doulas in the United States. Thus, DONA's language use and approach to childbirth support are extremely influential. The doula workshops offered by DONA usually span two to three days (at least sixteen hours of instruction), during which time students learn different techniques of labor support through guidebooks, lectures, and videos; students also practice communication and hands-on skills for physical comfort with each other.

While doula support is beneficial to the health outcomes of birthing people, significant limitations remain. According to Morton, because doulas are not considered medical professionals, they would "complement but not overtly threaten or question ongoing medical management of childbirth."[43] Thus, doulas have the potential to "open the technocratic system [of childbirth], from the inside, to the possibility of widespread reform," but mainstream doula care often does not overtly challenge or question the medicalization of birth and the power imbalance between physicians and birthing and pregnant people in hospital settings.[44] As we will discuss further, mainstream doulas are trained to defer to the authority of medical staff, especially the obstetrician. This practice renders mainstream doula care less effective in promoting a fulfilling and empowering birth experience for nonnormative birthing people, who must navigate systemic discrimination and obstetric violence.[45] Obstetric violence refers to "abuse or mistreatment by a healthcare provider" during or in relation to pregnancy, childbearing, and the postpartum period.[46] Acts of obstetric violence include humiliation (e.g., by repeatedly and purposefully misgendering a TGNC person or by making racist assumptions about a birthing person), coercion, and assault (e.g., performing an episiotomy or vaginal exam without the birthing person's consent or against their wishes). Birthing people who are the most vulnerable to medical mistreatment—Black women and people who are publicly insured or uninsured—can benefit significantly from having a doula present at their birth. Unfortunately, these groups of birthing people tend not to have doula support because of their socioeconomic status.[47]

Against Gender Essentialism   89

Gender Tension in Birthwork

In addition to the clients mainstream doulas serve, doulas as a profession are also deeply gendered and racialized. *Doula* is an ancient Greek word that refers to a "*female* attendant for the new mother."[48] Davis-Floyd also defines doula as "a *female* companion, especially trained to give labor support."[49] A doula's role is commonly described in training workshops as "mothering the mother."[50] This gendered definition of doulas reflects mainstream assumptions that the birthing person and their birth companion are always women. As Morton notes in her research from 2014, the typical practicing doula in the US is "female, white, married, with children. She is likely to have a college degree or attended some college. . . . She is passionate about how birth can be an empowering, positive experience for women. She may or may not be a self-declared feminist."[51] In the three mainstream birth doula trainings Morton attended as part of her research, Morton observed that in training materials, pregnant and birthing people are referred to as either "moms" or "the generic woman" whose bodies "naturally know how to birth."[52] The trainers also encouraged students to make use of "women's natural intuitive knowledge" to provide care.[53] In addition to reinforcing the assumption that doulas and birthing people are by default women, this discourse also relies on gender essentialism and naturalism that treat pregnancy and birth as exclusively women's domain.

In recent years, as birthworkers and health care providers move toward gender inclusivity, the use of gender-neutral terms in pregnancy and birth care has generated much tension among midwives. One specific example is worthy of mention, both for how it reflects these struggles in general and for how it has made a durable impact on contemporary birthworker communities. In 2014, the Midwives Alliance of North America (MANA) revised their core competencies, which "establish the essential knowledge, clinical skills and critical thinking necessary for entry-level midwifery practice."[54] The goal of this revision was twofold: first, to align with the core competencies of the International Confederation of Midwives and the World Health

Organization; and second, to revise the language so that it would be "inclusive and welcoming to all who seek midwifery care."[55] The revisions provided a more intersectional framework for midwifery care by underscoring matters such as environmental risks, food insecurity, and the human rights concerns specific to LGBTQ+ communities and to communities of color. Of particular note for many within the midwifery community, the MANA revisions also affirmed gender diversity in the context of pregnancy and childbirth, using terms such as "pregnant person," "birthing person," or "parents" in lieu of "pregnant woman" or "mothers."

MANA's shift to gender-inclusive language ignited a firestorm. Under the banner of Woman-Centered Midwifery, a large group of birthworkers that included leaders of national repute cosigned an open letter denouncing MANA's decision. The open letter insisted on language that recognized women's primary role in reproduction as biological fact:

> There is life-giving power in female biology. As midwives we protect the lives of the life-givers: women, mothers, females, and their offspring [*sic*]. We must not become blinded to the biological material reality that connects us. If midwives lose sight of women's biological power, women as a class lose recognition of and connection to this power. We urge MANA to reconsider the erasure of women from the language of birth.[56]

This emphasis on the shared biology among women lies at the heart of Woman-Centered Midwifery as an organization. They describe themselves on their website as

> a group of gender-critical midwives, mothers, and birthworkers deeply troubled by the present cultural trend of enforcing socially-constructed sex-role stereotypes as the primary definitions of female and male. While we believe all people's dignity, civil rights and safety should be supported regardless of their gender identity or manner of self-expression, we understand humans as a sexually dimorphic species that conceive and give birth through the biological functions

Against Gender Essentialism 91

of males and females, not through gender identity. We understand that a "woman" is a mature human female and that only females are capable of conceiving, gestating, and birthing children. Because we stand in support of females, fully acknowledging their unique experiences, capacities and vulnerabilities, we stand in resistance to the cultural, legal, and medical erasure of biological females and their lived reality.[57]

The open letter and "About" page make clear Woman-Centered Midwifery's attachment to the cis, white system of gender and sex dimorphism. Implicit in the letter is also the biological-essentialist and trans-antagonistic assumption that people who possess the organs to become pregnant *must* be women and that womanhood, in turn, is defined by one's ability to procreate. As discussed in chapter 1, this framework erases trans and nonbinary people's right to self-determination. Further, it mobilizes the anti-gender tactic of competing rights by evoking the supposed "erasure of biological females," while dismissing the concerns raised by trans and nonbinary people. By stating that "women have a right to bodily autonomy and to speak about their bodies and lives without the demand that we couch this self-expression in language which suits the agenda of others who were not born female," Woman-Centered Midwifery suggests a hierarchy of rights that puts cis women at the top.[58] As Emi Koyama has cogently articulated, white trans-antagonistic feminism has historically functioned under the assumption that "continuation of struggle against sexism requires silent compliance with all other oppressions."[59] This logic is harmful not only to trans people but also to Black people and other people of color whose experiences of anti-Blackness and racism are deprioritized. Our analysis of the criticisms Representative Cori Bush received for using gender-neutral language to discuss racial disparities in birth outcomes (see chapter 1) illustrates how an insistence on using woman-centered language functions to reinscribe Black people into a white supremacist gender framework that sees them primarily as disposable bodies for labor and reproduction.

MANA released a public statement authored by Elephant Circle in

92   *Doing Gender Justice*

response to the open letter, titled simply "Position Statement on Gender Inclusive Language." The statement defended the use of gender-inclusive language in birthwork in order to better serve and affirm a range of families. It also insisted that a refined understanding of sex and gender matters for *all* families, as the rich diversity of sex and gender that one might encounter in birth is not limited to serving LGBTQ+-identified parents but also includes, for example, the provision of compassionate and competent care to intersex infants.

Elephant Circle's response to Woman-Centered Midwifery was not the only one. Numerous midwives and doulas, organized under the name Birth for Every Body, released a response to Woman-Centered Midwifery's open letter to MANA.[60] Noting the harm and confusion resulting from the original open letter, Birth for Every Body's response was written "to explain why and how the Open Letter is harmful to transgender, genderqueer and intersex people, why midwifery documents should be gender inclusive, and why people of all genders should be welcomed into midwifery care."[61] The response offers various points of critique to debunk the biologically essentialist claims in the open letter, provides educational resources related to sex/gender and sexuality, and encourages birthworkers to educate themselves and initiate conversations with others about how to support trans, intersex, and nonbinary people during pregnancy and birth. Most importantly, Birth for Every Body's response counters the anti-gender narratives that remain prevalent in pregnancy and birth care. By firmly asserting that midwives care for *all* people and not just cis women, the response recognizes the right for people of different gender identities to access holistic midwifery care.

RJ Critiques of Mainstream Doula Trainings

In this section, we draw on our interviews with RJ doulas and Sharon's participant-observation data in order to elaborate how mainstream doula trainings fuel gender exclusion. RJ doulas—some of them queer-identified—regularly witness and confront cishet normativity in mainstream birthworker training and discourse. Their experience and critiques illustrate the need for more inclusive alternatives that would better equip birthworkers to serve queer and/or gender-non-conforming birthing people.

Sharon's participant observation at a DONA birth doula training in 2018 echoed Morton's findings with regard to demographics. In the DONA workshop, all but one of the students in class were cishet, married, and educated white women who had given birth before; most students expressed that they intended to serve clients who were from similar social backgrounds. At the beginning of the workshop, the instructor—a cishet white woman who was a seasoned childbirth educator and doula trainer—explained that she would be using a variety of terms to refer to the client base. The terms she used included the gender-neutral "birthing people." She further noted that she used the word "family" to refer to various kinship arrangements and structures. Despite the instructor's initial mindfulness on using inclusive language, during the workshop she frequently reverted to heteronormative language that assumed the birthing person was always a cis woman. In addition, course materials, such as the assigned textbooks, workshop manual, and videos, did not discuss the specific needs of queer, trans, and nonbinary birthing people, nor did they include any images of queer families. In an interview, Vicki, a queer and polyamorous full-spectrum doula, remarked that going to a childbirth education class that refers to parents as "mommies" and "daddies" can be "very dysphoric" for gender-nonconforming and genderqueer parents who do not always feel comfortable bringing their gender up with their instructors.

Other interviewees who received DONA training also remarked on the lack of discussions surrounding trans and queer birth and parenting. Beverly, a queer RJ birth doula, was initially skeptical of DONA's approach to queer and trans inclusivity:

> I've heard from people that [DONA] might not be accepting [of], say, lesbian couples, or surrogates, or transgender birthing people. . . . Their stuff all uses the feminine pronouns, so I was hesitant but also wanted to get the training done quickly, and knew that I am capable of making those adjustments myself, even if they don't come

> at this training from the same intersectional perspective that I do, I can bring that to it with my academic training.

While Beverly found the workshop to be a good learning experience overall, she witnessed fellow participants—most of them white working mothers hoping to start careers as doulas—expressing exclusionary views toward nonnormative and marginalized birthing people, such as Black women, queer and trans people, poor people, and people with substance use disorders: many announced that they could not work with clients from those populations.

The two trainers at Beverly's workshop responded to these exclusionary views differently. The one who was, as Beverly described, more social justice oriented, called out the participants' biases explicitly and encouraged critical reflection. The other trainer merely advised the participants not to take on clients from social backgrounds that made them uncomfortable. Tara Brooke, a DONA-trained doula who later founded a more inclusive and radical doula organization, remarked that DONA was not progressive and that the organization and workshops they offered mostly treated advocacy for birthing clients as taboo. In the DONA workshop manual, directly communicating the client's preferences to their health care providers is listed as an unacceptable action. Instead, trainees are instructed to encourage their clients to ask their own questions and express their preferences and concerns to their providers. This protocol severely limits the doula's ability to support clients who are systematically disempowered in medical birth settings, as medical staff are not always receptive to their needs.[62] By discouraging doulas from speaking directly to medical providers, doulas could not leverage their knowledge and social capital to help advocate for their marginalized clients.

Other RJ doulas expressed in interviews that their DONA training did not give them sufficient education on serving marginalized birthing people. Some of them subsequently enrolled in more radical doula-training workshops that were built upon intersectional reproductive justice principles. Stevie Merino, a queer Boricua and Chamorro doula and the cofounder of Doula of Color Training, noted that many of her trainees had previously received mainstream training from DONA but had experienced alienation due to their positionality as queer people of color. Merino herself attended a BIPOC-centered doula training that was taught by a queer instructor. Similar to Sharon's DONA trainer, Merino's instructor used gender-inclusive language but "sort of switched on and off, [and was] not really talking specifically or intentionally about serving this population or even being birthworkers who maybe identify as queer or trans." Merino's experience highlights the lack of intersectional birthworker training that refuses a piecemeal approach to people's identities and reproductive experiences.

In response to these deficits, RJ doulas have been promoting a more intersectional and inclusive framework that incorporates the reproductive experiences of pregnant and birthing people who claim a range of identities. In the next section, we analyze how RJ doulas are actively working to transform the birth world and affirm queer families through birthworker education and direct service.

Reproductive Justice Doulas and Queer Care

In 2007, the queer full-spectrum doula and activist Miriam Zoila Pérez started the blog *Radical Doula*, and later they published a seminal primer titled *The Radical Doula Guide*. In both, Pérez made clear the connection between political activism and birthwork. As Pérez puts it:

> I wanted to talk about why I was pro-choice and a birth doula, why I was queer and gender non-conforming and a birth doula, why I was Latina and the child of immigrants and a doula. I wanted to document the ways in which all of my identities and perspectives came together, and how they informed my work as a doula.[63]

For Pérez, it is important for birthworkers to understand the connections between birth activism, doula care, and other social justice issues. Pérez's blog features profiles of self-identified radical doulas, all of whom are people of color and white allies who are committed to providing nonjudgmental care to all pregnant and birthing people.

Pérez's work is an apt introduction to this section, as they have been a leading figure in the two arenas in which RJ doulas enact

96   Doing Gender Justice

change: direct care and educational efforts. In what follows, we highlight rhetorical strategies that span the development of inclusive birthworker curricula and ongoing education and the direct care for birthing people. This dual emphasis reflects the reality of work as an RJ doula; many doulas found that, as they worked to transform doula care for queer, transmasculine, and nonbinary clients, they were increasingly called upon to do educational work so that other birthworkers might adopt better practices for supporting LGBTQ+ families.

Within these two arenas, we elaborate on three themes that characterize RJ doulas' rhetorical efforts to dismantle exclusionary heteronormative language and practices in birth and pregnancy: (1) advocacy, (2) radical inclusion and nonjudgmental care, and (3) self-reflexivity. Given their liminal status in medical birth settings, RJ doulas perform advocacy for marginalized people through different tactics based on the specific contexts: while some would directly intervene in a situation where their clients did not feel comfortable speaking up, others deployed what Yam calls "soft advocacy" to promote more gender-inclusive practices.[64] Radical inclusion and nonjudgmental care were expressed in myriad ways, for example, in the creative use of language to center queer and BIPOC family formation. Meanwhile, in this context, self-reflexivity was embodied as a capacity to deeply listen to experiences from marginalized positionalities and to consider how identity, social location, and life experiences have shaped one's attitudes, beliefs, and behaviors.

Challenging the Dominant Culture and Discourse through Birthworker Education

In order to promote inclusive care, RJ activists and birthworkers began establishing doula organizations that disrupt gender-essentialist discourse in birthwork services and training. We interviewed the cofounders and educators of four such organizations: Doula Training International (DTI), Cornerstone Doula Trainings (Cornerstone), Doula of Color Training, and Birthing Advocacy Doula Trainings (BADT). All developed curricula that prompt students to consider the politics of birthwork and reproduction in an intersectional manner. These trainings tended to attract queer, nonbinary, and trans students who might otherwise feel alienized in more mainstream workshops.

First, radical doulas recognize the inherently political nature of birthwork and embrace advocacy as an essential dimension of doula care. Tara Brooke, the cofounder of DTI with Gina Giordano, is a white woman first trained by DONA. After working as a birth doula for several years, she became disillusioned by DONA's insistence that a doula be "a fly on the wall" in the birthing room rather than be an advocate. Brooke realized that in many circumstances, doulas could advocate for their clients in ways that could prevent obstetric violence and emotional trauma—which is especially important for marginalized birthing people who are subjected to systemic violence and discrimination in medical institutions. Brooke was not alone in feeling frustrated about mainstream approaches to doula work, specifically the restrictions on advocacy. Sabia Wade, a Black queer birthworker who founded BADT, echoed her frustration. Wade mentioned that given her firsthand experience of medical racism, she understood the importance for community doulas to advocate alongside their marginalized clients. Advocacy, for Wade, was an essential component of birthing support.

This belief that advocacy is fundamental is embraced by DTI, BADT, Cornerstone, and Doula of Color Training. Founded in 2011, DTI developed a doula-training curriculum that departs from mainstream curricula in its use of the RJ framework and its focus on the politics of reproduction and birthwork in ways that underscore the necessity of advocacy in particular settings. Additionally, DTI offers scholarships to people of color, and it started a Trans Health Initiative in 2015, which provides free in-person training and a nine-month mentorship to trans doulas. Brooke noted that DTI leadership frequently revisited and revised their curricula to be more inclusive and reflective of the wide range of reproductive experiences and bodies that birthworkers may encounter. The organization made the shift from woman-centered to gender-neutral language in all their materials. They also removed Gaskin's canonical work from the reading list and added

Trevor MacDonald's *Where's the Mother? Stories from a Transgender Dad* to the list for all certifying doulas. By changing the texts being assigned to student doulas, DTI and other doula educators who choose to do so are rewriting the canon of birthworker education.[65]

BADT has also been using advocacy to challenge exclusions in mainstream birth discourse and practices. For Sabia Wade, birthwork, activism, and social justice are interconnected. The mission statement of BADT reflects her commitment to educating birthworkers about such connections: "We not only train our students to serve their clients using the best practices available, we also provide them with a wide perspective of disparities, inequalities, policies and rights, and prepare them to be active partners in the movement to change birth and reproductive health culture locally, nationally and globally."[66] In addition to full-spectrum doula and childbirth educator trainings, BADT offers courses and workshops on queer and trans reproductive support, racism and privilege in birthwork, and birth and disability. Workshops such as these help doulas in training to develop a critical intersectional understanding of reproduction and birth—a necessary foundation for doing RJ birthwork and being an effective advocate for marginalized birthing people.

Stevie Merino's Doula of Color Training (DCT) underscores similar commitments in describing DCT's curriculum and goal. In an interview with the authors, Merino said, "There will be knowledge shares from POC midwives, doulas, herbalists, healers, abortion companions, etc. We will discuss birthwork as activism, trauma informed care, birth disparities, how to support pregnant people through all pregnancy outcomes, inclusive language, and so much more." Merino noted that when promoting the training on social media, the training would "uplift queer and trans voices, and use inclusive language." In addition to attracting queer and trans people to the training, Merino also wanted to train cishet birthworkers to better serve queer people and people of color:

> [It is a] very revolutionary, intentional act that we don't want to just attract queer and trans people. We want cisgender heterosexual

Against Gender Essentialism   99

people to also be forced to be uncomfortable and to sit in this space of them needing to get right. And [it's revolutionary] because you cannot say that you serve and uplift families and birthing people of color, if you're not also talking about the queer and trans experience.

The doula training Merino helped design and facilitate encourages students to consider the politics of birth through an intersectional lens. It critically considers the needs and experiences of queer and trans birthing people of color, including determining when intervention in medicalized birth settings might be necessary.

Cornerstone Doula Training similarly recognizes the political power of birthwork. They are committed to examining the connotations and histories of language in birth discourse, and more recently, they decided to move away from the term *doula* because of its gendered connotation. Like DTI, Cornerstone also offers scholarships to people of color and LGBTQ+ students to help diversify the demographics of birthworkers in the United States. These scholarship and mentorship programs are important because marginalized birthworkers often do not see themselves reflected or valued in mainstream training. These four organizations—BADT, DCT, DTI, and Cornerstone—all collaborate with Black, disabled, and/or queer activists and birthworkers to offer workshops and panels on topics supporting queer and trans birthing people, people with substance use disorders, and survivors of sexual violence. For example, Cornerstone collaborated with the trans birth activist and educator Trystan Reese to host a workshop for doulas. In the workshop, Reese drew on his own pregnancy and birth experiences as a trans man to illustrate the medical trauma common among TGNC people. In this workshop and in other similar ones, participants listened to the firsthand experiences of TGNC parents, but they also learned about current research on trans birth and concrete skills for supporting TGNC birthing people in medical contexts. In her interview with us, Merino mentioned a guest lecturer on abortion support that centered trans and queer narratives and did not address cisgender people much at all. By highlighting the abortion experiences of trans and queer people, the lecture challenged the widely held assumptions that only women need access to abortion care, and it provided insight into the specific needs of trans and queer communities in terms of abortion care. In sum, RJ doulas are reimagining the scope of birthwork and birthworker education to make advocacy and political awareness central to care for pregnant and birthing people.

Second, RJ doulas insist on radical inclusion and nonjudgmental care. This commitment is manifest in their transformation of educational curricula to center open, collaborative, and culturally competent care that is sensitive, in particular, to gendered language and the needs of gender-nonconforming clients. For example, in *The Radical Doula Guide*, Pérez sees gender-essentialist discourse—such as women's unique ability to tap into "feminine wisdom and instincts" during birth—as a historical response to sexism in obstetrics. In other words, by promulgating woman-centered, gender-essentialist arguments, midwives—who are commonly women—were working to challenge the patriarchal authority of obstetricians. Pérez argues, however, that "fighting gender essentialism with more gender essentialism" is "dangerous and damaging," as it has been used to dismiss women and exclude men and genderqueer people in doula work.[67] Pérez urges their readers not to "rely on ideas that imply biologically based gender differences."[68] Pérez's argument is a deft critique of the subsequent pushback against it by midwives, including Ina May Gaskin, who identify as "woman-centered," as it articulates why perpetuating gender essentialism not only excludes queer, trans, and nonbinary people but also further entrenches women in misogynist and sexist ideologies.

Other birthworkers are building on Pérez's commitment to radical inclusion, shifting curricula and using language in creative and expansive ways. In 2017, Tara Brooke and Gina Giordano started Born into This, an annual conference for birthworkers, doulas, and health care professionals. The conference featured panels and talks on reproductive justice and birthwork, birthworkers as activists, and gender biases and essentialism in mainstream birth culture. In 2019, the conference featured a panel titled "They/Them/Theirs," facilitated by Emma Robinson, a Black cisgender RJ activist, and in conversation

Against Gender Essentialism   101

with three birthworkers/educators on the transmasculine spectrum: Pérez, Trystan Reese, and Mac Brydum. The panelists discussed criticisms of gender-neutral language as mounted by woman-centered reproductive advocates. Noting his own desire to get pregnant in the near future, Brydum elaborated on his use of gender-neutral language: "I'm not here to take away from the amazing, powerful things that women's bodies can do that my body also happens to be able to do . . . the point is that there's more room for all of us. That inclusion is the goal." Robinson expanded on this note, positing that gender inclusivity was never a zero-sum game between women and queer and trans people: "We have to figure out a way to make sure that everybody is seen, because there are enough seats at this table. Like, if we are all sitting at this table, no one's going to be invisible. Women don't instantly become invisible because we say 'parents.'" For the reproductive justice activists and birthworkers, it is both possible and necessary to recognize the shared struggles and oppression that women, trans, and nonbinary birthing people face.

This insistence on shifting language and curricula is echoed in other places. In 2020, Brooke and Giordano published a short book titled *Born into This: A Creative Guide through Reproductive Health*, which covers the full spectrum of reproductive experiences. The target audience of the text is wide: "A young adult looking for more education and information around reproductive health, a birth professional, a reproductive justice advocate or someone who is pregnant for the first (or third) time looking to learn more about a birthing person's body."[69] *Born into This* differs significantly from canonical guidebooks on pregnancy and health. In addition to assuming that pregnant and birthing people are always women, as Marika Seigel points out, mainstream pregnancy and birth manuals also frequently perpetuate the technological system of childbirth, in which the birthing body is seen as always on the brink of malfunction. Especially when a pregnant person miscarries or has a difficult birth, their body is often framed as the source of the problem. More expansive in scope than the canonical guidebooks, *Born into This* contains chapters on miscarriage, loss, abortion, fertility, postpartum care, and menopause, in addition to several chapters on pregnancy and labor. The two beginning chapters and the conclusion introduce readers to the concepts of reproductive health, reproductive rights, and reproductive justice, while offering an introductory primer on gender, sex, and sexuality. Moreover, this sensibility is woven throughout the book. For example, when discussing infant feeding, Brooke and Giordano are mindful in explaining why and how they use "chestfeeding," "bodyfeeding," and "breastfeeding" to reflect different people's relationship to their body parts and their preferred language. The text, in other words, consistently demonstrates an attunement toward queer and trans experiences and needs.

Radical inclusion and nonjudgmental care are evidenced also in a willingness to challenge the dominant assumption that doulas are always women. Educators from reproductive justice doula organizations normalized the use of preferred pronouns and encouraged students to examine their language use and biases. For instance, Merino expected students in her training to mirror the gender-inclusive language she and other teachers used. This framework made the space more inclusive for queer, trans, and nonbinary trainees, but as Simone—a seasoned DTI trainer—pointed out, it also provided an opportunity for others to identify their biases and examine their gendered assumptions about doula work: "Because if a person identifies as perhaps as a 'he' instead of a 'she,' and you're used to being in a room full of women because we're doulas and birthworkers, you have to be mindful of your language from the very beginning as being respectful of the way the person identifies." Echoing Merino, Brooke remarked that DTI's curriculum was meant to be somewhat uncomfortable for students because the course challenged dominant gendered and racist assumptions about pregnancy and birth.

While most students who sought training at reproductive justice–oriented doula organizations tended to identify with the organization's intersectional RJ approach, they were not always comfortable with gender inclusivity in birth. Brooke observed that in more socially conservative regions of the United States, DTI trainers encountered resistance from attendees toward trans pregnancy and birth. Similarly, the cofounder and executive director of Cornerstone, Nickie Tilsner, pointed out that while she had not experienced much pushback from students on supporting genderqueer, trans, and nonbinary birthing people, students sometimes had a difficult time "wrapping their minds around, like, birth not being a woman thing."

This willingness to sit with and engage discomfort highlights the third significant rhetorical strategy that emerged from our data: self-reflexivity. For instance, Simone mentioned that in training workshops predominantly composed of white students, students often perpetuated white savior discourse when speaking about serving racialized communities. Hence, RJ doulas often find ways to prompt others to consider their own positionality, beliefs, and biases. For example, Brooke and Giordano's *Born into This* situates sex, gender, and sexuality as existing on a spectrum and subsequently invites readers to think of these categories and their accompanying language as fluid and changing. Before and after that chapter, the reader is encouraged to freewrite to the following prompts: "How has your gender influenced your life experiences? Has your gender presentation changed during your life? What are some ways in your life you already use gender neutral terms? Where could you start using more?"[70] This journaling exercise is intended to cultivate greater awareness of and sensitivity to the diversity of gendered experiences in the world and to empower doulas to better meet the needs of trans, nonbinary, and queer families in particular.

RJ birthwork educators also used their position in the context of doula training to facilitate meaningful exploration of cultural beliefs and biases. Mainstream doula-training programs often avoided these conversations, recommending instead that trainees refrain from working with populations that make them feel uncomfortable. Reproductive justice educators, however, take a different approach, one that emphasizes self-reflexivity, awareness, and the possibility of growth or change. The DTI trainer Simone stated that when a trainee expressed discomfort about serving a particular population, she would ask the trainee to consider where their hesitation was coming from and to examine their biases. As Simone recounted, some trainees experienced moments of revelation when they confronted their feelings about nonnormative birthing people. Before the workshop, these trainees were not aware of the biases they harbored. In her Doula of Color Training, Merino also invited her students to engage with deep questions about why and how they might wish to serve particular birthing people and/or communities. This critical reflection includes asking whether one is best positioned to serve particular communities:

> I do a lot of lactation trainings and discussions with other lactation professionals. And a lot of people will ask, well, I want to serve queer and trans families in lactation. What should I do as an ally? And my number one controversial response is you should refer them to someone who actually knows how to work with queer and trans people. And a lot of allies, of course, get in their feelings and center themselves . . . but there are people who are in these populations, who are battle tested and able to support in a good way, right?

For Merino, critical self-reflection is crucial and entails knowing the limits of one's capacity to serve clients at a particular moment in time.

The full-spectrum doula training that Sharon attended included similar value-clarification activities that were meant to prompt self-reflexivity. Participants were given a worksheet on which they evaluated on a scale from 1 to 5 their comfort level supporting different pregnant people during an abortion. The list included thirty-six marginalized subject positions, such as fat people; trans and gender-nonconforming people who want their doula to use their preferred pronouns; people who have mental health issues; disabled people; sex workers; undocumented immigrants; and people who are from different racial, cultural, or religious backgrounds. Similar to Merino's teaching, the instructors at this training suggested participants eschew taking on clients whom they rated as 1 on the scale, which was described on the worksheet as "I will never, ever, ever be comfortable/confident in a situation like this. It is not for me, and it never will be. I will avoid situations like this; this is a limit." For the instructors and the developers of the worksheet, not serving specific populations because of one's personal biases was a demonstration of accountability to oneself and others. The instructors then asked participants to

Against Gender Essentialism   105

review items they rated as 2 ("It would take considerable growth to be comfortable with this situation, but it's not out of the question. I would be considerably challenged by a situation like this"). The instructors encouraged the participants to review resources mentioned in the training manual and seek additional education. They also taught participants to build and learn from a network of doulas who were already equipped to serve those clients.

It is worth noting that this self-reflexivity exercise, in concert with recommendations to step away from serving particular clients as a doula, may raise concerns about exacerbating existing disparities in care, as marginalized pregnant and birthing people are already more likely to not receive adequate care. While this value-clarifying activity was valuable in preventing or reducing the harm doulas could cause, in other contexts this approach could exacerbate the marginalization vulnerable birthing and pregnant people face: for instance, currently in seven US states, medical providers can legally refuse to provide care to LGBTQ+ people on the basis of religious beliefs.[71] There are, however, crucial differences between these legislations and the self-reflexivity activities at RJ-informed doula trainings: prompting individuals who are already inclined to practice justice-oriented birthwork to clarify their values serves a different aim and has categorically different outcomes than legislating and thus granting state sanctions to homo- and transphobic medical practices. There is no simple, absolute answer to this conundrum: a harm reduction approach to birth care, however, prompts us to consider whether it would be more harmful to not have a doula at all or to have one who cannot provide nonjudgmental care.

Distinct from the canonical pregnancy guidebooks and DONA's training manual, the resource binder provided by the community full-spectrum doula training included extensive examples and scenarios from trans, queer, and nonbinary people. In a worksheet developed by the Bay Area Doula Project, participants were asked to work through different challenging scenarios as doulas. The scenarios included a genderqueer eighteen-year-old who wanted a medication abortion despite their partner's desire to continue the pregnancy; a thirty-two-year-old trans man who felt nervous about seeking an aspiration abortion in a clinic, as he did not feel comfortable with medical providers; and a cisgender woman who was polyamorous and was supported by her female partner. Without spectacularizing queer and trans pregnant people, these questions were crucial in preparing trainees to become full-spectrum doulas who recognize the diversity of reproductive experiences—specifically those experiences of people who are stigmatized or marginalized by right-wing transphobic and anti-queer discourse. By inviting participants to consider the abortion experiences of queer, trans, and nonbinary people who disrupt heteronormativity, this activity reminded full-spectrum doula trainees of the radical political potential of birthwork, while encouraging them to examine any feelings arising as they worked through these scenarios.

Similar prompts to encourage self-reflexivity are embedded in workshops that RJ birthworkers and educators offer to birth professionals, including medical professionals, in a range of settings. Several of these prompts also discuss privilege in an intersectional framework, encouraging participants to take stock of how they benefit from privilege and how they might leverage social capital to support marginalized people. For example, in a workshop led by a Black queer, nonbinary birthworker, the cis white trainees were asked how they could mobilize their social privilege in medical settings to support queer clients of color whose experiences and preferences were often dismissed by institutions. In a different workshop, the trans birth instructor remarked that trans pregnancy is increasingly treated as a "spectator sport" for birthworkers and journalists to generate social media attention, and the instructor reminded attendees to be mindful of their intention and positionality when serving trans pregnant people. Given the typical demographic of doulas in the United States (middle-class, cisgender, straight white women), these conversations within educational settings were significant in promoting more self-reflexivity among aspiring birthworkers who may not have much knowledge about or experience serving trans and queer clients.

Against Gender Essentialism   107

Inclusive Practices in Doula Work

In this section, we examine how RJ birthworkers deploy the rhetorical strategies of advocacy, radical inclusion, and self-reflexivity in doula work itself. Many RJ doulas view all aspects of their work—whether visible, overt, subtle, or behind-the-scenes—as a form of advocacy and activism, because providing nonjudgmental and inclusive care to those who regularly encounter violence at the hands of medical providers, the state, and culture writ large is a political act. For example, Gwen, a birth doula and midwife, expressed that in medical settings she practiced "feminist charting" when writing notes about patients in her midwifery practice: "When I'm writing notes about people, I like to include a lot of things about their life, how they're feeling emotionally, their decision-making process because I feel like it really humanizes them." Gwen observed that obstetricians would often focus solely on the anatomy of queer and trans patients. But by including emotional information about her clients, Gwen hoped that her notes would help promote more holistic care that does not reduce queer and trans people to their body parts. This insistence functions as a more subtle form of advocacy that prioritizes the interests of queer and trans patients over institutional norms.

RJ birthworkers' advocacy sometimes took a more direct route. Miranda, a white queer full-spectrum doula and midwife, stated that she would prepare her queer and trans clients for microaggressions that might occur in hospital birth settings so they would have time to ready themselves. Miranda's experience demonstrates that in addition to supporting clients before their medical appointments, queer RJ doulas often also engage in advocacy for their clients and mediate between their clients and medical staff during labor in hospital settings. For example, Miranda described how, in serving a lesbian couple, a nurse stopped both partners from entering the birthing tub. The nurse informed the couple that while the birthing person could enter the tub naked, the supportive partner must wear a swimsuit. Miranda noted that this particular policy on modesty was implemented out of the assumption that the partner of a birthing person would be someone with a penis. When Miranda noticed the couple beginning to shut down because neither had brought a swimsuit to the hospital, she defused the situation by asking the nurse, "We are all women here. Why could [the birthing person] be naked and her partner have to put on a swimsuit?" The nurse and the nonbirthing parent both then felt more comfortable about the situation, and she was able to accompany her wife into the tub. By inviting the nurse to consider the inapplicability of the hospital policy, Miranda simultaneously advocated for her client and disrupted mainstream gender assumptions about birth and family.

Sometimes advocacy takes the form of visibly aligning with a client's marginalized identity or experience in mainstream medical settings. For example, Miranda shared that she would occasionally and strategically out herself as queer to medical staff as a form of solidarity that would often deflect unwanted attention from her clients:

> I'm like, "Oh, well, my wife and I, you know, when we have babies, we're both going to call each other mom, and you know, we actually read this study that said that, you know, children actually know based on who is saying and how they're saying it who you're referring to when you say 'mom,' even if they have two moms, and so we'll just both call each other mom, and then when our kids differentiate, they differentiate however they want." I might throw that out there and [the clients] were like, "Yeah, yeah, we do that too."

In addition to educating the medical staff and placing herself in the conversation to (as Miranda put it) "take the heat off the family," Miranda also modeled preferred language and framing to medical staff. For instance, she would consistently use the correct pronouns for her queer clients and refer to their family as such, even when they did not resemble a normative heteronuclear family. In situations where medical staff consistently misgendered her clients or ignored her queer clients as equal parents, Miranda would remain in the birthing room the entire time in order to provide support.

This more subtle advocacy strategy was echoed across our interviews. Merino, who frequently serves masculine-of-center birthing

Against Gender Essentialism 109

people, noted that misgendering and deadnaming were common occurrences in medical settings, even when the client "had a full-on beard, and their partner [was] calling their name." In these instances, Merino saw her advocacy role as crucial in supporting the trans client. For Merino, advocacy did not need to be "guns blazing," but rather it needed to be "sustainable" in a way that would allow her "clients to be protected in their oxytocin bubble." This would include "gentle reminders" to health care workers about pronouns or queer family configurations, as well as open and ongoing conversations with clients to help them navigate their circumstances with her.

RJ birthworkers also emphasized radical inclusion as central to the provision of care—a commitment that included nonjudgmental care as well as a deep sensitivity to language. While nonjudgment should be the cornerstone of all reproductive care, our interviewees noted that this was especially true for clients who are systematically marginalized because of age, drug use, body shape, disability, race, class, gender, or sexuality. Monica, a birth doula, midwife, and childbirth educator, noted that she adopted a nonjudgmental approach in the childbirth classes she provided to pregnant people:

> My classes are really based on radical acceptance. And, like, radical non-judgment of people and their birth choices. I really strive to just give people information that is extremely non-judgmental . . . however you choose to do this is, like, it's completely up to you. You should have the right to make those choices, and you should have the right to not be pressured into birthing a certain way from any angle.

For Monica and all of our other interviewees, providing nonjudgmental care involves centering the client's desires and preferences and providing them with sound, accessible information from reliable sources so they can make their own decisions. Nonjudgmental birthwork enacts the reproductive justice principle that honors individuals' autonomy with regard to their own body and reproductive experiences.

Since gendered assumptions about birth and pregnancy are prevalent in mainstream discourse and medical infrastructure, birthworkers who want to provide inclusive services for trans, nonbinary, and queer people often have to reexamine the language and documents they use in their birth practice. In the interviews, Wade recommended that birthworkers include visual representations of queer and trans birthing people and families in their educational materials and on their websites. Monica, Wade, and Danie Crofoot, a queer doula who serves primarily LGBTQ+ people, used gender-neutral language in their client intake forms and included questions about pronouns and gender identity. Beyond pronouns, RJ doulas were attuned to the different language that queer, trans, and nonbinary people might use to describe their bodies. For example, "chestfeeding" might be a preferable description for feeding one's baby; "pelvic delivery" might reduce the dysphoria that can accompany descriptions of birth that reference female anatomy. Echoing the chapter on bodyfeeding in *Born into This*, queer birthworkers and educators encouraged their peers to ask and pay attention to how their clients referred to their bodies.

All interviewees remarked on the importance of using language that was gender-affirming to their clients. Gwen and Chaney, a Black queer full-spectrum doula and midwifery student, chose to use gender-neutral language in all settings, unless their clients preferred gender-specific wordings. Similarly, Pérez used both gender-neutral and specific language to accommodate their clients' diverse identities:

> For some people, their identity as a woman or man is really, really important and that's beautiful and valid. And some of those people are trans too, and they want that language. I think for me, it's like, how do we use both types of language in the way we talk about people that are getting birth so that, um, people feel seen across the identity spectrum?

For Pérez, using gender-neutral language such as "birthing people" as a default did not erase the reproductive experiences of women. At the same time, Pérez also believed that birthworkers should feel comfortable using "women" to refer to clients who identified as such.[72] Like Gwen, Monica, and Chaney, Pérez recommended that birth professionals never assume a client's identity and preferred language, but rather they should ask and listen openly: "We just listen to people about who they are, and then we mirror that back to them. And that's, for me, such a part of what it means to be a doula."

The emphasis on listening underscores the third key theme we identified across this work: self-reflexivity. RJ doulas embodied this commitment to reflecting on their own assumptions by leading, first and foremost, with questions, centering the clients' understanding of their own needs, and resisting the impulse to make too many assumptions. For example, on her intake form, Monica would ask clients to share, at their own discretion, any affirming and/or nonaffirming experiences they'd had with medical providers, and she would then initiate open conversation about how she could best support them given their identities. Many of our interviewees noted that this kind of self-reflexivity from birthworkers was unfortunately rare. Assumptions in reproductive health care settings are commonplace. RJ doulas, however, worked actively to avoid making assumptions about their clients' gender identity, pronouns, anatomy, and relationship status and practice. RJ doulas underscored the importance of asking questions only on a need-to-know basis and leading with open-ended questions. Gwen, a birth doula and midwife, described a wellness visit with a young cisgender woman who described a particular physical ailment that worsened after sex. Gwen followed up by saying, "Tell me a little bit more about the kinds of people you have sex with and their genders and anatomy." This open-ended, unassuming question was a catalyst, said Gwen: "It came out that she had three partners, and one of them was a cis man, one was a trans woman, and one was a cis woman. And, she ended up having chlamydia, and we ended up treating all of her partners . . . [which] could have easily been missed if someone hadn't taken the time to ask those questions." This example is a clear illustration of how cishet cultural norms and expectations undergird reproductive health care and how accessible, comprehensive health care pivots on a provider's self-reflexivity—in short, on their willingness or capacity to think broadly about gender, sexuality, and intimacy.

Self-reflexivity is also informed by deep listening to the needs and comfort of a client. In an interview, Vicki recounted a time when she was supporting a nonbinary client:

> I work with a non-gendered [birth parent] who had chosen not to get into [their gender identity] with the staff because they thought it would compromise their care. So [when] I'm in the room, just us in the room, I'm using "they" pronouns for them. And then when the nurse comes, I switch over to using "she" pronouns. And when the nurse leaves the room, I go back to using "they" pronouns. So being comfortable to do that respects the choice that individual is making.

Vicki's support demonstrates cultural competency and fluency regarding queer and trans care, which must be tailored to a client's needs and preferences, particularly within hospital settings. RJ doulas who advocated for their clients often emphasized the need to adapt their tactics to ensure a calm atmosphere in the space to avoid further distressing the birthing client.[73] Beyond birth settings, RJ doulas are aware of the potential postpartum challenges that might be amplified for LGBTQ+-identified people. Miranda noted that queer and trans parents had a much higher risk of developing postpartum anxiety and mood disorders; birth support, hence, should continue in the postpartum period. Trans- and nonbinary-inclusive full-spectrum and postpartum doulas have an integral role to play in supporting the formation of queer families. Their capacity for self-reflexivity and critical awareness is foundational to providing this support.

Conclusion

The history of reproduction and childbirth in white Western contexts has long reflected binary understandings of sex and gender, and it also reflects the legacies of cissexism, misogyny, racism, and the cultural primacy assigned to nuclear-family formation. This chapter examines how reproductive justice birthworkers—many of them queer and/or people of color—engage in practices that disrupt gender essentialism through the multifaceted rhetorical strategies of advocacy,

Against Gender Essentialism   113

radical inclusion, and self-reflexivity. Moreover, in embracing a non-judgmental approach to the full spectrum of reproductive experiences—from fertility, pregnancy, and birth to abortion and miscarriage—RJ doulas challenge not only exclusionary practices of birth but also the normative ideals of family as they actively craft spaces for queer families to grow and thrive.

Moreover, RJ doulas' efforts are potentially resonant and meaningful beyond the immediate health care needs of those who identify as trans, nonbinary, and queer. For instance, the increased scholarship in medical anthropology and gender studies has drawn attention to the ways in which Black women experience obstetric racism and misogynoir when navigating prenatal and birth care.[74] Some of our interviewees stated that their experiences of racism and marginalization in health care settings were what first motivated them to become doulas. A birth care practice that insists on advocacy, inclusion, and self-reflexivity is thus one that benefits a range of people in the context of reproduction and childbirth—a process fundamentally marked by profound vulnerability and needing deep care in kind. Adjacent to, but not part of, formalized reproductive care systems, doulas are uniquely positioned to provide support informed by reproductive justice principles. In doing so, they are also prompting other providers to consider how they, too, might participate in creating more just spaces for birth—not only for people of varying genders and familial configurations but also for people who struggle to be recognized and affirmed within dominant cultural contexts.

By challenging cishet norms in mainstream birth and pregnancy practices, RJ doulas participate in broader cultural debates about the definition of family, prompting critical reflection and urging expansion. Family justice is intimately connected with reproductive justice because reproductive freedom necessarily entails creating families that challenge white Western heteronuclear norms. By advocating for the freedom of queer, trans, and nonbinary people to birth on their own terms, RJ doulas are creating the space for familial self-determination. In the next chapter, we pivot to consider the voices and firsthand experiences of queer families—in particular, families that include one or more trans or nonbinary parent—highlighting how public discourse and mainstream reproductive practices regarding gender come to bear on the lives of queer families and noting how queer families push back.

CHAPTER THREE

Reimagining Family and Kin

Queer and Trans Reproductive Storytelling

I come from a legacy of queer and trans people who left roadmaps of how to survive for the next generation, which means I am called to leave roadmaps of how to survive for the generation that comes after me. And, my body holds an inherent dignity, and to recognize my inherent dignity I need to see myself reflected in the world around me, to fight for people like me to be a part of the cultural archive of existence, which means that your body holds this inherent dignity as well, and you have the right to see yourself reflected and your stories documented as well.
—GROVER WEHMAN-BROWN

Storytelling is a core aspect of reproductive justice practice because attending to someone else's story invites us to shift the lens.
—LORETTA ROSS and RICKIE SOLINGER

Content notice: Pages 122–130 contain content related to the systemic forms of violence that TGNC and LGBTQ+ communities experience. The content in this section may be emotionally difficult, particularly for queer, trans, nonbinary, and gender-nonconforming individuals.

GABBY RIVERA DESCRIBES herself as "a Bronx-born, queer Puerto Rican author on a mission to create the wildest, most fun stories ever."[1] Rivera is an accomplished writer whose work includes the critically acclaimed *Juliet Takes a Breath* and Marvel's *America* series, and she is the creator and host of the *Joy Uprising* (formerly *Joy Revolution*) podcast. In 2021, Rivera appeared as a guest on *The Intersectional Fer-*

tility Podcast, which is dedicated to fertility and family formation for LGBTQ+ and BIPOC people and hosted by its creator, the queer, non-binary Latinx acupuncturist Josie Rodriguez-Bouchier. In one of the most popular episodes of the podcast to date,[2] Rivera shares her intimate thoughts on creating family as a gender-nonconforming person with characteristic wit and perceptivity:

> I'm butch presenting, like shorter hair, tattoos, chubby papi-mami. Anyone that would see me and my girlfriend together, she's super high femme, you would imagine, "Oh, she's going to carry." There's such a gendered stigma around who is allowed to be pregnant, you know, and all of that is so silly and unnecessary. So, for me as a butch presenting person, my identity is still very much, like, full of femininity and softness. And it's the combination of all those things and other genderful feelings that I experience, that made it of course, "I'm definitely going to carry this baby." If I can, then I shall and I will because I don't know, I think it's going to be this beautiful experience and this wacky wild ride, and I'm always in it for the ride.[3]

Broadcasting to *The Intersectional Fertility Podcast* audience, Rivera offers both a critique of dominant gender regimes and a fierce corrective through her queer reproductive embodiment. She names the stigma attached to pregnancy outside of cisgender femininity, undercutting its power with succinct descriptors ("silly and unnecessary") and offering instead an expansive articulation of both gender and pregnancy itself. Rivera describes the richness of her queer butch identity as "genderful," embracing the possibility of carrying a pregnancy as a "beautiful" and "wacky wild ride." In so doing, she offers listeners a powerful counterstory for trans and gender-nonconforming (TGNC) parenting and queer family formation—one that, in the spirit of Aja Martinez's work,[4] contests and rewrites dominant narratives about family itself.[5]

Rivera's storytelling provides a powerful representative anecdote for the opening of this chapter, focused as we are on queer (counter)-storytelling, deliberative empathy, and the rhetorical possibilities for reproductive justice. In what follows, we examine the public narratives

Reimagining Family and Kin   117

authored by TGNC parents that center their experiences of reproduction and family formation outside of binary gender.[6] Previous chapters focused on the forms of gender-inclusive creativity and resistance that emerge in public discourse as well as in health care settings. This chapter expands those analyses by taking an additional locale into account and exploring how TGNC parents and communities use public storytelling to craft more inhabitable worlds. We highlight how they rhetorically negotiate their environments, drawing on strategies aimed at addressing dominant cisgender audiences, as well as strategies that aim to affirm and offer resources to other TGNC parents and communities. Of particular interest for our project are those moments in which TGNC parents' storytelling exceeds an insistence on liberal trans inclusion, edging us instead toward a deep interrogation of the gender binary as a critical component of reproductive justice world-making (see the introduction).

We assemble and analyze a vast archive of public storytelling, including published memoirs, documentaries, podcasts, blog posts, and interviews with trans, nonbinary, and gender-nonconforming parents. Because this book is centered on questions of *gender* and pregnancy— and not questions of sexuality and pregnancy, although they are related— we have explicitly crafted an archive that centers the voices and experiences of trans and gender-nonconforming birthing parents. Many are authored or produced, in fact, by TGNC parents themselves. While these stories often dovetail with those of other queer families, TGNC parents' narratives offer unique insights into how pregnancy, birth, and family formation are sites of intense gender normativity as well as creativity and invention. These accounts simultaneously bear witness to systemic exclusions and violence while also insisting that other worlds are possible. They draw on various rhetorical strategies to foster trans inclusivity, at a minimum, or to perhaps bring about more radical transformation in dominant forms of kinship and care. As Loretta Ross and Rickie Solinger note, storytelling is a key component of reproductive justice praxis; thus, the narratives of TGNC parents prompt us to "shift the lens" through rhetorically savvy enactments of resistance and solidarity toward a more capacious understanding of kin.[7]

This chapter proceeds as follows. We first offer an overview of our archive and the recent sociopolitical contexts that have shaped the reproductive and familial experiences of trans, nonbinary, and gender-nonconforming people. Next, we turn to two complementary critical frameworks that inform our inquiry: that of Shui-yin Sharon Yam's deliberative empathy and Aja Martinez's counterstory.[8] We detail how these two frameworks—each concerned with how marginalized rhetors use storytelling for survival and creative redress—are usefully understood in conversation with one another. Finally, drawing upon both deliberative empathy and counterstory, we engage our primary-source archive, exploring how TGNC storytellers utilize distinct rhetorical strategies in order to address specific audiences and exigencies.[9] While some TGNC narrative impulses are deeply assimilatory in nature, utilizing strategies that normalize TGNC reproduction and families to claim social and political inclusion, so too do these narratives contain significant moments of resistance, challenge, and critique. Thus, in addition to calls for state recognition and/or inclusion grounded in a human rights framework, TGNC storytellers adopt strategies of deliberative empathy to prompt the possibility of political solidarity with mainstream audiences, and they embrace counterstory to challenge and rewrite dominant configurations of kin. Not only is this the necessary survival work of making TGNC lives and families visible as lives that matter, but it is also a point of departure for imagining a future more fully rooted in reproductive justice.

Against the Grain: An Archive of TGNC Storytelling in Context

We assembled a variety of materials in order to capture the breadth of TGNC storytelling—and with particular attention paid to the voices of TGNC storytellers who occupy other marginalized positionalities. Our archive includes artifacts from the US, Canada, and the UK and includes a range of genres, from memoirs and documentaries to podcasts, blog posts, and published interviews with trans, nonbinary, and gender-nonconforming parents. Our primary-source materials span diverse genres and media, are situated in Western, English-speaking contexts, and target audiences that are interested in marginalized communities' experiences of pregnancy, birth, and parenting. This particular emphasis on trans pregnancy and birth means that trans-feminine experiences of motherhood and/or parenting are not a focal point here, although these voices are represented as they surface in our archive, and we note trans maternal experience as a rich site of inquiry in its own right.[10] Our archival commitment to thinking across various storytelling platforms reflects how queer and trans storytell-ers broadcast their experiences, how audiences might seek them out, and how more accessible forms of storytelling—like podcasting, as opposed to memoir—allow more room for BIPOC, trans, and non-binary voices to be heard. Taken together, these stories allow us to toggle between TGNC parents' experiences of the intimate/personal and their experiences of the public/political to provide insight into how parents navigate the various liminalities of gender, reproduction, and family formation.

Our archive includes six recent documentary films, including three features: *A Womb of Their Own* (2017); *A Deal with the Universe* (2018), and *Seahorse* (2019),[11] as well as three short videos: *Pregnant Dad: Giving Birth as a Transgender Man* (2017), *My Trans Life: Trans Couple Pause Transition to Become Parents* (2017), and *Raising My Baby Gender Neutral* (2018).[12] Most of the selected documentaries were pro-duced in the United Kingdom and feature a single family's story, ex-cept for *A Womb of Their Own*, which focuses on the United States and weaves together the stories of six TGNC birthing parents (and in some cases, their partners/co-parents). Some films, such as *Seahorse* and the shorts, are widely available to stream online; others, such as *A Womb of Their Own*, we could acquire only through our university library. We also include five memoirs penned by TGNC birthing par-ents in our archive: Thomas Beatie's *Labor of Love: The Story of One Man's Extraordinary Pregnancy* (2008), Karleen Pendleton Jiménez's *How to Get a Girl Pregnant* (2011), A. K. Summers's *Pregnant Butch:*

Nine Long Months Spent in Drag (2014), Trevor MacDonald's *Where's the Mother? Stories from a Transgender Dad* (2016), and Krys Malcolm Belc's *The Natural Mother of the Child: A Memoir of Nonbinary Parenthood* (2021).[13] These memoirs span niche (Trans Canada Press) and more established (Seal Press) publishing houses and incorporate a range of visual material, from personal photographs and legal documents to the graphic memoir genre as a whole. Each is also readily available for purchase in multiple formats through large online retailers.

While films and memoirs represent the heightened visibility of TGNC pregnancy and parenting narratives in broader public arenas, many center white TGNC parents, which reflects the multiple marginalization that queer people of color experience in dominant culture. Hence, we supplement our analysis of texts published in more mainstream outlets with podcasts, blogs, and other storytelling platforms that broaden accessibility and provide greater opportunities to attend to the voices of queer people of color in particular. Every podcast we analyze was created by, for, and with TGNC birthing people and parents. Some episodes included in our study are drawn from podcasts conceptualized for broader audiences: BIPOC birthing people (*Birth Stories in Color*), trans people (*TransLash*), and parents and primary caregivers (*The Longest Shortest Time*; *The Double Shift*).[14] Others are drawn from podcasts devoted specifically to TGNC conception, pregnancy, birth, and parenting (*Masculine Birth Ritual*), as well as LGBTQ+ fertility and reproductive health care (*The Intersectional Fertility Podcast*).[15] We also drew into our archive the public storytelling of trans, nonbinary, and gender-nonconforming parents that appears in edited volumes (such as Syrus Marcus Ware's "Confessions of a Black Pregnant Dad") and on popular blogs on parenting (e.g., Aren Aizura on *Mutha Magazine*; Andrew Rich on *Romper*) and LGBTQ+ culture (e.g., Grover Wehman-Brown on *Autostraddle*).[16] Finally, we deepen this public-facing archive with secondary materials that foreground the voices and personal experiences of trans, nonbinary, and gender-nonconforming parents, including the ethnographic work of scholars such as Miles Feroli, Trevor MacDonald, and Michelle Walks.[17] The stories highlighted in this study reveal steady and

Reimagining Family and Kin   121

skillful navigations of the narrow social, legal, medical, and cultural infrastructures that shape normative notions of family.

This rhetorical situation is shaped by a sociopolitical landscape that presents numerous significant barriers for TGNC family formation, even as most trans people report wanting to have children and 25%–50% of trans adults in the United States already do.[18] The specific structural hurdles may vary across nation-states, but TGNC struggles—as well as anti-trans hostilities and violence—are networked across borders (see chapter 1) and are therefore characterized by several broader themes, as we elaborate below. Please note that the following may prove distressing in detailing the numerous structural hostilities that LGBTQ+, and specifically TGNC, communities must navigate on a regular basis.

Challenges to TGNC reproduction and family formation include at least three distinct arenas of disparity—knowledge structures, health care structures, and legal structures—all of which are compounded by other oppressive forces, such as racism, xenophobia, ableism, classism, and wealth disparities. First, systems of knowledge and knowledge production create structural barriers to TGNC reproduction and family formation in myriad ways. Despite evidence to the contrary, there is a widespread assumption within Western medical communities that TGNC individuals do not want to have biogenetic children; relatedly, there are limited data and research on gender transition and fertility.[19] This gap creates an information vacuum in which health care practitioners provide gender-affirming care that is often inattentive to fertility preservation or that relies on cultural norms and assumptions in the absence of more concrete information and guidance.[20] While fertility preservation options do exist, people seeking gender-affirming care are frequently ill-advised in matters of reproduction and fertility.[21] Medical providers may fail to address reproductive options such as fertility preservation through gamete storage, or they may fail to advise patients pursuing chest masculinization that subsequent pregnancies may alter chest size or appearance.[22] Despite clear and growing evidence that hormonal transition does not necessarily result in permanent sterility, providers often caution patients to the contrary and underscore permanent sterilization as a side effect of transition.[23] Thus, as many voices within our archive attest, TGNC people are frequently misled by health care providers, and so they undertake informal and independent research (often through queer digital networks) and educate providers about their reproductive health care needs and circumstances.

Still, all of these matters assume a supportive health care provider—a luxury that many TGNC people do not have, particularly if they are also working class, of color, or disabled. Similar to other marginalized communities that have struggled against abusive medical practices, LGBTQ+ people have reason to be cautious in their encounters with established Western medicine, given its history of hostility toward and experimentation on queer and trans bodies. Providers can and do refuse care to LGBTQ+ people. Approximately 29% of trans people have experienced denial of medical care;[24] our archive confirmed stories of medical gatekeeping as a common refrain among trans and nonbinary birthing people. Thomas Beatie notes in his memoir that, for medical providers, "My gender identity was the problem."[25] When an ethics committee voted to refuse Beatie's fertility care, they cited concerns over his "psychological health" and what he would "tell the baby"; the committee concluded, "You know, Thomas, just because you can have a baby doesn't mean that you should."[26] Beatie's testimony evidences the overt forms of transphobia shaping fertility clinic policies, which include eugenic assertions of binary sex/gender and assumptions about who is "fit" for parenthood. For TGNC parents and queer families more broadly, who are more likely to need some form of assisted reproduction in order to create families, the deprivation of reproductive care is significant, severe, and entirely legal.

Those individuals who are not turned away experience medical harm and trauma at rates disproportionate to their straight cis white peers.[27] Recent research indicates that nearly half of trans adults—and 68% of BIPOC trans adults—experience mistreatment or discrimination from a health care provider, including intentional misgendering, deadnaming, and verbal or physical abuse. As a result, trans patients report high rates of medical avoidance and delay in seeking care.[28]

Pregnancy, however, prompts many TGNC people to interface with established medicine, particularly if those people are also managing chronic illness or are otherwise considered too high risk for at-home or birthing center care. Consistent with broader patterns of medical harm, a recent study conducted by the Center for Health Justice found that "LGBTQ+ birthing people reported worse birthing experiences than cisgender, heterosexual birthing people . . . [and more] complications following childbirth."[29] Even outside of traditional medical settings, the production of knowledge/power persists—childbirth classes and pregnancy books almost exclusively cater to cisgender women and straight families, making it difficult to gather information from vetted sources and fueling the general experience of alienation of TGNC people during pregnancy and birth.[30]

As we discuss in the chapter on radical birthworkers (see chapter 2), many LGBTQ+ and BIPOC doulas are taking matters into their own hands to address the poverty of care within traditional settings by offering gender-affirming nonjudgmental support to those for whom hospital-based birth settings are the only option. Still, and perhaps unsurprisingly, our archive contains numerous testimonies from TGNC birthing parents seeking care adjacent to or outside of this system altogether. Many people relayed stories of empowerment made possible through less medicalized forms of perinatal care. As the nonbinary single parent J Carroll explains on the *Masculine Birth Ritual* podcast, "I had an all-queer birthing team. And so I had a midwife who was queer and . . . my Doula identifies as trans. . . . I felt safe with them, because they mentally understood who I was and my situation, but they were also in that community as well."[31] Similarly, the birthing parent Charlie King Miller reflects on the decision to work with a home birth midwife: "The experience of pregnancy in birth is a really deep and intimate one . . . if somebody can't figure out that they need to ask your pronoun or use the right name, there's no way to get to that intimate space with them."[32] This story represents a common refrain among TGNC birthing parents, underscoring how "small" gestures—like respecting names, asking for pronouns, acknowledging partners, and so on—are critical to creating safe and supportive re-

124   *Doing Gender Justice*

productive health care settings. While some TGNC advocates have raised noteworthy concerns about the trend toward at-home birthing care, it remains clear that avoidance of mainstream medical spaces is warranted and common among TGNC birthing parents.

Moreover, health care systems as a whole often reflect broader cultural norms and values. The primacy of white cisgender femininity and the heteronuclear family abounds in Western health care contexts, surfacing in poorly designed intake forms and feminized depictions of pregnancy, as well as in more overt displays of homophobia and transphobia.[33] A few examples suffice to illustrate the gendered architecture of health care itself. As some of our interviewees from chapter 2 noted, the most widely used health care records system in the United States, which was developed by Epic Systems, compromises providers' ability to serve trans and nonbinary birthing people well simply by virtue of its interface and organization of data. The software segments data in ways that render information especially critical to LGBTQ+ people far less visible to teams of providers. Moreover, the ability to access appropriate charting for pregnancy is contingent on how sex/gender identity is marked in the system. Thus, medical charting becomes a site where erasure of queer identity and experience regularly takes place.

Medical insurance presents another set of complications and failings for those fortunate enough to access it.[34] For example, some insurance companies insist that anyone receiving perinatal care and coverage be tagged as "female" and/or "woman" in medical records and insurance documents. Having to change this information is unnecessary, onerous, and—for many patients—deeply distressing, but it can also prove logistically impossible if the timing of these changes does not serendipitously collide with the annual window within which individuals are able to renew or revise their insurance options during open enrollment. The insurance failings may extend to the baby as well; for example, if a family is covered through the non-birthing parent's policy, enrolling a baby on the health care plan may prove difficult in the absence of a state-recognized relationship (see more on this on the following pages). Climate aggressions exacerbate these inhospi-

Reimagining Family and Kin   125

table structures: for example, overt displays of transphobia can lead trans and nonbinary people to seek home birth care at disproportionately high rates, and obstetric racism has produced profound racial disparities in pregnancy-related mortality, particularly for Black and Indigenous women and for birthing people who are more likely to die than their white peers because of complications related to pregnancy and childbirth.[35] And of course, access to biogenetic reproduction for many TGNC families pivots on wealth. Assisted reproduction is extremely expensive, and families that lack eggs or sperm must go to great lengths—financial and otherwise—to conceive, often in ways that necessitate greater intimacy with highly medicalized settings.[36]

Finally, the legal architecture of family has persistently undermined or even barred family creation for nonnormative bodies and people through marriage laws, eugenic population control policies, racist immigration laws, and family separation.[37] This is a trend that has endured for centuries, since the earliest years of the colonization of the Americas. For example, in order to establish white wealth and power in the colonial states, marriage was prohibited between slaves, interracial marriage was made illegal, and white women's fidelity to their husbands was strictly enforced—a codification of "family" in the interests of nation building.[38] Native American genocide was perpetuated not only through massacre, land grabs, and disease but also through sexual and reproductive violence, including sterilization, abuse, and the forced removal of children from Native communities.[39] Restrictive immigration policies in concert with anti-miscegenation laws in the late nineteenth and early twentieth centuries barred the possibility of family formation for East Asian immigrants in particular, and it codified immigrant women's sexuality in general as a threat to national security.[40] Eugenic sterilization programs throughout the twentieth century in the United States targeted low-income Black, Indigenous, and Latinx women—as well as queer people, poor people, and people with disabilities and mental health conditions—thus robbing entire communities of their capacity to have children. Family separation— a mainstay of US racial terror—persists into the early twenty-first century through for-profit carceral systems of immigration enforcement and the foster care system, targeting low-income children of color for state removal in what Dorothy Roberts terms "family policing."[41] In short, the definition of *family* has long turned on a white supremacist vision of nation in which the ability to create and nurture familial bonds is a privilege of white wealth and biogenetic, heteronuclear kinship.

Even as the state has persistently imposed its racist vision of belonging on the most intimate dimensions of everyday life, so too has a series of more recent US Supreme Court decisions broadened access to family formation and legibility. The Supreme Court affirmed the right to interracial marriage in 1967 (*Loving v. Virginia*), the right to same-sex marriage in 2015 (*Obergefell v. Hodges*), and the right of same-sex married couples to appear on a child's birth certificate in 2017 (*Pavan v. Smith*). In 2023, the Supreme Court upheld the Indian Child Welfare Act (*Haaland v. Brackeen*), which safeguards Native children from forced removal and assimilation. Still, state recognition of family and reproductive rights remains precarious. The 2022 *Dobbs v. Jackson* ruling by the Supreme Court overturned federal recognition of the human right to safe and legal abortion care. Justice Clarence Thomas also used this opportunity to suggest that the US Supreme Court would do well to revisit constitutional protections for birth control and the right to marry as well. The National Center for Lesbian Rights notes that recent protections still do not guarantee legal parental rights for same-sex couples and thus "encourages non-biological and non-adoptive parents to get an adoption or parentage judgment, even if you are named on your child's birth certificate."[42] This lack of protections leaves many parents in legal limbo as they navigate narrow birth certificate nomenclature and second-parent adoption requirements—that is, assuming they possess the time and financial resources to do so.[43]

Legal recognition for TGNC parents in particular often pivots on adhering to binary sex/gender and/or essentialist notions of parenthood. Consider, for example, the strict codification of parenting nomenclature on birth certificates, medical records, insurance policies, and the like. The state-sanctioned architecture of the family in the

United States seldom recognizes anything beyond "mother" and "father" and sutures pregnancy to motherhood regardless of the sex/gender of the gestational parent. Many storytellers within our archive describe the frustration of navigating the legal system as a TGNC parent rendered invisible by the state. Krys Malcolm Belc explains that seeing *mother* "on every form, phrased that way—*the natural mother of the child*—made me cringe. It made me rage. My relationship with Samson could be natural without my having to stand up in court and say I was a mother."[44] Many echoed this sentiment, underscoring the psychological toll of navigating institutional constraints and the significant sense of familial precarity that this often engenders. This illegibility is more acute for unmarried same-sex couples and families with more than two intended parents, a set of hurdles also compounded by cultural stigma and invisibility.

In the years since we began writing this book, we have borne witness to an intensifying legal climate of state-sanctioned hostility toward queer, trans, and nonbinary people across the United States, as states ban gender-inclusive curricula in schools, access to public facilities, trans kids' participation in athletics, and gender-affirming health care. The year 2023 marked an all-time high in anti-LGBTQ+ legislation, with at least seventy-five bills passed in states across the country—more than double that of 2022, previously the worst year on record. The sharp rise in legislative attacks prompted Human Rights Campaign to declare—for the very first time in its forty-year history as an advocacy organization—a state of emergency for LGBTQ+ Americans at the opening of Pride Month in June 2023.[45] Although anti-trans and anti-LGBTQ+ bills do not reflect the majority US public opinion, this hostile climate persists, thus compounding existing hardships for TGNC families and parents.

In this context, the significance of queer and trans storytelling is ever more radical and resonant. And indeed, in spite of the numerous barriers and inhospitabilities, TGNC parents continue to voice their experiences, rich with gender complexity and nuance. For the remainder of this chapter, we explore how the stories of TGNC parents echo across distinct registers, embracing dual address as a rhetorical strategy for engaging with myriad audiences, including those within and beyond queer community enclaves. By dual address, we refer to the means by which TGNC storytellers might speak to and with multiple audiences simultaneously. More specifically, in our archive we found evidence that TGNC storytellers use dual address in order to build alliances with dominant audiences and communities while simultaneously offering affirmation and supportive resources to queer and trans parents. Understanding public address in this way is steeped in considerations of both text and audience. In terms of the former, rhetorical scholars have long asserted the polysemy of language; as Robin Jensen notes, "Language contain[s] multiple meanings as intended by authors or interpreted by audiences."[46] This textual ambiguity and dexterity can offer a site of invention, a vehicle through which storytellers might navigate ambivalent or even contradictory beliefs within a single audience.[47] Moreover, textual interpretation and resonance may rely in no small part on audiences as cocreators of meaning. Thus, rhetorical scholars have also attended to audience—what constitutes an audience and how storytellers and other public speakers might strategically invoke or otherwise engage with multiple communities at once. Scholars distinguish a rhetorical audience from a general audience insofar as a rhetorical audience is both open to influence and capable of enacting change.[48] Moreover, audiences are not monolithic: they might include insiders and outsiders, meaning those individuals who are addressed—directly or indirectly—and those who are invoked. Audiences may, in fact, be brought into being through discourse itself.

For scholars of movements and/or counterpublics,[49] dual address allows rhetorical actions for social change to appeal to different audiences to accomplish different objectives. For instance, a counterpublic speech may be directed internally to define and concretize a collective identity and consciousness among its members; the same social-change rhetors may also engage in rhetorical acts that target an external audience, persuading them to challenge the status quo or to act in solidarity with the movement.[50] For the purposes of this study, we draw on the tradition of rhetorical criticism that offers critical discernment of audiences both within and outside a given community, noting how

Reimagining Family and Kin   129

marginalized rhetors in particular adopt dual address to speak to and with multiple audiences, sometimes simultaneously. This orientation feels particularly appropriate for a model of reproductive justice that centers those experiences and perspectives that have historically been ignored or overlooked—those that embody the spirit of resistance, critical interrogation, and movement toward a more just vision of collective life (see chapter 2).

Our archive is rich with myriad examples. We aim less at comprehensive synthesis and summary and more at foregrounding an analysis that critically accounts for politically potent rhetorical strategies that radically reimagine family and kin and the relationship between gender and reproduction. More specifically, we focus on two rhetorical strategies that consistently punctuate our archive: deliberative empathy and counterstory.[51] Each of these strategies stretches the rhetorical imagination beyond familiar strategies of persuasion and identification in order to obtain recognition from the dominant public. Martinez defines *counterstory* as a narrative form and methodology for disrupting and rewriting dominant systems and narratives in spaces such as the classroom. Yam defines *deliberative empathy* as a rhetorical effect evoked by the telling of marginalized familial stories that foster coalitions and solidarities across difference. In other words, while both rhetorical strategies focus on storytelling from the margins, the two differ in their orientation to audiences and intended political outcomes. In what follows, we elaborate each of these rhetorical concepts and highlight how, when used to analyze dual address in the context of counterstorytelling, these theories complement and extend one another in ways that reveal the mechanisms of resistance and empowerment.

Deliberative Empathy and Counterstory

Despite the different intended effects and audiences, at the heart of deliberative empathy and counterstory are acts of storytelling from the margins. Reproductive justice scholars and activists have argued that storytelling is "a vehicle for social and personal transformation."[52] As Solinger argues, through storytelling, marginalized rhetors perform their full humanity, demanding the audience to see them as "real and whole, [as] a person who must be heard."[53] Other feminist scholars offer a similar understanding about the political and ethical significance of storytelling: by sharing their stories with others and seeing that their narratives are valued by others, storytellers receive the validation that their experience and personhood are worthy of attention and recognition from others.[54] Being heard and recognized on their own terms gives marginalized storytellers both discursive and political agency. Storytelling also helps create spaces for collective social change. Extending Hannah Arendt's observations that we are all simultaneously agentic subjects with autonomy and objects who are subjugated to forces and conditions beyond our control, the anthropologist Michael Jackson posits that storytelling is always intersubjective and politically meaningful; it functions as "a modality of working with others to transform what is given, or what simply befalls us, into forms of life, experience, and meaning that are collectively viable."[55]

Informed by the conundrum of how marginalized communities can receive recognition on their own terms without conforming to dominant state models, Shui-yin Sharon Yam examines storytelling from the margins as a way to promote what she calls "deliberative empathy" among audiences who occupy a more dominant positionality. For Yam, deliberative empathy is "a productive emotion and rhetorical effect that prompts dominant subjects to engage in transformative deliberation"—a form of deliberation that decenters achieving consensus and focuses instead on an "ongoing intersubjective engagement" between the marginalized storyteller and their dominant audiences.[56] It is important to note that we understand dominance as contextual and contingent rather than absolute and unchanging. While a cis straight married woman may occupy a more dominant position than a nonmonogamous trans person of color in the context of normative reproduction and family-making, they are *both* harmed by compulsory hetero- and cisnormativities, albeit in different ways. By prompting more dominant audiences to see how their interests and experiences align with those of the marginalized rhetor's, stories that

Reimagining Family and Kin   131

evoke deliberative empathy carry the potential of creating coalition moments across different positionalities and lived experiences.

We draw on deliberative empathy in our analysis of TGNC parents' reproductive and familial stories because this concept illustrates a productive way of sharing their experiences and engaging with mainstream audiences without assimilating into dominant institutions and narratives. Building on Arendt's concept of *inter-est*, which denotes overlapping interests and desires that politically and ethically connect otherwise distinct and separate individuals, deliberative empathy focuses on developing an affective relationship between the storyteller and audience to promote intersubjectivity and coalition through shared interests while actively recognizing and respecting the storyteller's alterity. Stories that evoke deliberative empathy offer marginalized rhetors the opportunity to illuminate conditions of structural exclusion and harm, including how such conditions may also entrap dominant audiences. By doing so, deliberative empathy fosters a form of relationship between mainstream audiences and the marginalized rhetors that refuses assimilation and the erasure of difference. Deliberative empathy encourages storytellers and audiences to engage with each other as interlocutors in order to promote political coalition and recognition "based not on the identification of sameness, but on an awareness of intersubjectivity" and shared struggles.[57] In this way, stories that evoke deliberative empathy echo Fred Moten's understanding of coalition against oppressive structures: "The coalition emerges out of your recognition that it's fucked up for you, in the same way that we've recognized that it's fucked up for us. . . . I just need you to recognize that this shit is killing you, too, however much more softly."[58] In other words, marginalized storytellers do not have to bear the burden of relaying their experiences in a way that makes them entirely resonant to the mainstream audience.[59] Rather, the audience shoulders some of the responsibility to critically recognize how the storyteller's struggles intersect with theirs.

Like deliberative empathy, counterstory considers the power of storytelling from the margins, theorizing how marginalized voices might intervene in dominant discourse and ideology. While deliberative empathy considers how this kind of storytelling cultivates a co-alitional space wherein privilege and power are renegotiated, counterstory considers how storytelling from the margins can challenge and rewrite dominant narratives. Aja Martinez theorizes counterstory as both methodology and method. In other words, counterstory is a theoretical framework for understanding how narratives confront dominant tropes from minoritized perspectives, as well as a tool kit for challenging tropes through counterstory genres that include narrated dialogue, fantasy/allegory, and autobiographic reflection. Intrinsically oppositional to dominant racist ideologies and institutions in its orientation, counterstory is, in Martinez's definition, a "theoretically grounded research approach" indebted to numerous fields, but it is most deeply rooted in the lineage of critical race theory and theorized in the context of higher education. Counterstory "empowers the minoritized through the formation of stories that disrupt the erasures embedded in standardized majoritarian methodologies."[60] However, Martinez is explicit in explaining that not all marginalized narratives are counterstory: in addition to expressing one's minoritized subjectivity and experience to critique dominant ideologies, counterstory should also be accessible to a wide range of public audiences beyond academia and should include the storyteller's critical self-reflection of their own privilege.

Two aspects of our engagement with counterstory as methodology and method distinguish it from Martinez's original use. First, Martinez focuses on the possibilities of counterstory for transformational change in the classroom, the university, and the discipline of rhetoric and writing studies. Our focus is, of course, aimed at public-facing storytelling contexts primarily outside of academe. Still, the power of Martinez's theorization of counterstory is not tethered to conditions exclusive to higher education. Under the right set of conditions and in keeping with the spirit of the original critical framework, there is great potential import in this method "for telling stories of those people whose experiences are not often told, and . . . to expose, analyze, and challenge majoritarian stories of racialized privilege."[61] Drawing on counterstory to consider the public storytelling practices of TGNC

Reimagining Family and Kin　　133

parents is appropriate because many of them not only center trans, nonbinary, and gender-nonconforming voices but also actively amplify Black, Indigenous, Latinx, and Asian and Pacific Islander storytelling as they interrogate long-standing histories of colonization and white supremacist racial terror.

The commitment to antiracism anchors the capacity for counterstory to traverse contexts beyond those exclusive to communities of color. Martinez notes this explicitly: "While there are indeed many marginal/ized narratives, the measure remains whether the tellers and stories subscribe to CRT's [critical race theory's] tenets, particularly in their critique of a dominant ideology (e.g., liberalism, whiteness, color blindness) and their sustained focus on social justice as an objective."[62] Second, then, and relatedly in our engagement of TGNC storytelling through counterstory, we stretch the boundaries of Martinez's theory to include gender nonconformity as a potential locus of inquiry. This is, at once, an expansion of Martinez's original work as well as, we argue, a deepening of its fidelity to critical race and ethnic studies. As we explored in earlier chapters of this book, gender itself is racialized all the way down. In the words of Khye Tyson, a Black nonbinary doula, a birth educator, and one of our interview participants: "Gender is a racist concept." Thus, drawing on critical race and decolonial theorists, we root our understanding of counterstory in this expansive interrogation of how gender and race are deeply entangled, building on work that clarifies how binary gender has long functioned as a weapon of white supremacist colonization and integrating this critique more explicitly into reproductive justice struggle and frameworks. Just as counterstory offers a critical lens through which to understand TGNC storytellers and their rhetorical strategies, so too does a consideration of TGNC counterstory expand our understanding of how counterstory itself functions.

We see deliberative empathy and counterstory as complementary in helping us unpack the different rhetorical effects TGNC birth stories have on the mainstream public and on people within the queer community. In practice, as marginalized rhetors deploy these two concepts within their storytelling, the concepts build on one another to

134   *Doing Gender Justice*

simultaneously sustain a radical space of affirmation and transformation among marginalized people and to expand the coalitional potential between marginalized communities and those in the mainstream public. While counterstory is defined as both a research methodology and rhetorical tactic deployed by marginalized rhetors to tell and understand their experiences of marginalization and resistance on their own terms, we posit that it can also be deployed to promote deliberative empathy among mainstream audiences. Since deliberative empathy does not hinge upon assimilation into dominant institutions or upon identification that erases the alterity of marginalized rhetors, it is not incongruent with the overarching tenets of counterstory. In short, deliberative empathy and counterstory work together in ways that both amplify and create conditions of possibility for one another. Placing these concepts in conversation throughout our analysis allows us to offer a richer, more robust rhetorical account of the stakes and political possibilities of storytelling from the margins.

The Rhetorical Possibilities of TGNC Storytelling

Our analysis is not aimed at providing a comprehensive overview of all significant themes that emerge within this vast archive of TGNC storytelling. Many stories within this archive deploy assimilatory rhetorical moves to foster identification with the mainstream citizenry and/or to secure state recognition. An emphasis on identification and state recognition, as many have pointed out, tends to reify dominant exclusionary institutions, while giving further valence to oppressive ideologies and practices.[63] Common strategies that are used to gain legitimacy in the eyes of the state and the mainstream public include reinscribing the significance of biogenetic kin and asserting one's resemblance to the dominant ideal of the middle-class, heteronuclear family. While these strategies stem from the need to survive and remain safe in contexts historically hostile to TGNC parents and nonnormative families, they give primacy to state institutions, gender ideologies, and familial structures that are exclusionary and based on colonial and racist ideologies (see the introduction).

Acknowledging the rhetorical constraints and systemic oppressions

Reimagining Family and Kin   135

faced by marginalized communities, we understand that transformative movements for social change do not progress in a linear way: while they carve out spaces of resistance and joy for communities who have experienced significant violence from dominant institutions and oppressive ideologies, they sometimes do get drawn back into the logics of the state. Rather than dismissing and casting out all assimilatory rhetorical moves as unfit for a transformative movement, we follow the footsteps of queer activists of color who practice harm reduction and transformative justice to eschew purity politics and moral perfectionism. Hence, we continue to analyze TGNC reproductive stories that may traffic in dominant logics alongside narratives that more critically challenge racist, colonial state ideologies. In what follows, we first perform a rhetorical analysis on TGNC parent stories that target a dominant mainstream audience. When analyzing assimilatory discourse, we identify moments of more radical possibility—places in which the rhetor decenters inclusion and assimilation to promote deliberative empathy or recognition on their own terms. Afterward, we read narratives that are created by and for TGNC parents to uplift each other's reproductive experiences, share resources, and grant each other recognition beyond the confines of state institutions and dominant ideologies.

Engaging Dominant Audiences

Within our archive, certain storytelling formats are more acutely attuned to speaking with and to dominant audiences. Those platforms with broad circulation—namely, popular-press memoirs, feature documentaries, and prominent parenting podcasts—afford marginalized rhetors the opportunity to situate TGNC birth and parenting within legible or otherwise assimilatory frameworks, while also occasionally adopting rhetorical strategies for cultivating deliberative empathy. Among these artifacts, many TGNC storytellers promote identification by situating their own experiences of pregnancy and parenting within hegemonic reproductive frameworks (middle-class, white nuclear-family ideal) while, at the same time, layering the complexity of gender and queerness onto those experiences. In so doing, TGNC rhetors can underscore their shared struggle and experience with dominant audiences even as they insist on clarifying places of difference—cultivating spaces of deliberative empathy, where the possibility of coalition is made real, and in turn stretching/expanding the edges of legible family formation.

We would be remiss if we did not mention the first widely circulated TGNC pregnancy and birth story: Thomas Beatie's memoir *Labor of Love: The Story of One Man's Extraordinary Pregnancy*. Published in 2008, just months following a mainstream media firestorm surrounding his pregnancy, *Labor of Love* deploys numerous assimilatory rhetorical strategies through appeals to mythic norms of gender, race, reproduction, and family. This is done in part through Beatie's adherence to reproductive homo- and heteronormativity in his adult life (as we discuss below), as well as through his narration of his tumultuous childhood and queer coming-of-age. Beatie recounts the trauma of growing up in an abusive home and the devastating loss of his mother to suicide in ways that—regardless of intent—function to mobilize tropes of white women's victimization, the violence perpetrated by men of color, and Asian American masculinity as harsh and stoic. While we critique his amplification of racialized stereotypes and assimilatory rhetorical moves in *Labor of Love*, we do not intend to police Beatie's representation of his experience, nor do we aim to dismiss or condone the violence he experienced at the hands of his father. Rather, we attempt to engage meaningfully with how the dominant logics of gender, sexuality, race, and family are at work with the TGNC narratives that circulate widely beyond LGBTQ+ enclaves, asking how they work to establish identification with mainstream audiences and to what rhetorical effect.

Beatie's story is undoubtedly complex; its narrative arc, however, moves steadily toward white, middle-class normativity. Throughout the latter part of his memoir, Beatie articulates his steady, loving relationship and home life with his white cisgender wife, Nancy, through culturally resonant forms of hegemonic familialism. The narration of Beatie's childhood alongside the suburban middle-class life he and Nancy have built work to bolster the clarion call of mainstream LGBTQ+

Reimagining Family and Kin   137

advocacy—"love makes a family"—through an unsettling juxtaposition replete with gendered and racialized stereotypes. In describing his journey to parenthood, Beatie emphasizes common cultural tropes about familial longing, naturalizing the yearning for children as "a fundamental imperative of families everywhere."[64] This claim renders Beatie's reproductive desire and family more legitimate in the eyes of mainstream audiences by adhering to a pronatalist ideology common among middle-class white Americans. In addition to fueling racialized stigma, the claim also risks giving valence to the exclusion that nonnormative families and kinship arrangements face—namely, voluntary kin ties not based on the birth of biological children, the practice of other-mothering, and people who either cannot or do not want to have children.

In addition to describing his desire to have biological children, Beatie also deploys assimilatory techniques to discuss his family formation. He frames his family life as typical, even boring in its banality: "We take walks around the lake and hold hands, we work hard and try to save money, we were thrilled to buy our first home together, and we practically live in Costco. And then, like millions of happy couples, we decided to have a family. In these things we are no different from anyone else. Our dreams are white-picket dreams."[65] Here, Beatie offers a narration of his reproductive desires as consonant with those of "anyone else"—as pedestrian, mundane, universal. Even as Beatie offers an extensive accounting of trans identity and experience, so too does he emphatically underscore how much his family resembles mainstream middle-class white American households in a narrative structure that foregrounds sameness even as it clarifies difference. For instance, he notes that his gender transition had nothing "to do with my desire to have a child. . . . My wife and I are in love and we wanted to start a family together. Anyone out there who is in love, or who has had a child, can certainly understand this."[66] Throughout *Labor of Love*, Beatie chronicles the challenges unique to TGNC family formation, including medical gatekeeping, legal obstacles, and struggles for trans (and trans pregnancy) acceptance within LGBTQ+ communities. He also takes great care to situate the specifics of TGNC families within a context legible to dominant audiences by describing the search for durable love, the desire for marriage, the experience of fertility challenges, and the hope for children. These rhetorical attempts to render TGNC families legible and assimilable—as "white picket" and just like "anyone else"—are direct entreaties to mainstream audiences, actively nurturing the conditions for empathy that might yield greater trans acceptance and inclusion.

While the dominant narrative themes throughout *Labor of Love* are deeply assimilatory, Beatie does engage the possibilities of deliberative empathy as he offers audiences new ways of contemplating gendered configurations of pregnancy and parenting. In a particularly compelling moment toward the end of his memoir, in a chapter titled "Manternity," Beatie writes: "I believe that being pregnant will make me a better father; I'm not quite sure in what ways yet, but I know it will. I feel such an incredible bond forming between us—in a way, it's the ultimate father-daughter bond."[67] The reference to bonding, of course, reflects common cultural beliefs that afford privilege and primacy to biogenetic kin. Still, in this simple declaration, Beatie reroutes the significance of this biogenetic tie in order to assert other (nonnormative) narratives about gender, reproduction, and family. He invites his audience to reconsider what it means for fathers to bond with their daughters; how a gestational tie to another human life might shape the relationship itself; and how a father bearing life might rewrite all manner of taken-for-granted relationships within the family unit. In a move decidedly un-assimilatory, Beatie leverages earlier moments of identification with the mainstream audience in order to nurture the possibility that straight, cisgender audiences might reflect on the narrowness of the prescribed familial bonds that shape their own experience. In so doing, he invites mainstream audiences to consider how gestational fatherhood might offer insights into their own circumstances, crafting moments of coalitional possibility across gender identity and family formation.

Another text within our archive is *Seahorse: The Dad Who Gave Birth*—one of the most widely acclaimed documentaries of TGNC pregnancy to date—which provides a clear and resonant example of

Reimagining Family and Kin   139

using assimilatory tropes alongside tactics that evoke deliberative empathy. The name of the film itself—titled in reference to male gestation in the animal kingdom—normalizes TGNC pregnancy and birth through direct ties to the "natural" world, a narrative and assimilatory theme that anchors the entire film. Premiering at Tribeca Film Festival to rave reviews in 2019, *Seahorse* has been hailed as "nuanced, tender," and "moving"[68] in mainstream media outlets. Earning a 100% rating on Rotten Tomatoes, the film was described by top critics as "a vital, fascinating story," one that shatters stereotypes and "underscores the fact that however atypical our lives may be, we have more in common than not."[69] The film documents the journey of Freddy McConnell, a thirty-year-old white gay trans man who pursues pregnancy and parenting, at first with a Black trans romantic partner but eventually on his own. Speaking to *The Guardian* upon the release of the film, McConnell describes his decision to document his journey through the lens of identification and empathy: "I think empathy is key in convincing people that trans people are actually quite normal, and live lives that are not sensational or scary.... Hopefully people will come away thinking they've seen something relatable, a universal story about love and family and wanting to have kids."[70] Indeed, relatability and universality ground the narrative arc and central themes of the film, as McConnell's trans pregnancy is folded into normative ideals and beliefs. For example, throughout the documentary, McConnell situates his pregnancy within a familiar set of tropes about reproductive desire and natalism—noting at the outset of the film that he has always wanted to have children and that using his own gamete and carrying his own child is the most "pragmatic" option available to him.

However, it is important to recognize that TGNC parents do not always have the privilege—and should not always be expected—to resist familial and legal norms. Gametes and gestational surrogacy are both expensive, rendering them inaccessible to many TGNC parents. And as we noted earlier, TGNC parents face significant precarity because their parentage and/or guardianship of their children is frequently questioned by the state. At the same time, when such reproductive decisions are not situated within a critique of structural barriers, they risk reinforcing the harmful belief that biogenetically related children are more valuable.

In addition to the pronatalist ideologies affirmed through McConnell's narrative, dominant understandings of family are nurtured in the film by the presence of McConnell's mother, Esme, who becomes his primary support person throughout his pregnancy. Esme's unequivocal support for her son helps to translate his experiences to mainstream audiences, naturalizing his pregnancy by situating it within a more typical family unit. She articulates her support for her son through the lens of maternal protection: "You just worry for your child. You want them to be happy." In the same breath, she offers audiences a framework for understanding McConnell's experiences as "a brave and amazing thing to do. It's much braver than we can imagine. I'm in awe of him basically."[71] Through this rendering of McConnell's journey, TGNC pregnancy is tethered to hegemonic understandings of family and reproduction—namely, the strong desire to have a child, the powerful impulse to protect one's child, the parent-child bond, the human longing for love through gestation, and the reproduction of (biogenetic) kin. The effect is largely about trans inclusion and assimilation—an ideological stretching of dominant beliefs to incorporate TGNC parents, while simultaneously mobilizing tropes that render other familial desires or configurations, such as the desire to not have children or to create family outside of biogenetic reproduction, perhaps less legible or legitimate.

The narrative structure of *Seahorse* toggles between frameworks that emphasize normative reproduction on the one hand and the unique qualities of TGNC conception, pregnancy, and birth on the other. Queer theorists have long critiqued assimilatory moves such as those described above as capitulating to normativity in ways that blunt the radical import of queerness. While our archive contains countless examples of what some might call assimilatory rhetorical moves, we understand the forms of strategic assimilation invoked here as creative and, in many ways, rhetorically savvy enactments of survival, particularly when paired with curations of deliberative empathy. For example, like other TGNC reproductive narratives, *Seahorse* repeatedly highlights the complexities TGNC people face when trying to have a biological child. Early in the documentary, CJ, a Black nonbinary person and McConnell's romantic partner at the time, laments that there are only four Black sperm donors available, noting how white couples do not have to consider whether they will be able to find (and afford) gametes that match their ethnic heritage or racial identity. This exchange between McConnell and CJ taps into familiar terrain, as the expense of assisted reproduction continues to occupy considerable airtime in dominant media outlets; mainstream audiences may have even experienced this financial hardship directly. While the film does not dive much deeper into complex ethical and political questions about the selection of gamete donors and the purchase of sperm—questions that scholars have examined at length—it does prompt the audience to consider how race shapes access to reproductive technologies and how TGNC people of color, especially those who are working class, face additional burdens when trying to have a child.[72]

In another example prompting deliberative empathy, McConnell walks along the shore in his tranquil coastal town in Kent, England, vocalizing his experience of pregnancy. In a passage worth quoting at length, he speaks simultaneously to concerns both universal and specific:

> I thought [pregnancy] would feel more of a kind of natural thing because it's my body, but actually I'm surprised by the extent to which I feel like a man who is doing something really odd. I did not expect to feel this uncomfortable, and I think if all men got pregnant, then, like, my god, pregnancy would be taken so much more seriously and talked about, and I would have known what to expect because it would be this thing that men have to suffer through. No one tells you that morning sickness isn't just in the morning, and no one tells you that you have to eat to feel better but then that doesn't work half the time and that you're just going to feel like an emotional disaster zone all the time. Fuck. This is fucking awful. If men had to go through this all the time, you'd just never hear the end of it.[73]

Here, McConnell narrates his pregnancy through the lens of alienation—as someone who is physically capable of gestating a child but who also experiences a heightened sense of estrangement in the process. This might have provided an opportunity to delve deeper into gender and pregnancy in a way that was tailored to trans experience, but McConnell opts instead to connect the gendered dimensions of reproduction to structural critiques of sexism and misogyny. He offers a broad critique of heteronormativity in reproduction, clarifying how it constrains TGNC experience while also highlighting structural critiques of sexism and misogyny writ large. He highlights how the physical and emotional challenges of pregnancy are minimized in public culture and rendered invisible in contexts that center cisgender men's experiences and needs.

Throughout the film, McConnell's remarks about his pregnancy experiences offer ample opportunities for anyone who has gestated a child to relate directly to his experience, while also weaving TGNC-specific references into his story. Framed thus, his struggles function both to highlight chasms between cis experiences and trans experiences and to simultaneously offer generative sites of deliberative empathy, wherein audiences are invited to reflect on the broader structural conditions that shape reproduction and family. And, as he identifies spaces of congruency, so too does McConnell integrate additional intimate details related to TGNC concerns, such as the difficulty of attending work while visibly pregnant and his heightened gender dysphoria in general. His story also underscores queer family formation, pairing the biogenetic with single parenting as a gay trans dad and cultivating an ongoing relationship with his ex (CJ), who is an active parent to the child of an extended family-of-origin member. Stretching the boundary of reproductive legibility by weaving together the pedestrian and unique, *Seahorse* locates ample space for coalitional alignments between cis- and TGNC-identified parents, between biogenetic and adoptive parents, and between families configured across various lines of difference—spaces in which to nurture deliberative empathy and its political power.

Film reviews of *Seahorse* in mainstream media outlets reflect the

Reimagining Family and Kin   143

effects this film has on the wider public audience. Specifically, they illustrate how the film prompts some to experience a more critical form of empathy rather than merely identification. For example, in a review published in *The Guardian*, Charles Bramesco writes, "We all share universals like hurt and hope, it's just that their expression differs for McConnell. Like the act of childbirth itself, something that has happened trillions of times and yet always feels intimately personal, he's one of us and one of a kind."[74] This comment suggests that Bramesco is inching toward deliberative empathy as he simultaneously recognizes the shared and distinct experiences and feelings. The remark, however, betrays that the film may not be effective in prompting mainstream audience members to critically consider how transphobia, gender normativity, and cisnormativity in reproduction negatively affect cis people as well. Bramesco's remark about McConnell being "one of a kind" reveals that, for some, the documentary poses a spotlight effect—a narrow focus of affective energy on an individual at a personal level—that limits the audience's ability to engage in structural critique and collective action.

A review published in the *Portland Observer* offers greater critical insight. In it, the film critic Darleen Ortega reflects on two scenes in the film in which McConnell interacts with cis woman friends and relatives. In the first scene, he is surrounded by a group of older white cis women, who are attempting to support him. As the women enthusiastically share their own experiences of pregnancy, parenthood, and birth, McConnell looks visibly uneasy and remains mostly quiet. In the second scene, McConnell's relatives are angered quickly when McConnell rejects a normative understanding of the reproductive experience. Ortega considers this scene significant in prompting the audience to examine "the ways in which our fear and assumptions keep us from appropriate curiosity—which requires us to hold our assumptions much more loosely than we are prone to do.... Freddie's [*sic*] experience also made me reflect on how pregnant women actually do experience some similar dynamics."[75] Ortega's reflection suggests that the film has prompted her to examine the coalitional potential between cis and trans pregnant people.

Despite the film's evocation of deliberative empathy in several moments, the ending of *Seahorse* is overwhelmed by the trope of an innocent white baby. About halfway into the film, McConnell reveals that he is no longer in a relationship with CJ. Not wanting to use the sperm that CJ has purchased, McConnell purchases his own. In the film, McConnell does not explicitly explain how he chooses another donor, nor does the film address the racial politics of assisted reproduction from this point forward. The silence about race and gamete selection becomes somewhat problematic toward the end of the film: after zooming in on a seahorse, a naturalizing image, the camera then offers close-up shots of a white baby's hand, feet, cheeks, and hazy blue eyes. The bright white light surrounding these shots emphasizes the innocence of the white baby. The film then zooms out a bit to show McConnell's face against his baby's, emphasizing a phenotypic likeness between the two. Without a more critical discussion about the racial politics of gamete selection in queer reproduction, these last few scenes reify dominant logics of biological reproduction and family-making by prompting the audience to validate McConnell's father-child relationship through the lens of biogenetic kin ties and whiteness.

Similar patterns of crafting deliberative empathy emerge in TGNC narratives featured in episodes of popular parenting podcasts such as *The Double Shift* and *The Longest Shortest Time*. While both podcasts have recently ceased producing new episodes, each is still widely circulated and critically acclaimed. Launched in 2010 by the journalist Hillary Frank and in production for over nine years, *The Longest Shortest Time* is perhaps one of the best-known parenting podcasts to date. In addition to being named one of the fifty top podcasts by *The Atlantic* and *Time*, it has also garnered numerous awards, including from "New York Festival's World's Best Radio, The Academy of Podcasters, the Webbys, and the Third Coast International Festival."[76] *The Double Shift*, airing new episodes regularly from its launch in 2019 until its hiatus in 2022, is described by its creator as a storytelling podcast that centers motherhood. *The Double Shift* is a featured pick across multiple platforms and, according to its website, is "ranked in the top 2% of downloads for all podcasts."[77]

When mainstream parenting podcasts feature TGNC storytellers, their stories are rooted firmly alongside the stories of cisgender heteronuclear families by design. Narrative alignments that normalize TGNC families are often emphasized to promote identification—for example, discussing with TGNC parents the chaos of family life or the ineffable love one has for their children.[78] The stories told by TGNC parents are structured in ways that toggle back and forth between familiar or otherwise legible contexts—contexts aimed at eliciting identification with straight, cisgender podcast listeners give way to contexts more particular to TGNC experiences, which need greater explication for mainstream audiences but occasionally offer sites of deliberative empathy and/or counterstory. For example, appearing on an episode of *The Double Shift* in 2019, a birth dad named Ted explained his experience in ways that invite audiences to reflect broadly on gender, reproduction, and labor. Ted transitioned after giving birth to five children; in his experience, he notes that pregnancy, breastfeeding, and parenting are "not super gendered experiences." He states: "Maybe I loved being pregnant because finally my body was good for something. . . . And breastfeeding is just endlessly convenient and I like the connection. So for me, it's more the connection with my kids, it's not really gendered."[79] By delinking gender from reproduction and reproductive labor, Ted deploys a counterstory tactic that denaturalizes gender assumptions and challenges common presuppositions about gender, reproduction, and labor that render minoritized people and families inferior.

This theme echoes across our archive—and, in particular, among stories circulating within counterpublic media enclaves. A number of TGNC storytellers underscore pregnancy as wide enough for many gendered experiences and as an opportunity to experience the body not as a site of alienation but rather as something useful and powerful in the creation of human life. Moreover, in this moment, counterstory functions in tandem with the evocation of deliberative empathy. For mainstream audiences, Ted's reflection offers an opportunity to reflect on *how* pregnancy and reproduction are gendered in dominant culture and the extent to which that is accurate or otherwise necessary.

Even as he claims a position that, by his admission, may be unpopular (e.g., by asserting that pregnancy is not necessarily gendered), he invites identification with his audience when he asserts the parent-child bond created through the intimacies of biological reproduction. Ted uses feminine language to describe bodyfeeding, and in so doing he refigures feminized reproductive processes as gender neutral, thereby inviting mainstream audiences to reconsider the gendering of reproductive and care labor writ large. Delinking femininity and pregnancy, for example, might invite us to question how femininity is unnecessarily mapped onto all manner of things linked with children and child-rearing, fueling uneven distributions of labor within the nuclear family unit and beyond. Questioning how gestation and parenting are naturalized as feminine, in other words, invites broader critiques of how reproductive and care labor are deeply—and yet unnecessarily—gendered in turn.

In the first of what became a popular series of episodes on the award-winning podcast *The Longest Shortest Time*, trans gay dad Trystan Reese draws on deliberative empathy and counterstory to describe his first few months as a parent to two small children. His narration is attuned to the familiar emotional terrain of parenting, even as his circumstances differed from many. For Reese and his family, gender was not the only—or even the most significant—marker of difference. His children entered his life abruptly and in crisis through the US foster system, as the biological children of his partner's sister with nowhere else to go. Reese is clear that his family's origin story is complicated because it was predicated on someone else's loss: "We wanted to prepare and get ourselves ready, get our lives ready, be a parent to someone where everyone felt great about it. Not where one person had to experience the trauma of losing her kids. We don't take that lightly."[80] In this moment, Reese shifts into counterstory, and in lieu of upholding dominant figurations of adoption as child rescue, he offers some structural critique of the systems that informed his children's separation from their birth parents, which include poverty, addiction, and violence. He underscores these conditions briefly in the context of describing the intense process of healing for his young

Reimagining Family and Kin   147

children, who had been subject to horrific abuse. This is a delicate negotiation, for Reese is speaking with an audience most likely unfamiliar with queer and trans people in general, which is to say nothing of queer and trans parenting. Even as he is tasked with justifying his right to exist as a trans person and his worth as a parent—which he does attend to at length—Reese is careful not to erase how structural forms of violence shaped how his family came to be.

Reese also narrates his experiences in ways that prompt deliberative empathy. In narrating his family's origin story, Reese situates the legal and cultural precarity of LGBTQ+ and foster parenting within dominant frameworks of enduring parental love and fierce protection for children:

> We lived with that terror [of state removal] every single day. There were three months when we didn't have any legal rights at all. And at any point their biological parents could've showed up and said, "Never mind. Give them back." And we would've lost them. It was like building the plane while flying it. It's like we're trying to parent these deeply traumatized kids while also defending our right to parent them at the same time . . . if you have no legal rights to a kid, you can't put them in school. You can't take them to a doctor, you can't put them in preschool, you can't do almost anything with them. And as gay parents it's harder 'cause if we were a straight couple, we could just show up at a school and enroll them and no one would ask for proof. But because we're gay parents, you automatically know these are not your biological kids, show us the paperwork.[81]

Reese tenderly weaves in accounts of difference rooted in queer experience as well as the experience of fostering children. In so doing, he offers mainstream cisgender audiences an opportunity for deliberative empathy—an opportunity to interrogate how the state violently surveilles and intervenes in the lives of some families (much more so than in others) and how LGBTQ+ people have long been excluded from legal, social, and cultural recognition and rights. He reveals how the basic rights and responsibilities that many parents take for granted—such as enrolling a child in school or daycare or taking them to the

148   *Doing Gender Justice*

doctor—are in fact mired in biogenetic, heteronuclear, and racially homogeneous familial privilege, even as he crafts alignments with other cis and/or straight parents by articulating the pedestrian concerns and tasks of child-rearing. Reese's narrative thus nurtures deliberative empathy and the conditions for coalitional possibility and political solidarity.

When TGNC storytellers engage with mainstream audiences, their narratives work to underscore shared commitments, often in ways that echo white cisgender heteronuclear reproduction and family. The effect is an emphasis on trans inclusion and assimilation, which broadens how we imagine family even as it doubles down on some of its normative exclusions and constraints. The logic of inclusion and assimilation is complicated, however, by repeated rhetorical entreaties for deliberative empathy and, occasionally, counterstory as well. But delving deeper into our archive and focusing on media created *by* and *for* LGBTQ+ (and often BIPOC) communities will offer greater nuance in showing how TGNC stories circulate and function in public spaces. In what follows, we turn to TGNC narratives created by and for TGNC people and which draw more heavily on counterstory.

Counterstorytelling by and for Queer Communities

Circulating at the edges of dominant media, in smaller enclaves created *by* and *for* trans and gender-nonconforming communities, podcasts and digital magazines offer spaces cultivated explicitly for TGNC birthers and parents. Josie Rodriguez-Bouchier, the founder and host of *The Intersectional Fertility Podcast*, underscores how this orientation distinguishes these media spaces. In the inaugural episode of their podcast, they note, "There is a significant difference between 'all are welcome here' and 'this was created with you in mind.' . . . Qmmunity [*sic*], all of this was created with you in mind. Welcome."[82] Within these enclave spaces, the possibility of TGNC counterstory more fully emerges. Committed to cultural critique and transformation, TGNC counterstory voices and affirms reproductive experiences that run against the grain and, significantly, creates space for the joy, resilience, and radical possibility of queer family formation. In this final section, we illustrate how TGNC storytellers challenge and rewrite dominant narratives about pregnancy, parenting, and family writ large through counterstory. In what follows, we begin by clarifying how counterstory itself is a catalyst for the creation of TGNC parenting media. We then detail how TGNC counterstorytellers challenge dominant narratives by uplifting one another's reproductive experiences, sharing resources, and granting one another recognition beyond the confines of state institutions and dominant ideologies.

Counterstory is an explicit and formative impulse for TGNC storytellers, both in the desire to tell their own stories and, for some, in the creation of media outlets that curate and circulate similar stories. Throughout our archive, across varied platforms and mediums, TGNC counterstorytellers were expressly motivated by a desire to cultivate space for nuanced conversations and resource exchange about TGNC pregnancy and parenting. In the opening episode of the groundbreaking podcast *Masculine Birth Ritual*, white transmasculine parent and creator/host Grover Wehman-Brown states, "This podcast is an offering to community, an attempt to fill the void of stories, imagery, and collective imagination about what it feels and looks like for masculine of center people to conceive, carry, birth, and nurture humans with and through our bodies."[83] For Wehman-Brown, this curation of transmasculine storytelling was not abstract but was in fact rooted in their own experience, and it was expressly articulated to the project of gender liberation, birth justice, and antiracism:

> I had an unexpectedly difficult and gender-isolating pregnancy, then a very complicated, long, life-threatening birth. . . . And as I was healing physically and healing from the most acute trauma, I kept thinking "What the fuck are you going to do with your survival?" I wanted to create access to the stories I needed but there were very few readily accessible when I was pregnant in 2014. I wanted to create the project so that MoC [masculine of center] pregnancy and birth was understood by listeners—especially white MoC listeners like myself—as part of wider Birth Justice movements led by Black, Brown, and Indigenous women and nonbinary and trans leaders.[84]

150   Doing Gender Justice

Counterstory is thus built into the foundation of Wehman-Brown's project. It is oppositional by nature, a challenge to dominant myths and norms, and is rooted in an intersectional politic that draws on the legacy of antiracist and decolonial struggles for justice. Echoing the dual function of counterstory as both resistance and in-group affirmation, the podcast itself is articulated in myriad ways as a resource, affirmation, and mode of community survival.

Rodriguez-Bouchier draws their inspiration for *The Intersectional Fertility Podcast* from a counterstorytelling impulse as well, describing the podcast as a significant facet of their health- and justice-based activism. Realizing their complicity in a system of harm within traditional reproductive health care settings, Rodriguez-Bouchier states: "As a fertility acupuncturist, my new path and calling emerged loud and clear to create liberatory and intersectional spaces for queer, trans and non-binary folks, especially people of color in reproductive health-care and everywhere."[85] Rodriguez-Bouchier characterizes their podcast in terms that resonate with the oppositional orientation of counterstorytelling, focusing on "recenter[ing] queer, trans, and non-binary folks in the reproductive health care realm."[86] Indeed, Rodriguez-Bouchier notes, *re*-centering signals how queer, trans, and nonbinary people have always been present in reproductive health care settings and struggles, and moreover, it shows that the work of reproductive justice pivots on decolonial understandings of sex, gender, and reproduction. Thus, for TGNC podcasters like Wehman-Brown and Rodriguez-Bouchier, counterstorytelling is the formative impulse. Curated niche media by and for TGNC communities offer both resistance and solidarity—opportunities to challenge narrow ideologies and rewrite how we collectively envision pregnancy, parenting, and kin.

One of the primary ways TGNC parents use counterstory is to affirm one another's reproductive experiences and, in particular, the expansive complexity of gender-diverse family formation. Decentering state recognition in favor of affirming one another's experiences, TGNC counterstorytellers focus on articulating the experience of reproduction as intensely diverse; this includes voicing dysphoria and hardship, as well as what Rivera refers to as the "genderful," complex,

Reimagining Family and Kin 151

and empowering. While nearly all of the stories told by TGNC parents discuss pregnancy and/or parenting beyond and outside of gender binaries, counterstorytellers offer messier accounts of gender in the context of pregnancy and parenting for those audiences imagined as smaller and, especially, LGBTQ+ identified. These accounts include how binary gender is often imposed on TGNC birthing people and parents in ways that are harmful and violent, as TGNC storytellers detail experiences of medical gatekeeping, social isolation, and exclusions—both from the dominant birth and parenting culture and from within queer and trans communities. In other words, the structural constraints outlined earlier in this chapter have a direct impact, as the voices in our archive attest. We focus here, however, on a prominent, if perhaps unexpected, set of counterstory articulations. Many TGNC individuals use counterstory to insist that the violence of binary gender is not the exclusive—or even most prominent—dimension of queering reproduction. Thus, TGNC counterstorytellers reframe pregnancy and parenting in order to affirm the desire to reproduce, as well as reframing the myriad possibilities of embodiment that reproduction might entail.

TGNC counterstories rearticulate a gender-expansive framework for pregnancy and parenting that goes against the grain of mainstream representation. This rearticulation challenges the narrow understandings of TGNC pregnancy as always already misaligned and thus dysphoric. Jacoby Ballard, a white genderqueer birth parent and featured guest on the podcast *Masculine Birth Ritual*, noted this succinctly: "As a trans person, there's a lot of complicated feelings, I think, for a lot of masculine identified or genderqueer people or trans guys about carrying a child."[87] Counterstorytellers discuss gender dysphoria as one of many possible experiences with pregnancy and birth, affirming the challenge of gender fluidity in binary cultural settings while also voicing experiences of joy and empowerment. In the next breath, Ballard continues: "Just the experience of pushing, I feel made it all worth it to me. So it's this pure experience of the power of my body and just energy moving through me that I wouldn't give back for anything."[88] Thus, Ballard narrates childbirth as a site of embodied empowerment that shifts the entire terrain of their gestational experience. Consistent across our archive, counterstorytellers attest to a wide range of TGNC experiences in order to reframe reproduction as a rich site of gender diversity and to affirm the desire of TGNC individuals to have a child in the first place.

Destabilizing strong cultural associations between femininity and reproduction, many TGNC storytellers use counterstory to rearticulate pregnancy and parenting as wide enough for myriad gendered experiences. As Krys Malcolm Belc writes in his memoir, *The Natural Mother of the Child: A Memoir of Nonbinary Parenthood*, "Nothing about being pregnant made me feel feminine. This body is what it is: not quite man, not quite woman, but with the parts to create and shape life. To expel and care for that life. Creating Samson, given such a strong name because I felt I had done something strong, made me ready to be me."[89] The strength and gender fluidity that Belc associates with his pregnancy echoes across our archive. The documentary filmmaker Cyn Lubow underscores pregnancy and parenting as demanding competence, courage, strength, and endurance: "All kinds of things that might actually be, you know, considered more masculine. . . . I was fully myself in doing those things. I was all of my intimate, emotional, nurturing self and I was also all of my powerful, tough, strong [self]."[90] In moments like these, TGNC counterstorytellers contest white supremacist colonial understandings of binary gender through a retelling of reproduction itself. The resistance to hegemonic narratives here is at least twofold. First, the resistance challenges naturalized associations between (white) femininity and reproduction— associations that reduce femininity to weakness, as directly opposed to masculine strength and courage. Articulating the full spectrum of demands entailed in pregnancy and parenting, TGNC counterstorytellers defy the binary logics that tether narrow understandings of gender to reproduction. Second, and perhaps even more significantly, they simultaneously resist transphobic narratives that position TGNC bodies as deficient or pathological. Instead, TGNC counterstorytellers

Reimagining Family and Kin 153

insist on narrating their bodies as creative, powerful, and nourishing—an embodiment of the rich diversity of human life and experience.

Indeed, some storytellers use counterstory to recast reproduction as trans—as a unique possibility in the constellation of transmasculine experience. Mac Brydum describes this sentiment in his interview with *Masculine Birth Ritual* as follows: "I really want to carry a pregnancy. That's an experience that is interesting to me and how neat to be able to use the body that I have to do something really cool . . . for myself, there's never been an incongruence with being a man and being very binary-identified and carrying a pregnancy."[91] Nonbinary parent J Carroll concurs: "I don't see being pregnant and birthing and laboring as a feminine thing. So I think in that way, it wasn't dysphoric for me . . . my body is able to grow a human. And I am not feminine, so it can't be a feminine ailment."[92] Building on the aforementioned critiques of pregnancy as inherently feminine and of trans bodies as deficient, TGNC counterstory reframes pregnancy as trans embodiment, adding another welcome dimension to the diversity and complexity of TGNC experience.

These rearticulations of reproduction as being gender expansive function as trans affirmation in multiple ways. While our archive and analysis focus on the pregnancy and birth narratives and experiences of TGNC people, it is also important to note the intimate connections among gender, family-making, and the decision *not* to get pregnant. Reading an early draft of this chapter, Natalie's partner, V, noted how their decision to forgo pregnancy—while also wholeheartedly embracing parenting—had everything to do with gender: "I became increasingly aware of not only the suffocatingly heteronormative spaces that pregnancy occupies, but the physical changes to my body that I felt would take a toll on my mental health. . . . I will never know what harms I have avoided, but I do know that I can show up every day as a parent confident in who I am and the body I occupy."[93] We include this here not only to mark the magnitude of TGNC counterstorytelling possibility but also to acknowledge and honor the act of refusal—the insistence of protecting oneself from harm as a sacred political act. While a fuller exploration exceeds the parameters of this study, we simply wish to note here that some parents deliberately reject the biophysiological dimensions of reproduction as an act of trans embodiment and survival, investing queer reproductive love in the act of parenting beyond biogenetics. This, too, is a radical act.

Thus, the decision to embrace pregnancy created an exigency for TGNC counterstorytelling to affirm not only the *experience* of but also the very *desire* for pregnancy and parenting. Rae Goodman-Lucker voices this sentiment on an episode of *Masculine Birth Ritual*: "I always wanted to be pregnant and give birth and have that experience . . . it's such a core experience of being a person. Obviously not everyone has it, but it's one of the things that's available and I don't know. I wanted to have done it, to know what that is."[94] Through counterstory, Goodman-Lucker challenges long-standing eugenic assumptions about who can and should desire pregnancy. In a similar vein, when asked for any advice for listeners of *The Intersectional Fertility Podcast*, the writer Gabby Rivera chooses to address the audience directly with a related affirmation of queer desire: "If you're a solo, queer, butch of color, you should know that you are allowed to want a child, to want to conceive a child. . . . You are allowed to take up space and to create the family that you want, that you dream about."[95] Through counterstory, TGNC individuals powerfully rearticulate the terrain of available reproductive experience; in so doing, they affirm a range of TGNC kinship desires and embodiments.

As TGNC parents articulate a broad spectrum of experience, they use counterstory to affirm gender-expansive reproduction and family formation while also underscoring the infinite unfixity of gender itself. Against the dominant grain of binary gender, which assumes fixity and rigidity, many emphasize that reproduction can be a site of gender's unfolding. Reflecting on their reproductive journeys, some TGNC parents underscore just how surprisingly fluid and unstable gender can be. As the graphic novelist A. K. Summers describes in *Pregnant Butch*: "I feel like my *masculinity* got stretched along with my whatchamacallit. I'm a more flexible and resilient butch now."[96] Goodman-Lucker relays that pregnancy created an opportunity to explore feeling more at home in femininity.[97] Belc's memoir provides an extended

Reimagining Family and Kin 155

meditation on how having his son offered Belc clarity about his gender identity and gave him the courage to live as his authentic self.[98] TGNC parents repeatedly use counterstory to unsettle gender in myriad ways; in so doing, they offer "possibility models" for parenting beyond the binary.[99]

As TGNC parents rearticulate their reproductive and familial experiences on their own terms, some use counterstorytelling as a means to rearticulate the process of family formation or even the meaning of family and kin itself. To be clear, and as evidenced in our exploration of deliberative empathy, our archive attests to powerful TGNC storytelling that focuses on trans inclusion in our collective vision of "family." Many TGNC stories do not necessarily unsettle dominant figurations of kin; indeed, many TGNC storytellers assert legibility by claiming biogenetic or nuclear family forms. As noted above, we understand this impulse as a form of impure politics[100]—as an often conscious and savvy technique of survival in a world profoundly hostile to trans, nonbinary, and gender-nonconforming lives. Still, for the purposes of this chapter and in the spirit of counterstory, we also wish to highlight those spaces in which TGNC parents narrate family against the grain of dominant culture, providing small glimpses of worlds perhaps possible. As queer-identified midwife Sara Ceiba Flores succinctly states in an interview aired twice on *The Intersectional Fertility Podcast*, "Actually, no, we're not just like everybody else and that's our gift. That's our strength. That's sacred, that's beautiful. And so, we don't have to conceive in a cis-het linear model either."[101] In this way, TGNC storytellers use counterstory to articulate alternative— and in some cases, radically transformative—visions of reproduction and kin.

TGNC counterstorytellers celebrate queer resilience and invention and the capacity to reimagine reproduction and family. For example, some TGNC parents find that even supposedly neutral terms— "pregnancy" in particular—feel intensely feminine. Summers playfully relays this sentiment in a small single column of graphic art, writing, "Incidentally, is there a term we can use other than 'pregnancy'? It's always made me feel squeamish . . . there's always knocked up? Up a tree? In a pickle? Chockfull o' kitties? G-gravid? Big with child? No no no! I guess I could invent my own term."[102] This extended meditation is situated alongside a larger exploration of transmasculine pregnancy fashion, in which Summers playfully sketches out the use of suspenders and smoking jackets to support a gestating body. In so doing, Summers invites audiences to quite literally visualize pregnancy differently—to rearticulate its linguistic investments alongside its pedestrian appearance. Summers's reimagining considers the challenges that linguistic creativity might present for legibility, within medical contexts in particular: "What is the reason for your visit today? / Fetal corpulence / Excuse me? / Uterine glut / Whuh? / Ok. Preggy eggy weggy / Oh! Why didn't you say so?!" This reflection underscores both the challenge of legibility within these contexts and the capacity for creativity and linguistic dexterity. In this way, counterstory works to foster imagination, offering a space for active collaboration with readers that might prompt new, more capacious articulations of pregnancy.

Some TGNC parents discussed how they did, in fact, invent new words to describe the experience of gestation. Jacoby Ballard co-authored a "germination proclamation" with their wife as a quick reference for friends and family, answering frequently asked questions and explaining their linguistic choices in the following way: "I called it a germination rather than pregnancy. Because that was a word that resonated more, is kind of non-gendered. And I'm also an herbalist. And so it kind of had a sweetness of identifying with my plant friends."[103] And indeed, the language surrounding reproduction is rapidly expanding, with cues taken from TGNC counterstorytellers. Flores underscores how attending to individuals' naming and linguistic desires can help to reimagine gender-affirming care; their storytelling playfully and intentionally offers listeners of *The Intersectional Fertility Podcast* new vocabularies to prompt queer understandings of reproduction:

> We understand that there's a need for a warm environment for the
> egg to become fertilized and then grow. Which many people call

Reimagining Family and Kin   157

the womb, or the uterus, or the baby holder. There's lots of different words. But I don't think that that has to mean that that person who's carrying a baby growing in their body, has to even identify with being pregnant . . . that piece has really been a gift to me, by working with trans men, who are really ready to be dads, can't wait to be dads, and happen to have a place for a baby to grow inside of their body. But don't identify as pregnant people at all.[104]

As Flores points out, even terms widely assumed to be gender inclusive (e.g., "pregnant person") may not resonate across the gender spectrum. For some, like Flores's clients and Summers, there is a binary residue to a term like "pregnancy" that renders it too rigid to capture the experience of TGNC reproduction well or more fully. Indeed, many storytellers named how being labeled "pregnant" resulted in being regularly misgendered—not only by strangers but also by friends, family, and coworkers who had previously respected their gender identity. These forms of linguistic creativity through counterstory reflect TGNC parents' continued commitment to unsettling gender and the ongoing opportunities for radical reimagining and reinvention of reproduction itself. Consistent with themes we explore earlier in this book, the way we use language to describe gender and reproduction is never fixed but rather is up for reinvention and reinterpretation (see chapter 1).

TGNC counterstorytellers' reimagining of dominant reproductive practice extends beyond conception and gestation to question assumptions about parenting practice and the relationship between family and community. TGNC parents use counterstory to narrate the complexity of gender in child-rearing, for example. Max, a white nonbinary parent featured in the short film *Raising My Baby Gender Neutral: Max and River*, notes that gender-neutral child-rearing is a form of resistance to the cultural expectations that others might map onto their child: "The meaning of raising a gender neutral child is just giving them the ability to have the freedom to choose themselves, without any constricted ideas of what their gender will be."[105] Moreover, TGNC counterstorytellers underscore that gender-expansive parenting is re-

158   *Doing Gender Justice*

sponsive, first and foremost, to the child. Wehman-Brown explains, "As my oldest daughter started to really assert her own gender . . . she didn't want to be called by those gender-neutral terms. She wanted to be my daughter and was proud to be my daughter. . . . I quickly had to school up on the complexities of what mainstream gender stuff is so that I could parent her well."[106] Here, Wehman-Brown offers a mode of parenting with and alongside their daughter that centers her needs and recognition and permits the fluency of gender to move in and out of forms of recognition granted by the state or mainstream audiences.

Gender in the context of parenting, however, is not the only site of challenge and critique, as TGNC counterstorytellers rearticulate parenting as informed by and part of social justice work. For example, Ballard uses counterstory to expose commonplace ableism in reproductive contexts. They underscore how they are guided by queer and disability frameworks to welcome "whatever being comes," which is personally important to Ballard because of their gender identity:

> Ways of the world haven't welcomed me. And also that of my partner who is disabled. And when she was born, she was not welcomed; there was an idea that something was wrong. And so from that night of insemination up to the current day, we've been trying to catch ourselves on any kind of expectations that we have of the child. If one of us says, "I can't wait to go hiking with this being," then the other one will usually say, "Or get them into the outdoors in whatever way is possible." Or one of us says, "I can't wait to hear what his voice singing sounds like," the other one might say, "I'm excited to hear whatever sounds he can make and however he expresses themselves."[107]

Ballard uses counterstory, particularly with its emphasis on personal experience, to critique dominant, ableist beliefs about human worth that regularly shape reproductive and familial cultural contexts. In this way, Ballard rearticulates the value of human life, delinked from notions of individualism, capacity, and self-reliance, and aims to promote another way of being in the world for themselves and their family.

Reimagining Family and Kin   159

In another example of how counterstorytellers link reproduction and parenting to the project of liberation, Black trans mother LaSaia Wade discusses her conception and parenting journey with award-winning journalist and trans activist Imara Jones in a Mother's Day episode of Jones's podcast *TransLash*. Wade situates her decision to become a parent and the intention she brings to it within a liberation framework:

> This is the pinnacle of a child being liberated from all types of chains. The understanding that trans people cannot give birth or have kids. The understanding that queer people cannot give birth or have kids. The understanding that Black queer and trans people and the parents fighting are freedom fighters too. . . . I am excited to see this little liberated mind just to be able to give all types of pushback.[108]

Wade relays this as queer generational wisdom, passed down from her own "gay mother" on the journey to becoming a mother. Rather than nurture a dominant form of reproduction, vested in the continuation of a white supremacist heteropatriarchial nation, Wade envisions a distinct form of futurity in which children "raised by us [Black trans elders] are able to live with chains that we have broken" and continue to "give all types of pushback" toward liberation. Thus, many TGNC counterstorytellers rearticulate parenting—especially for trans and nonbinary BIPOC people—as a radical possibility and transformation.

Wade's reflection points us to a final observation; namely, that counterstory as transformation is articulated at the level of reimagining family and community kin. Many TGNC counterstorytellers celebrate how LGBTQ+ and BIPOC communities have long nurtured chosen families beyond their families of origin as a form of communal survival. This rich history includes numerous and diverse chosen family forms, from tight-knit friend circles to the culture of house drag balls and activist enclaves like Sylvia Rivera and Marsha P. Johnson's STAR House (for Street Transvestite Action Revolutionaries). Thus, it is not uncommon for TGNC storytellers to critique the dominant forms of state recognition that obscure and refuse the capaciousness of queer kin. For example, Belc notes in his memoir that many LGBTQ+ people find the legal necessity of second-parent adoption offensive, a form of erasure for the nongestational parent in particular. For Belc, however, "the one always being erased was the boys' donor, a friend whose intimate bond with our family had to be minimized as much as possible in this process. These repeated renunciations bothered me as much as Anna's and my having to adopt our own children."[109] Here, Belc describes the legal architecture of family as intensely narrow, not only in its binary assertion of gendered parentage, but also in its limited scope of recognition for various forms of kin. Belc's counterstory works to resist parenting within the nuclear unit and to reimagine it as tethered to a broader social and communal web of life.

Counterstory is also leveraged to interrogate exclusions often embedded within queer configurations of kin. Counterstoryteller Rabbi Elliot Kukla gently urges this reflection for his audience; he notes how many trans, nonbinary, and gender-nonconforming people come to parenting children through the experience of parenting one another through trauma. In his words, "I've always understood queerness as being a lot about communal survival. And I would love to see us really have better ways to support each other in parenting."[110] Indeed, a number of TGNC counterstorytellers delicately recount the surprising failures of chosen family to show up in the context of pregnancy and parenting. These stories prompt their audiences to reconsider what it means to create chosen family and how to welcome babies and children in ways that are sustainable and sustaining. Trans doula and educator Mac Brydum explains that because kids are sometimes excluded from the fabric of queer life, it may take proactive education to "support your friends or your chosen family member in this journey . . . [and to] envision this kid growing up with this really rich, interesting queer family around them."[111] In a related example that highlights the deficiency of current care structures, Flores articulates some of the challenges that chosen families and queer communities must

Reimagining Family and Kin   161

grapple with in order to show up meaningfully for TGNC birthing people, including building supportive systems:

> Can somebody go from working outside of the home to working inside the home? Can somebody go from needing to commute on public transportation to getting rideshares? Or can crowdsourcing be done to help with financial support for folks? Because, if they literally need to essentially, hibernate for the time in which they need to change their gender-affirming hormones to survive, to live, then, it's those of us who don't have that lived experience, it's our obligation to actually rally in support and leverage the privilege we have.[112]

Counterstories, in these moments, offer loving critiques of how conceptualizing queer chosen family has often excluded the forms of care necessary for those who birth and parent children, as well as for small children themselves. In so doing, they rearticulate the meaning of queer community and engagement, building on a long legacy of queer and BIPOC elders providing safety and sanctuary for their chosen kin.

The reflections of TGNC counterstorytellers underscore the need for steady cultivation of care for parents and children in LGBTQ+ community enclaves. For Ballard and their partner, a written document (the "germination proclamation") shared with close friends and family served as an explicit "instruction manual for communities and families of how to love us in this moment" and as "a manifesto of how we're going to be in the germination period and how we want to be as parents and how we want to ask our communities to rally around us. And so since then people really have shown up in the ways that we've asked them to."[113] Thus, TGNC counterstorytellers affirm the beauty and brilliance of queer chosen family, even as they challenge how it is often configured in LGBTQ+ enclaves. Working at the edges of family—suturing chosen and biogenetic forms of kin—TGNC parents use counterstory to curate possibilities for building more caring and inhabitable worlds.

162   *Doing Gender Justice*

Conclusion

The storytelling of trans, nonbinary, and gender-nonconforming pregnant and parenting people offers a critical window onto the contemporary politics of gender and reproduction in Western contexts. As those within reproductive justice communities strive for a world in which all people can determine when, whether, and with whom they create a family—a world in which we are all afforded bodily autonomy and ensured safe, sustainable environments for our children, families, and communities—the efforts of TGNC storytellers to craft more inhabitable worlds of queer thriving are paramount. As TGNC individuals share their experiences with mainstream and enclave audiences, they creatively adopt rhetorical strategies to move beyond narrow configurations of pregnancy and kin. Their stories offer new expressions of queer embodiment—insisting, for example, on reproduction as trans and on the creative capacity of language to expand our understanding. Drawing on deliberative empathy and counterstory, their stories edge us closer to a world where reproductive justice is made possible.

Reimagining Family and Kin 163

CONCLUSION

Deepening Intersectional and Coalitional Reproductive Justice

WE ARE WRITING this book at a time when anti-trans legislation and right-wing attacks against women, BIPOC, and trans and gender-nonconforming (TGNC) people are relentless. As such, it is important for us to write a book that does not just unveil and critique the insidious connections among white supremacy, gender binary, and reproduction. Rather, we want to also amplify the rhetorical performances of queer TGNC communities and their accomplices, uplifting the ways they invent and deploy different tactics to advocate for reproductive justice at the personal and structural levels and to empower each other through acts of care and coalition. Throughout *Doing Gender Justice*, we demonstrate the elasticity and fluidity of language in relation to how we understand gender and reproduction: while dominant right-wing discourse has mobilized gendered language to convince the public that the sex/gender binary is a priori and immutable, TGNC people and reproductive justice activists have repeatedly demonstrated the expansive capacity of language to challenge and dismantle long-standing logics of white supremacy and coloniality.

In this concluding chapter, we first highlight the key themes that run through the previous chapters. Since the confluence of gender justice, trans justice, and reproductive justice has ramifications for different stakeholders, we will then articulate key lessons that pertain, respectively, to rhetorical scholars, reproductive justice activists and practitioners, and reproductive health care providers. We do not posit these lessons as fixed and exhaustive; rather, we hope they may be generative of new conversations, tactics, and coalitions.

Reproductive Justice and the Politics of Gender

In *Doing Gender Justice*, we began by historicizing and situating the construction of binary sex/gender in relation to logics of coloniality, white supremacy, and anti-Black and anti-Indigenous racism. We then examined how dominant constructions of gender, family, and reproduction have come to bear on mainstream public discourse, fueling the right-wing anti-gender movement, lending legitimacy to anti-trans beliefs and policies, and brutally dismissing and erasing the reproductive desires and lived experiences of TGNC people. At the same time, to demonstrate the constructedness of gender and the ways in which language can be adapted, reinvented, and mobilized to construct a more just world, we explored the rhetorical praxis of reproductive justice–informed birthworkers, health care providers, and TGNC parents who have chosen to share their narratives and experiences with their community and the broader public. While our analysis traverses different rhetorical contexts and scales, several key themes repeatedly emerged as salient.

First, *dominant constructions and performances of binary gender and reproduction uphold colonial white supremacist logics.* Despite extensive scholarly accounts on the colonial and racist history of the gender binary (see the introduction), gender categories remain deeply yoked to essentialist and hierarchical understanding of the body. Indigenous scholars and activists remind us that rigid categories and hierarchies have long been used to perpetuate colonial violence.[1] Similarly, Black trans feminist scholars and activists name how binary sex/gender continues to function as a weapon of racial domination and control. Under this schema, the bodies of Black, Indigenous, and other people of color are always already rendered nonnormative, queer, and aberrant. While BIPOC bodies are seen as threatening and abject, their reproductive labor has consistently been exploited by systems of racial capitalism, even long after the end of chattel slavery in the United States. The deep connections between white supremacy and trans antagonism are illustrated saliently by the transnational anti-gender movement (see chapter 1)—an umbrella movement that simultaneously undermines the humanity of BIPOC, women, and TGNC people.

Second, *TGNC reproduction, kin formation, and parenting are always already disruptive.* The nation is premised on long-standing hierarchies of race and gender to which struggles over reproductive control are indebted. In other words, control over definitions of *motherhood* and *family* have long ensured the perpetuation of white supremacist colonial patriarchy, and, importantly, the gender binary itself is a cornerstone of this nation-building project. Reproduction and kin ties that defy the hetero- and homonormative logic of a nuclear family are inherently disruptive to the status quo and to the ongoing project of white supremacist nation building. Attacks on TGNC parents and families, hence, need to be understood within the context of structural racism, patriarchy, and nationalism, wherein the only acceptable form of kinship is a biological nuclear family sustained by the undervalued reproductive labor of cisgender white women. Understanding the disruptiveness of TGNC reproduction and kin formation is key to how we strategize about resistance and social change: rather than organizing in ways that silo the lived experiences and interests of BIPOC, TGNC people, and women, we need coalitional advocacy that takes into account shared struggles.

Third, *state recognition and liberal politics of inclusion are not sustainable solutions to gender, racial, and reproductive injustice.* Advocating for minoritized communities to gain state recognition, mainstream visibility, and inclusion has long been a key emphasis in liberal politics. While securing state recognition does ameliorate some of the precarious conditions that marginalized communities face, relying on the state and other dominant institutions to confer legitimacy is incremental at best and may, in fact, obfuscate the need to question the logic of sex, gender, and familial classification by the state in the first place.[2] Take, for example, legal recognition of parentage. Birth certificates vary widely in their use of state-sanctioned nomenclature, but the traditional language refers to two parents ("mother" and "father"); this has been expanded in some states in recent years to include additional options (e.g., "parent"). The state acknowledges no more or no less than two parents and almost universally insists on a birthing parent being designated as "mother." TGNC parents note the narrowness of legal recognition in capturing the breadth of queer relationality and kin (see chapter 3), revealing state investments in biogenetic family, heteronormativity, and binary gender. Fighting for inclusion and recognition on all these varied fronts is, thus, a necessary—and also insufficient—tactic for survival. These strategies alone cannot fully remediate a system designed to promote the welfare of some families and the systematic destruction of others. Promoting intersectional and coalitional gender, reproductive, and racial justice requires the dismantling of the very ideologies that form the foundation of dominant cultural institutions.

Finally, grassroots networks of care and rhetorical inventiveness are key to empowerment and radical social change. *Doing Gender Justice* is filled with examples of the inventive rhetorical tactics deployed by TGNC people and their accomplices to advocate for their reproductive desires and rights; empower themselves in the face of oppressive institutions; share resources and insights; and perhaps most importantly, render a deeply unjust world more livable. Notably, and in conversation with the above, these networks and strategies often operate outside of—and/or beyond—the state. They instead leverage the power of community to cultivate resource exchange and reciprocity, amplify the needs and demands of TGNC communities, and work to ensure that these needs are met. Harnessing the creative power of language, these communities participate in the deeply imaginative project of queer world-making.

In addition to these overarching themes, which are significant to all stakeholders committed to advancing coalitional and intersectional justice in reproduction, family-making, and gender, *Doing Gender Jus-*

tice also offers insights tailored to particular communities who have high stakes in this domain. In what follows, we discuss key takeaways for rhetorical scholars, reproductive justice activists, and health care providers.

For Rhetorical Scholars

First, we urge rhetorical scholars to decenter persuasion, an inheritance of the ancient Western Greco-Roman tradition and one that continues to loom large in the field of rhetorical studies. Persuasion, however, is a vexed enterprise. Our study suggests that rhetorical scholars would do well to question its primacy in our critical and worldmaking endeavors. In chapter 3, for example, we trace how arguments deemed most persuasive to a mainstream audience often risk reifying the oppressive logics that have caused marginalized communities harm. More specifically, while narratives that highlight the normativity of nuclear TGNC families may be expedient in securing mainstream visibility and support from a broad public audience, and certainly function as a mode of survival in a transphobic world, the uptake of these stories relies on their harsh constitutive outside. These stories prompt a narrow expansion of reproductive and familial legibility in ways that perpetuate harm to TGNC people, especially those of color, whose kin ties and reproductive desires defy the script of middle-class white normativity. Hence, rather than focusing on identifying the most effective means of persuasion, we urge scholars to amplify marginalized ways of knowing and communicating that do not treat persuasion as the main goal. Counterstory and deliberative empathy are two examples of this; each foreground distinct modes of public engagement with dominant discourse that refuse assimilation in favor of creating strategic alliances and rewriting mainstream narratives.

In addition, our study demonstrates that rhetorical analyses of tactics from the margins can be simultaneously critical, uplifting, and amplifying. As our analysis of TGNC personal narratives (see chapter 3) demonstrates, the TGNC parent community is not monolithic, nor are the rhetorical tactics they deploy: while some rhetorical performances seek to promote more radical transformative social change,

168   *Doing Gender Justice*

others primarily deploy assimilatory logic to render TGNC families legible to the state and the mainstream public. As critical rhetoricians, we grappled with how we could ethically analyze these myriad rhetorical tactics deployed by marginalized TGNC parents. On the one hand, we are wary of the tendency exhibited by dominant interlocutors who readily dismiss rhetorics from the margin as unruly, ineffective, and disrespectful. Hence, we seek to recognize rhetorical inventions from the margin on their own terms, uplifting the ways in which they disrupt the status quo. On the other hand, we believe that critical rhetorical scholarship ought to illuminate the political limitations of our objects of study, specifically the ways in which they perpetuate oppressive ideologies and perceptions. Being uncritically celebratory of rhetorical performances from the margin is antithetical to the overarching goal of justice for multiple reasons: not only does doing so foreclose opportunities for productive critique and revision, it also essentializes and tokenizes the identities of minoritized rhetors.

Relatedly, we recognize that marginalized rhetors are implicated in interlocking systems of oppression and power. Socialized into dominant ideologies and, significantly, forced to navigate precarious material conditions, they may decide to advocate for themselves through assimilatory rhetorical acts made legible to the state and the mainstream public. As an act of queer survival and joy, this too is radical. Thus, while we argue that critical rhetoricians ought to critique and unveil dominant logics and the harms they perpetuate, we see it also as our responsibility to deeply contextualize such rhetorical acts rather than individualizing, blaming, and shaming marginalized rhetors for deploying them. Promoting radical social change and justice through rhetorical analysis requires that we holistically contextualize and critically analyze the impetus and effects of rhetorical performances from the margin.

Finally, analyzing the rhetorics of reproductive and gender justice requires deftness in research methods and expansiveness in objects of study. When we first set out to examine gender and language in the context of reproduction, we focused primarily on debates about the use of woman-centered versus gender-neutral language. But we quickly

Conclusion   169

realized that in order to fully contextualize these debates and articulate their profound sociopolitical and cultural implications, we needed to expand our archive beyond discourse in the context of reproductive care. Since gender is inextricably connected to histories of colonialism, anti-Blackness, white supremacy, and racial capitalism, our examining of the confluence of gender and reproductive justice movements necessitates a more expansive and agile research approach: one that allows us to trace how intersecting ideologies inform rhetorical performances in different contexts and across different levels (e.g., from the domestic and familial to the institutional and state). By doing so, we are better positioned not only to reveal the ways in which trans antagonism becomes networked with racial and reproductive injustice but also to identify and amplify rhetorical tactics that dismantle these intersecting logics.

For Reproductive Justice Scholars and Activists

First and foremost: reproductive justice necessarily entails gender and trans justice. This may seem an obvious or even foregone conclusion. As we write, the visibility of trans-inclusive efforts are steadily on the rise across various cultural contexts—for example, in the uptick in gender-inclusive public restrooms, email signatures that denote pronouns, and the ubiquity of the new pride flag that explicitly celebrates BIPOC and trans communities. Many mainstream reproductive rights organizations have adopted language for reproductive care that embraces people across a spectrum of gender identities. Many activists and intellectuals have noted the collusion of right-wing policies that have targeted both gender-affirming care and abortion care; abortion *is*, in fact, gender-affirming care.

All of these things are true. To declare, however, that reproductive justice is trans justice is not simply a signaling of overlapping concerns regarding bodily sovereignty. Nor is it a straightforward recognition that LGBTQ+ communities, too, deserve compassionate reproductive and sexual health care. Rather, reproductive justice activism necessarily entails gender and trans justice because the gender binary is racist all the way down. Gender—and relatedly, sexuality—has long

170   Doing Gender Justice

been wielded as a weapon of colonization and racial stratification; it is a means of shoring up white supremacist patriarchy and ensuring its replication across generations. Control over sex and gender—both in their expression and culturally assigned expectations—is intimately entangled with strict scrutiny and control over reproduction itself and resides at the heart of reproducing the United States as a nation. Thus, there is no reproductive justice without gender justice. There is no reproductive justice without trans justice.

From here, we can embrace various rhetorical tactics and strategies to expand reproductive justice work. This book offers myriad examples of those people working at the edges of reproductive justice activism and intervention. In interviewing radical birthworkers and assembling an archive of TGNC parents' public storytelling, we amplify the exceptional creativity, imagination, and invention of those dedicated to actively crafting spaces for nonnormative families and communities to thrive in. If we consider trans and gender justice to be a critical growth edge for reproductive justice communities and scholarship, perhaps we can also consider the other edges of reproductive justice praxis, and with a similar set of curiosities. What lessons might be gleaned from these activists, birthworkers, and storytellers? How do they offer rhetorical templates for survival that might be adapted to other contexts, circumstances, and struggles? Where else might reproductive justice grow and expand; how might TGNC and BIPOC leaders guide us in this work?

For Health Care Workers

As we have detailed throughout this book, gendered and transphobic microaggressions and violence are embedded throughout dominant medical systems. This embedded violence shapes not only the everyday exchanges between patients and providers but also the way patients must navigate the health care system, from intake forms to insurance coverage and legal documents like birth certificates. *Doing Gender Justice* provides a holistic account of this system so health care workers and professionals can locate opportunities for intervention and redress that reside within their own sphere(s) of influence. As our study attests, there is no act too small—indeed, slight adjustments to established routines and discourse can go a long way in promoting safe and affirming reproductive health care spaces for TGNC parents and communities. For example, the storytelling of radical birthworkers and TGNC parents repeatedly underscores the significance of acknowledging gender diversity on medical intake forms, inquiring about pronouns and preferred names, refusing assumptions about parenting configurations, and so on. Their stories remind us that mirrors—the ability for TGNC birthing people and parents to see themselves reflected in contexts devoted to fertility, pregnancy, and reproduction—are paramount. Health care workers are invited to consider how the space of the clinic itself—the signage, the pamphlets, the art adorning the walls—collectively shape a story about who is valued, who is served, who belongs.

This reminder is not, however, an endorsement of cosmetic changes that signal but do not otherwise foster LGBTQ+ inclusivity. As one of our interviewees noted, this kind of window dressing, regardless of intent, can perpetuate additional harms by suggesting a kind of cultural competence not yet embraced in practice. Thus, our study urges those immersed in health care settings to consider the extent to which their services currently serve TGNC parents and families in ways that are culturally sensitive and tailored to trans, queer, and nonbinary needs and experiences. Conduct an audit! When and where do current practices fall short? Consider educational or consulting opportunities with TGNC reproductive educators, such as Khye Tyson, Jenna Brown, king yaa, or Trystan Reese, to benefit organizational cultures and client-patient relationships. Books by trans and queer health care workers such as *The Care We Dream Of* by Zena Sharman, *Queer Conception* by Kristin Liam Kali, and *Trans Bodies, Trans Selves* edited by Laura Erickson-Schroth can provide additional critical insight into our cis-centric health care system and the particular reproductive care needs of TGNC people and families. Hire TGNC consultants and health care staff; invest in culturally diverse materials and information for patients; work to build environments where parents across the gender spectrum can be seen, heard, and cared for.

Finally, TGNC patients benefit from client-centered care instead of a one-size-fits-all approach. Trans, queer, and nonbinary are not fixed or stable identities, and linguistic dexterity aids in offering health care that is responsive to a patient's needs. For example, common vernacular in reproductive health care might prompt discomfort or a sense of invisibility among TGNC patients. Which words do patients embrace or otherwise prefer for their own reproductive anatomy or processes? How can providers then adapt their care accordingly? Perhaps "pelvic birth" could be used in lieu of "vaginal birth," or "chestfeeding" in lieu of "breastfeeding." These are adaptations that can be adjusted in response to individual patient preferences by asking open-ended questions and mirroring patients' language. For example, "How do you plan to feed your baby?" prompts more responsive possibilities for parents, regardless of gender, than does the more commonplace "Do you plan to breastfeed?" Many of our radical birthworker interviewees reminded us that the unsettling of assumptions about gender, family formation, and language—and critically evaluating how patient-provider communication might be refined to avoid these assumptions—was, and remains, a cornerstone of TGNC care.

Listening for patient cues in these conversations is important, for even language that seems neutral may carry unwelcome valence. As one storyteller within our archive noted, not all who gestate a child identify as a pregnant person. This storyteller, a midwife, went on to note their work with many trans dads who are thrilled to become dads and quite willing to use their bodies in this way, but who do not identify as pregnant at all. TGNC parents in our archive offered additional ways to talk about pregnancy—for example, as gestation or simply as carrying. How might providers mirror the language that these patients use? In another example, some patients may embrace gender-specific or traditional parenting labels, but our archive attests quite clearly that not everyone who gives birth is a "mom." Parenting names are radically diverse within TGNC communities, inclusive of gender-specific referents (e.g., papa, dad), terms coined within a family (e.g., baba, mapa), or those that refer to heritage (e.g., nanay). Language, in short, is fluid and contingent. Health care workers' efforts to embrace an

Conclusion   *173*

additive approach to established language, to experiment with other expressions, and to willingly cocreate new descriptive lexicons with their patients curate a space for TGNC families to exist and thrive.

Doing Gender Justice

Building upon the insights of Black, Indigenous, queer, and trans feminist scholars and activists, we have demonstrated throughout our book that oppressive logics and systems are interconnected. Put differently, misogyny, binary sex/gender, trans antagonism, anti-Black racism, anti-Indigeneity, coloniality, and white supremacy are all threads that are woven into the same cloth. Hence, we need tactics of resistance and advocacy that are intersectional and coalitional in ways that recognize shared struggles across movements and across conditions of marginalization. These struggles against oppression do not exist only in the public political sphere. Rather, for minoritized people, especially for those who are multiply marginalized, these power dynamics inform their everyday experiences and relationships.

In *Doing Gender Justice*, we have focused extensively on domains, interactions, and relationships that are often considered private and deeply intimate: birth and pregnancy, reproductive health care, and family and kin. We foreground the ways in which these embodied and affective sites function as double-edged swords for TGNC people: On the one hand, they are tender and significant areas of people's lives and communities that hold the potential for radical transformation at the personal, collective, and structural levels. On the other hand, policed and tightly controlled by the state and other dominant institutions, these sites are also often sources of pain, trauma, and loss. We illuminate this tension throughout our analysis, contextualizing how TGNC parents, reproductive justice activists, and health care providers invent and deploy different rhetorical tactics to challenge, circumvent, and resist systems of oppression. It is important to also remember that not all rhetorical performances deployed by marginalized people center the state or other oppressive structures. Some of the most radical rhetorical praxis decenters the state and dominant logics and instead amplifies and makes room for care relations, practices, and resources that are meant to bring joy and affirmation to the marginalized rhetors themselves. We hope that *Doing Gender Justice* serves also as a record and reminder of the ways TGNC people and their allies have created radical spaces of care for themselves, for their kin, and for their broader communities—reclaiming this power as a collective birthright.

NOTES

Preface

1. This quote is from an art print Borealis designed. The full text states: "our freedoms and our friendships have much to say to each other. apparently, the words free and friend share linguistic roots in the meaning to love. no surprise, then, that systems of domination secure their position by separating us from each other—through competition, the private hells of the nuclear family, quotas for the production of crap, the terror of imperialism. no surprise, too, that our resistance is strongest through collaboration, mutual aid, imaginative reconfigurations of kinship, remembering our habits of reciprocity. to do the courageous and vulnerable work of making friends is to prefigure one of our manyfold rebirths as collective peoples. to share space, to break bread, to compare notes, to ask questions, to try, to listen, to offer, to eat, to study, to cavort, to scheme, to practice, to revolt together. may we be brave through the nervous anticipation of a new relationship and hold fast to softness through the sage slowness of an old one. may our friendly actions make collective autonomy the only hospitable outcome. may we mobilize the power of our shared capacities and believe in mutual liberation. may we take risks and defend each other. may we be fierce and relentless with our love." Another one of their posters that I display in my office reads: "May we reach towards kinship every moment that we are small things, which is to say that I hope we reach for each other every moment that the sun is on fire."

Introduction

1. Laura Briggs, *How All Politics Became Reproductive Politics: From Welfare Reform to Foreclosure to Trump* (Oakland: University of California Press, 2017); "About," *Woman-Centered Midwifery* (blog), June 13, 2015, https://womancenteredmidwifery.wordpress.com/about/.

2. Alicia D. Bonaparte, "Physicians' Discourse for Establishing Authoritative Knowledge in Birthing Work and Reducing the Presence of the Granny Midwife," *Journal of Historical Sociology* 28, no. 2 (2015): 166–94, https://doi.org/10.1111/johs.12045; Trevor MacDonald, "Transphobia in the Midwifery Community," Huffington Post, September 15, 2015, https://www.huffingtonpost.com/trevor-macdonald/transphobia-in-the-midwif_b_8131520.html.

3. "Open Letter to MANA," *Woman-Centered Midwifery* (blog), August 20, 2015, https://womancenteredmidwifery.wordpress.com/take-action/.

4. S. E. Smith, "Women Are Not the Only Ones Who Get Abortions," Rewire.News, March 1, 2019, https://rewire.news/article/2019/03/01/women-are-not-the-only-ones-who-get-abortions/; Katha Pollitt, "Who Has Abortions?," *The Nation*, March 13, 2015, https://www.thenation.com/article/archive/who-has-abortions/.

5. Marquis Bey, *Cistem Failure: Essays on Blackness and Cisgender* (Durham: Duke University Press Books, 2022).

6. Brooklyn Leo, "The Colonial/Modern [Cis]Gender System and Trans World Traveling," *Hypatia* 35, no. 3 (2020): 454–74, https://doi.org/10.1017/hyp.2020.27; Maria Lugones, "The Coloniality of Gender," *Worlds & Knowledges Otherwise* 2, no. 2 (Spring 2008): 1–17, https://globalstudies.trinity.duke.edu/sites/globalstudies.trinity.duke.edu/files/documents/v2d2_Lugones.pdf.

7. Deborah Miranda, "Extermination of the Joyas: Gendercide in Spanish California," *GLQ: A Journal of Lesbian and Gay Studies* 16, no. 1–2 (January 27, 2010): 253–84, https://doi.org/10.1215/10642684-2009-022.

8. Gregory D. Smithers, *Reclaiming Two-Spirits: Sexuality, Spiritual Renewal & Sovereignty in Native America* (Boston: Beacon Press, 2022); Alice Bushell, "Los Muxes: Disrupting The Colonial Gender Binary," *Human Rights Pulse*, June 11, 2021, https://www.humanrightspulse.com/mastercontentblog/los-muxes-disrupting-the-colonial-gender-binary.

9. Miranda, "Extermination of the Joyas."

10. Miranda, "Extermination of the Joyas."

11. Cathy J. Cohen, "Punks, Bulldaggers, and Welfare Queens: The Radical Potential of Queer Politics?," *GLQ: A Journal of Lesbian and Gay Studies* 3, no. 4 (May 1, 1997): 445, https://doi.org/10.1215/10642684-3-4-437; Bey, *Cistem Failure*; Leo, "Colonial/Modern [Cis]Gender System."

12. Cohen, "Punks, Bulldaggers, and Welfare Queens."

13. Loretta Ross and Rickie Solinger, *Reproductive Justice: An Introduction* (Oakland: University of California Press, 2017).

14. Shui-yin Sharon Yam, "Visualizing Birth Stories from the Margin: Toward a Reproductive Justice Model of Rhetorical Analysis," *Rhetoric Society Quarterly* 50, no. 1 (January 1, 2020): 22, https://doi.org/10.1080/02773945.2019.1682182.

15. Ross and Solinger, *Reproductive Justice*.

16. macfound, "Loretta J. Ross, Reproductive Justice and Human Rights Advocate | 2022 MacArthur Fellow," October 12, 2022, YouTube video, 2:20, https://www.youtube.com/watch?v=sF_9VktvSPA.

17. Jael Silliman et al., *Undivided Rights: Women of Color Organizing for Reproductive Justice*, 2nd ed. (Chicago: Haymarket Books, 2016).

18. Imani Gandy, "Why Losing Your Housing Is One of the Greatest Threats to Reproductive Health," Rewire.News, July 30, 2020, https://rewirenewsgroup.com/2020/07/30/why-losing-your-housing-is-one-of-the-greatest-threats-to-reproductive-health/; Alexis Pauline Gumbs, China Martens, and Mai'a Williams, eds., *Revolution-*

ary Mothering: Love on the Front Lines, illus. ed. (Oakland: PM Press, 2016); Miriam Zoila Pérez, *The Radical Doula Guide: A Political Primer* (2012), https://radicaldoula .com/the-radical-doula-guide/; Grover Wehman-Brown, "Bearing Life With and Alongside: On Masculinity, Pregnancy, and Medical Trauma," Autostraddle, November 19, 2018, https://www.autostraddle.com/bearing-life-with-and-alongside-on-masculinity -pregnancy-and-medical-trauma-438219/.

19. Khiara M. Bridges, *Reproducing Race: An Ethnography of Pregnancy as a Site of Racialization* (Berkeley: University of California Press, 2011); Dána-Ain Davis, *Reproductive Injustice* (New York: NYU Press, 2019); Patricia Zavella, *The Movement for Reproductive Justice: Empowering Women of Color through Social Activism* (New York: NYU Press, 2020); Ross and Solinger, *Reproductive Justice*; Dorothy Roberts, *Killing the Black Body: Race, Reproduction, and the Meaning of Liberty* (New York: Vintage, 1998); Rickie Solinger, *Pregnancy and Power: A Short History of Reproductive Politics in America* (New York: NYU Press, 2005).

20. Andrea Smith, "Beyond Pro-Choice versus Pro-Life: Women of Color and Reproductive Justice," *NWSA Journal* 17, no. 1 (March 15, 2005): 119–40.

21. Roberts, *Killing the Black Body*; Solinger, *Pregnancy and Power*.

22. Elizabeth C. Ghandakly and Rachel Fabi, "Sterilization in US Immigration and Customs Enforcement's (ICE's) Detention: Ethical Failures and Systemic Injustice," *American Journal of Public Health* 111, no. 5 (May 2021): 832–34, https://doi.org/10.2105 /AJPH.2021.306186.

23. Brianna Theobald, *Reproduction on the Reservation: Pregnancy, Childbirth, and Colonialism in the Long Twentieth Century* (Chapel Hill: University of North Carolina Press, 2019).

24. Zakiya Luna, *Reproductive Rights as Human Rights: Women of Color and the Fight for Reproductive Justice* (New York: NYU Press, 2020).

25. Ross and Solinger, *Reproductive Justice*, 71.

26. World Health Organization, *Interpreting Reproductive Health: ICPD + 5 Forum, The Hague, 8–12 February 1999* (World Health Organization, 1999), 15, https://iris.who .int/bitstream/handle/10665/64992/WHO_CHS_RHR_99.7.pdf.

27. World Health Organization, *Interpreting Reproductive Health*, 17.

28. World Health Organization, *Interpreting Reproductive Health*, 21.

29. Ritu Sadana, "Definition and Measurement of Reproductive Health," *Bulletin of the World Health Organization* 80 (2002): 407–9, https://doi.org/10.1590/S0042 -96862002000500013.

30. Katherine Rachlin, Jamison Green, and Emilia Lombardi, "Utilization of Health Care among Female-to-Male Transgender Individuals in the United States," *Journal of Homosexuality* 54, no. 3 (May 14, 2008): 243–58, https://doi.org/10.1080/00918360801982124.

31. Margaret Besse, Nik M. Lampe, and Emily S. Mann, "Experiences with Achieving Pregnancy and Giving Birth among Transgender Men: A Narrative Literature Review," *The Yale Journal of Biology and Medicine* 93, no. 4 (September 30, 2020): 517–28; Julia D. Sbragia and Beth Vottero, "Experiences of Transgender Men in Seeking Gynecological and Reproductive Health Care: A Qualitative Systematic Review,"

JBI Evidence Synthesis 18, no. 9 (September 2020): 1870–1931, https://doi.org/10.11124/JBISRIR-D-19-00347.

32. Lillian Faderman and Stuart Timmons, *Gay L.A.: A History of Sexual Outlaws, Power Politics, and Lipstick Lesbians* (Berkeley: University of California Press, 2009); C. Riley Snorton, *Black on Both Sides: A Racial History of Trans Identity*, 3rd ed. (Minneapolis: University of Minnesota Press, 2017); Susan Stryker, "Transgender Liberation," in *Transgender History: The Roots of Today's Revolution*, 2nd ed. (Berkeley: Seal Press, 2017), 59–90; Raquel Willis, "Trans Women Are Women. This Isn't a Debate," *The Root*, March 17, 2017, https://www.theroot.com/trans-women-are-women-this-isn-t-a-debate-1793202635.

33. Finn Enke, "Collective Memory and the Transfeminist 1970s," *TSQ: Transgender Studies Quarterly* 5, no. 1 (February 1, 2018): 9–29, https://doi.org/10.1215/23289252-4291502; Cristan Williams, "Radical Inclusion: Recounting the Trans Inclusive History of Radical Feminism," *TSQ: Transgender Studies Quarterly* 3, no. 1–2 (May 2016): 254–58, https://doi.org/10.1215/23289252-3334463.

34. Faderman and Timmons, *Gay L.A.*; Simon D. Elin Fisher, "Pauli Murray's Peter Panic: Perspectives from the Margins of Gender and Race in Jim Crow America," *TSQ: Transgender Studies Quarterly* 3, no. 1–2 (May 2016): 95–103, https://doi.org/10.1215/23289252-3334259.

35. Janice G. Raymond, *The Transsexual Empire: The Making of the She-Male*, Athene Series 39 (New York: Teachers College Press, 1994); Sandy Stone, "The Empire Strikes Back: A Posttranssexual Manifesto," *Camera Obscura: Feminism, Culture, and Media Studies* 10, no. 2 (29) (May 1, 1992): 150–76, https://doi.org/10.1215/02705346-10-2_29-150; Stryker, "Transgender Liberation."

36. Patricia Hill Collins and Sirma Bilge, *Intersectionality* (Cambridge, UK: Polity, 2016); Kimberle Crenshaw, "Demarginalizing the Intersection of Race and Sex: A Black Feminist Critique of Antidiscrimination Doctrine, Feminist Theory and Antiracist Politics," *University of Chicago Legal Forum* 1989, no. 1 (1989), https://chicagounbound.uchicago.edu/uclf/vol1989/iss1/8; "Kimberlé Crenshaw on Intersectionality, More than Two Decades Later," Columbia Law School, para. 4, accessed August 28, 2023, https://www.law.columbia.edu/news/archive/kimberle-crenshaw-intersectionality-more-two-decades-later.

37. Jasbir K. Puar, "'I Would Rather Be a Cyborg than a Goddess': Becoming-Intersectional in Assemblage Theory," *philoSOPHIA* 2, no. 1 (2012): 49–66, https://doi.org/10.1353/phi.2012.a486621; Marquis Bey, *Black Trans Feminism* (Durham: Duke University Press Books, 2022); Jennifer C. Nash, *Black Feminism Reimagined: After Intersectionality* (Durham: Duke University Press Books, 2019).

38. Jasbir K. Puar, *Terrorist Assemblages: Homonationalism in Queer Times* (Durham: Duke University Press, 2007), 213.

39. Bey, *Black Trans Feminism*.

40. "Advocacy Groups Rank States Based on Reproductive, Sexual Rights," National Organization for Women, June 2, 2006, https://now.org/read-this/advocacy_groups_rank_states_based_on_rep/.

41. Alex Berg, "Why Reproductive Justice Is an LGBTQ+ Rights Issue," *Out*, February 19, 2019, para. 6, https://www.out.com/out-exclusives/2019/2/19/why-reproductive-justice-lgbtq-rights-issue.

42. Bey, *Black Trans Feminism*, 61.

43. "The Aftermath of Dobbs: Putting the Movement for Reproductive Justice in Conversation with the Fight for Trans Justice," Events, Berkeley Law, accessed May 31, 2024, https://www.law.berkeley.edu/research/center-on-race-sexuality-culture/events/.

44. "Aftermath of Dobbs."

45. Laura Nixon, "The Right to (Trans) Parent: A Reproductive Justice Approach to Reproductive Rights, Fertility, and Family-Building Issues Facing Transgender People," *William & Mary Journal of Race, Gender, and Social Justice* 20, no. 1 (December 1, 2013): 73; Kimala Price, "Queering Reproductive Justice: Toward a Theory and Praxis for Building Intersectional Political Alliances," in *LGBTQ Politics: A Critical Reader*, ed. Marla Brettschneider, Susan Burgess, and Christine Keating (New York: NYU Press, 2017), 72–88; Kimala Price, "Queering Reproductive Justice in the Trump Era: A Note on Political Intersectionality," *Politics & Gender* 14, no. 4 (December 2018): 581–601, https://doi.org/10.1017/S1743923X18000776; Camisha Russell, "Rights-Holders or Refugees? Do Gay Men Need Reproductive Justice?," *Reproductive Biomedicine & Society Online* 7 (August 16, 2018): 131–40, https://doi.org/10.1016/j.rbms.2018.07.001; Marcin Smietana, Charis Thompson, and France Winddance Twine, "Making and Breaking Families—Reading Queer Reproductions, Stratified Reproduction and Reproductive Justice Together," *Reproductive Biomedicine & Society Online* 7 (November 2018): 112–30, https://doi.org/10.1016/j.rbms.2018.11.001; Judith Stacey, "Queer Reproductive Justice?," *Reproductive Biomedicine & Society Online* 7 (November 2018): 4–7, https://doi.org/10.1016/j.rbms.2018.06.004.

46. Price, "Queering Reproductive Justice in the Trump Era"; Russell, "Rights-Holders or Refugees?"; Marcin Smietana, "Procreative Consciousness in a Global Market: Gay Men's Paths to Surrogacy in the USA," *Reproductive Biomedicine & Society Online* 7 (November 2018): 101–11, https://doi.org/10.1016/j.rbms.2019.03.001; Judith Butler, "Is Kinship Always Already Heterosexual?," *Differences* 13, no. 1 (January 1, 2002): 14–44, https://doi.org/10.1215/10407391-13-1-14; Stacey, "Queer Reproductive Justice?"

47. Loretta J. Ross, *Understanding Reproductive Justice* (Atlanta: SisterSong Women of Color Reproductive Health Collective, May 2006), https://d3n8a8pro7vhmx.cloudfront.net/rrfp/pages/33/attachments/original/1456425809/Understanding_RJ_Sistersong.pdf.

48. Alyosxa Tudor, "Decolonizing Trans/Gender Studies? Teaching Gender, Race, and Sexuality in Times of the Rise of the Global Right," *TSQ: Transgender Studies Quarterly* 8, no. 2 (May 1, 2021): 238–56, https://doi.org/10.1215/23289252-8890523.

49. Judith Butler, *Gender Trouble: Feminism and the Subversion of Identity* (New York: Routledge, 2006).

50. Butler, *Gender Trouble*.

51. Heath Fogg Davis, *Beyond Trans: Does Gender Matter?* (New York: NYU Press, 2017), 50.

52. Davis, *Beyond Trans*; Julia Serano, *Whipping Girl: A Transsexual Woman on Sexism and the Scapegoating of Femininity*, 2nd ed. (Berkeley: Seal Press, 2016).

53. Cáel M. Keegan, "Getting Disciplined: What's Trans* About Queer Studies Now?," *Journal of Homosexuality* 67, no. 3 (2018): 390, https://doi.org/10.1080/00918369.2018.1530885.

54. Keegan, "Getting Disciplined."

55. Janet Halley, *Split Decisions: How and Why to Take a Break from Feminism* (Princeton, NJ: Princeton University Press, 2006); Jay Prosser, *Second Skins: The Body Narratives of Transsexuality* (New York: Columbia University Press, 1998); Keegan, "Getting Disciplined," 392.

56. Prosser, *Second Skins*, 59; Keegan, "Getting Disciplined," 392.

57. Serano, *Whipping Girl*.

58. Sheila Jeffreys, *Gender Hurts: A Feminist Analysis of the Politics of Transgenderism* (Abingdon, UK: Routledge, 2014); Ruth Barrett, *Female Erasure: What You Need To Know about Gender Politics' War on Women, the Female Sex and Human Rights* (Tidal Time Publishing, 2016).

59. Bey, *Black Trans Feminism*, 56.

60. Keegan, "Getting Disciplined," 387.

61. Bey, *Black Trans Feminism*, 53.

62. Lugones, "Coloniality of Gender"; Xhercis Méndez, "Notes toward a Decolonial Feminist Methodology: Revisiting the Race/Gender Matrix," *Trans-Scripts* 5 (2015): 41–59; Freya Schiwy, "Decolonization and the Question of Subjectivity," *Cultural Studies* 21, no. 2–3 (March 1, 2007): 271–94, https://doi.org/10.1080/09502380601162555; Greg Thomas, *The Sexual Demon of Colonial Power: Pan-African Embodiment and Erotic Schemes of Empire* (Bloomington: Indiana University Press, 2007).

63. Jules Gill-Peterson, *Histories of the Transgender Child*, 3rd ed. (Minneapolis: University of Minnesota Press, 2018).

64. Lugones, "Coloniality of Gender," 12.

65. María Lugones, "Heterosexualism and the Colonial/Modern Gender System," *Hypatia* 22, no. 1 (2007): 186–219, https://doi.org/10.1111/j.1527-2001.2007.tb01156.x; Oyeronke Oyewumi, *The Invention of Women: Making an African Sense of Western Gender Discourses* (Minneapolis: University of Minnesota Press, 1997).

66. Scott Lauria Morgensen, *Spaces between Us: Queer Settler Colonialism and Indigenous Decolonization* (Minneapolis: University of Minnesota Press, 2011); Kyla Schuller, *The Trouble with White Women: A Counterhistory of Feminism* (New York: Bold Type Books, 2021).

67. Dorothy E. Roberts, "Prison, Foster Care, and the Systemic Punishment of Black Mothers," *UCLA Law Review* 59 (2012): 1474–1500; Alys Eve Weinbaum, *The Afterlife of Reproductive Slavery: Biocapitalism and Black Feminism's Philosophy of History*, illus. ed. (Durham: Duke University Press Books, 2019).

68. Alyosxa Tudor, "Im/Possibilities of Refusing and Choosing Gender," *Feminist Theory* 20, no. 4 (December 1, 2019): 367, https://doi.org/10.1177/1464700119870640.

69. Kyla Schuller, *The Biopolitics of Feeling: Race, Sex, and Science in the Nineteenth Century*, illus. ed. (Durham: Duke University Press, 2017); Thomas, *Sexual Demon of Colonial Power*.

70. Schuller, *Biopolitics of Feeling*.

71. Morgensen, *Spaces between Us*, 32.

72. Lisa Lowe, *The Intimacies of Four Continents*, illus. ed. (Durham: Duke University Press Books, 2015), 33.

73. V. Jo Hsu, *Constellating Home: Trans and Queer Asian American Rhetorics* (Columbus: Ohio State University Press, 2022), 16.

74. Bethany Schneider, "Oklahobo: Following Craig Womack's American Indian and Queer Studies," *South Atlantic Quarterly* 106, no. 3 (July 1, 2007): 606, https://doi .org/10.1215/00382876-2007-018.

75. Miranda, "Extermination of the Joyas"; Scott Lauria Morgensen, "Settler Homonationalism: Theorizing Settler Colonialism within Queer Modernities," *GLQ: A Journal of Lesbian and Gay Studies* 16, no. 1–2 (April 1, 2010): 30, https://doi.org/10.1215 /10642684-2009-015; Mark Rifkin, "Romancing Kinship: A Queer Reading of Indian Education and Zitkala-Ša's American Indian Stories," *GLQ: A Journal of Lesbian and Gay Studies* 12, no. 1 (January 1, 2006): 27–59, https://doi.org/10.1215/10642684-12-1-27; Andrea Smith, *Conquest: Sexual Violence and American Indian Genocide*, repr. ed. (Durham: Duke University Press Books, 2015), https://doi.org/10.1215/9780822374817.

76. Miranda, "Extermination of the Joyas"; Smithers, *Reclaiming Two-Spirits*.

77. Smithers, *Reclaiming Two-Spirits*, 74.

78. Qwo-Li Driskill, "Stolen From Our Bodies: First Nations Two-Spirits/Queers and the Journey to a Sovereign Erotic," *Studies in American Indian Literatures* 16, no. 2 (2004): 50–64, https://doi.org/10.1353/ail.2004.0020; Brooklyn Leo, "Dancing with Shadows: Two Spirit Childhoods and the Carlisle Indian Boarding School," *Blog of the APA* (blog), December 6, 2021, https://blog.apaonline.org/2021/12/06/dancing-with -shadows-two-spirit-childhoods-and-the-carlisle-indian-boarding-school/.

79. Qwo-Li Driskill, "Doubleweaving Two-Spirit Critiques: Building Alliances between Native and Queer Studies," *GLQ: A Journal of Lesbian and Gay Studies* 16, no. 1–2 (April 1, 2010): 69–92, https://doi.org/10.1215/10642684-2009-013; Smithers, *Reclaiming Two-Spirits*.

80. Hsu, *Constellating Home*, 134.

81. Hortense J. Spillers, "Mama's Baby, Papa's Maybe: An American Grammar Book," *Diacritics* 17, no. 2 (1987): 65–81, https://doi.org/10.2307/464747.

82. Thomas, *Sexual Demon of Colonial Power*.

83. Eva Hayward and Che Gossett, "Impossibility of That," *Angelaki* 22, no. 2 (April 3, 2017): 18, https://doi.org/10.1080/0969725X.2017.1322814.

84. Snorton, *Black on Both Sides*, 12.

85. Snorton, *Black on Both Sides*, 24, 33.

86. Jack Halberstam, *Female Masculinity* (Durham: Duke University Press Books, 1998); Butler, *Gender Trouble*; Snorton, *Black on Both Sides*.

87. Marquis Bey, "The Trans*-Ness of Blackness, the Blackness of Trans*-Ness," *TSQ: Transgender Studies Quarterly* 4, no. 2 (May 1, 2017): 278, https://doi.org/10.1215/23289252-3815069.

88. Faye D. Ginsburg and Rayna Rapp, eds., *Conceiving the New World Order: The Global Politics of Reproduction* (Oakland: University of California Press, 1995), 3.

89. Chandan Reddy, *Freedom with Violence: Race, Sexuality, and the US State* (Durham: Duke University Press Books, 2011); Jennifer Wingard, *Branded Bodies, Rhetoric, and the Neoliberal Nation-State* (Lanham, MD: Lexington Books, 2013); Shui-yin Sharon Yam, *Inconvenient Strangers: Transnational Subjects and the Politics of Citizenship* (Columbus: Ohio State University Press, 2019).

90. Wingard, *Branded Bodies, Rhetoric, and the Neoliberal Nation-State*.

91. Natalie Fixmer-Oraiz, *Homeland Maternity: US Security Culture and the New Reproductive Regime*, Feminist Media Studies (Urbana: University of Illinois Press, 2019).

92. Schuyler Mitchell, "The Right's Creeping Pro-Natalist Rhetoric on Abortion and Trans Health Care," *The Intercept*, May 17, 2022, https://theintercept.com/2022/05/17/abortion-trans-health-care-pro-natalism-authoritarianism/.

93. Roberts, *Killing the Black Body*; Dorothy Roberts, *Torn Apart: How the Child Welfare System Destroys Black Families—and How Abolition Can Build a Safer World* (New York: Basic Books, 2022); Roberts, "Prison, Foster Care, and the Systemic Punishment of Black Mothers."

94. Dorothy Roberts, *Shattered Bonds: The Color of Child Welfare* (New York: Civitas Books, 2009).

95. Virginia Eubanks, *Automating Inequality*, repr. ed. (London: Picador, 2019).

96. Roberts, *Torn Apart*.

97. Leo R. Chávez, *Anchor Babies and the Challenge of Birthright Citizenship* (Stanford, CA: Stanford Briefs, 2017); Eithne Luibhéid, *Pregnant on Arrival: Making the Illegal Immigrant* (Minneapolis: University of Minnesota Press, 2013).

98. Victoria Bekiempis, "More Immigrant Women Say They Were Abused by Ice Gynecologist," *The Guardian*, December 22, 2020, sec. US news, https://www.theguardian.com/us-news/2020/dec/22/ice-gynecologist-hysterectomies-georgia.

99. Maya Manian, "Immigration Detention and Coerced Sterilization: History Tragically Repeats Itself | ACLU," American Civil Liberties Union, September 29, 2020, https://www.aclu.org/news/immigrants-rights/immigration-detention-and-coerced-sterilization-history-tragically-repeats-itself; Jessica Enoch, "Survival Stories: Feminist Historiographic Approaches to Ghicana Rhetorics of Sterilization Abuse," *Rhetoric Society Quarterly* 35, no. 3 (June 1, 2005): 5–30, https://doi.org/10.1080/02773940509391314; Elena R. Gutiérrez, *Fertile Matters: The Politics of Mexican-Origin Women's Reproduction* (Austin: University of Texas Press, 2008).

100. Shani King, "U.S. Immigration Law and the Traditional Nuclear Conception of Family: Toward a Functional Definition of Family That Protects Children's Fundamental Human Rights," *UF Law Faculty Publications*, October 1, 2009, https://scholarship.law.ufl.edu/facultypub/20.

101. King, "U.S. Immigration Law."

102. Wingard, *Branded Bodies, Rhetoric, and the Neoliberal Nation-State.*

103. Zavella, *Movement for Reproductive Justice.*

104. Nicole Trujillo-Pagán, "Crossed out by LatinX: Gender Neutrality and Genderblind Sexism," *Latino Studies* 16, no. 3 (October 1, 2018): 397, https://doi.org /10.1057/s41276-018-0138-7.

105. Trujillo-Pagán, "Crossed out by LatinX," 397.

106. Bey, *Black Trans Feminism*; Bey, *Cistem Failure.*

107. Bey, *Black Trans Feminism*, xiv.

108. María Lugones, "Toward a Decolonial Feminism," *Hypatia* 25, no. 4 (2010): 742–59.

109. Méndez, "Notes toward a Decolonial Feminist Methodology," 49.

110. Personal communication, 2020.

111. Personal communication, 2020.

112. Bey, *Cistem Failure*, 66.

113. Méndez, "Notes toward a Decolonial Feminist Methodology."

114. Emi Koyama, "Whose Feminism Is It Anyway? The Unspoken Racism of the Trans Inclusion Debate," *The Sociological Review* 68, no. 4 (July 1, 2020): 735–44, https://doi.org/10.1177/0038026120934685.

115. Personal communication, 2020.

116. Alyosxa Tudor, "Im/Possibilities of Refusing and Choosing Gender," 272.

117. Bey, *Black Trans Feminism*; Kai M. Green, "The Essential I/Eye in We: A Black TransFeminist Approach to Ethnographic Film," *Black Camera* 6, no. 2 (2015): 187–200, https://doi.org/10.2979/blackcamera.6.2.187; Eric A. Stanley and Nat Smith, eds., *Captive Genders: Trans Embodiment and the Prison Industrial Complex*, 2nd ed. (Oakland, CA: AK Press, 2015).

118. Leo, "Colonial/Modern [Cis]Gender System," 2.

119. Ross and Solinger, *Reproductive Justice*, 22.

120. Uma Narayan, "Essence of Culture and a Sense of History: A Feminist Critique of Cultural Essentialism," *Hypatia* 13, no. 2 (1998): 35, https://doi.org/10.1111 /j.1527-2001.1998.tb01227.x.

121. Aja Y. Martinez, *Counterstory: The Rhetoric and Writing of Critical Race Theory* (Champaign, IL: National Council of Teachers of English, 2020).

122. Michael Middleton et al., *Participatory Critical Rhetoric: Theoretical and Methodological Foundations for Studying Rhetoric In Situ* (Lanham, MD: Lexington Books, 2015).

123. Raymie E. McKerrow, "Critical Rhetoric: Theory and Praxis," *Communication Monographs* 56, no. 2 (June 1, 1989): 91, https://doi.org/10.1080/03637758909390253.

124. Middleton et al., *Participatory Critical Rhetoric*, 11.

Chapter 1: Networking Arguments

1. "Mapping Attacks on LGBTQ Rights in U.S. State Legislatures," LGBTQ Rights, American Civil Liberties Union, April 18, 2023, https://www.aclu.org/legislative-attacks -on-lgbtq-rights.

2. Jude Ellison S. Doyle, "What's So Scary about 'Birthing People'?," *Medium*, May 11, 2021, para. 2, https://judedoyle.medium.com/whats-so-scary-about-birthing-people-8fb489397f1b.

3. Monica Hesse, "Ketanji Brown Jackson Did Define 'Woman' at Her Confirmation Hearing," *Washington Post*, March 25, 2022, https://www.washingtonpost.com/lifestyle/2022/03/25/ketanji-brown-jackson-woman/.

4. The Rubin Report, "Far-Left Professor Melts Down When Hawley Refuses to Ignore Reality | Direct Message | Rubin Report," July 13, 2022, YouTube video, 59:18, https://www.youtube.com/watch?v=m_ITfZmbOhk; Caroline Wharton, "Senator Hawley Finds That UC Berkeley Professor Doesn't Know What a Woman Is," Student for Life Action, July 14, 2022, https://www.studentsforlifeaction.org/senator-hawley-finds-that-uc-berkeley-professor-doesnt-know-what-a-woman-is/.

5. Our Readers and Katha Pollitt, "Does Talking about 'Women' Exclude Transgender People From the Fight for Abortion Rights?," *The Nation*, April 22, 2015, https://www.thenation.com/article/archive/letters-505/; Katha Pollitt, "Who Has Abortions?," *The Nation*, March 13, 2015, https://www.thenation.com/article/archive/who-has-abortions/; S. E. Smith, "Women Are Not the Only Ones Who Get Abortions," Rewire.News, March 1, 2019, https://rewire.news/article/2019/03/01/women-are-not-the-only-ones-who-get-abortions/.

6. Michael Powell, "A Vanishing Word in Abortion Debate: 'Women,'" *New York Times*, June 8, 2022, sec. U.S., https://www.nytimes.com/2022/06/08/us/women-gender-aclu-abortion.html.

7. Emma Green, "The Culture War over 'Pregnant People,'" *The Atlantic*, September 17, 2021, https://www.theatlantic.com/politics/archive/2021/09/pregnant-people-gender-identity/620031/; Sarah Ditum, "Trans Rights Should Not Come at the Cost of Women's Fragile Gains," *The Economist*, July 5, 2018, https://www.economist.com/open-future/2018/07/05/trans-rights-should-not-come-at-the-cost-of-womens-fragile-gains; Glosswitch, "The Problem with Talking about 'Pregnant People,'" *New Statesman*, September 29, 2015, https://www.newstatesman.com/politics/2015/09/what-s-matter-talking-about-pregnant-people; Kieran Gair, "Gender-Neutral Terms May Put Mothers at Risk," *The Times*, February 14, 2024, sec. News, https://www.thetimes.co.uk/article/gender-neutral-terms-could-have-serious-implications-for-mothers-t67p9r7lr.

8. Damjan Denkovski, Nina Bernarding, and Kristina Lunz, *Power over Rights: Understanding and Countering the Transnational Anti-gender Movement*, vol. 1 (Berlin: Centre for Feminist Foreign Policy, March 2021), https://static1.squarespace.com/static/57cd7cd9d482e9784e4ccc34/t/60c865e5f8c3ce53222039e3/1623746023308/PowerOverRights_Volume1_web.pdf.

9. Emi Koyama, "Whose Feminism Is It Anyway? The Unspoken Racism of the Trans Inclusion Debate," *The Sociological Review* 68, no. 4 (July 1, 2020): 735–44, https://doi.org/10.1177/0038026120934685; Kyla Schuller, *The Trouble with White Women: A Counterhistory of Feminism* (New York: Bold Type Books, 2021); Alyosxa

186   *Notes to Pages 35–36*

Tudor, "Decolonizing Trans/Gender Studies? Teaching Gender, Race, and Sexuality in Times of the Rise of the Global Right," *TSQ: Transgender Studies Quarterly* 8, no. 2 (May 1, 2021): 238–56, https://doi.org/10.1215/23289252-8890523.

10. María Lugones, "Heterosexualism and the Colonial/Modern Gender System," *Hypatia* 22, no. 1 (2007): 186–219, https://doi.org/10.1111/j.1527-2001.2007.tb01156.x; Maria Lugones, "The Coloniality of Gender," *Worlds & Knowledges Otherwise* 2, no. 2 (Spring 2008): 1–17, https://globalstudies.trinity.duke.edu/sites/globalstudies.trinity .duke.edu/files/documents/v2d2_Lugones.pdf.

11. Schuller, *Trouble with White Women*; Xhercis Méndez, "Notes Toward a De-colonial Feminist Methodology: Revisiting the Race/Gender Matrix," *Trans-Scripts* 5 (2015): 41–59.

12. Anjali Vats, "Mapping Property," *Quarterly Journal of Speech* 105, no. 4 (October 2, 2019): 511, https://doi.org/10.1080/00335630.2019.1666347.

13. Raymie E. McKerrow, "Critical Rhetoric: Theory and Praxis," *Communication Monographs* 56 (1989): 91–111, https://doi.org/10.1080/03637758909390253; Martha Cooper, "A Feminist Glance at Critical Rhetoric," in *Making and Unmaking the Prospects for Rhetoric*, eds. Theresa Enos and Richard McNabb (Mahwah, NJ: LEP, 1997), 99–106; Michael K. Middleton et al., *Participatory Critical Rhetoric: Theoretical and Methodological Foundations for Studying Rhetoric in Situ* (Lanham, MD: Lexington Books, 2015); Kent A. Ono and John M. Sloop, "Commitment to Telos—a Sustained Critical Rhetoric," *Communication Monographs* 59 (1992): 48–60.

14. Karma R. Chávez, "Border (In)Securities: Normative and Differential Belonging in LGBTQ and Immigrant Rights Discourse," *Communication and Critical/Cultural Studies* 7, no. 2 (June 1, 2010): 136–55, https://doi.org/10.1080/14791421003763291; Tamika L. Carey, "Necessary Adjustments: Black Women's Rhetorical Impatience," *Rhetoric Review* 39, no. 3 (July 2, 2020): 269–86, https://doi.org/10.1080/07350198.2020 .1764745; Darrel Enck-Wanzer, "Tropicalizing East Harlem: Rhetorical Agency, Cultural Citizenship, and Nuyorican Cultural Production," *Communication Theory* 21, no. 4 (2011): 344–67, https://doi.org/10.1111/j.1468-2885.2011.01390.x; V. Jo Hsu, "Irreducible Damage: The Affective Drift of Race, Gender, and Disability in Anti-trans Rhetorics," *Rhetoric Society Quarterly* 52, no. 1 (January 1, 2022): 62–77, https://doi.org/10.1080/027 73945.2021.1990381; V. Jo Hsu, *Constellating Home: Trans and Queer Asian American Rhetorics* (Columbus: Ohio State University Press, 2022); GPat Patterson and Leland G. Spencer, "Toward Trans Rhetorical Agency: A Critical Analysis of Trans Topics in Rhetoric and Composition and Communication Scholarship," *Peitho* 22, no. 4 (2020), https://www.academia.edu/download/64189894/Patterson&Spencer20.pdf; Lisa A. Flores, "The Rhetorical 'Realness' of Race, or Why Critical Race Rhetoricians Need Performance Studies," *Text and Performance Quarterly* 34, no. 1 (January 2, 2014): 94–96, https://doi.org/10.1080/10462937.2013.849356.

15. Walter D. Mignolo, *Local Histories/Global Designs: Coloniality, Subaltern Knowledges, and Border Thinking*, rev. ed. (Princeton, NJ: Princeton University Press, 2012), 68.

16. Jason Willick, "The Man Who Discovered 'Culture Wars,'" *Wall Street Journal*, May 25, 2018, https://www.wsj.com/articles/the-man-who-discovered-culture-wars -1527286035.

17. James Davison Hunter, *Culture Wars: The Struggle to Define America* (New York: BasicBooks, 1991).

18. Patrick Joseph Buchanan, "Culture War Speech: Address to the Republican National Convention," Voices of Democracy, para. 39, https://voicesofdemocracy.umd .edu/buchanan-culture-war-speech-speech-text/.

19. Joy Rohde, "Police Militarization Is a Legacy of Cold War Paranoia," *The Conversation*, October 22, 2014, http://theconversation.com/police-militarization-is-a -legacy-of-cold-war-paranoia-32251; Natalie Fixmer-Oraiz, *Homeland Maternity: US Security Culture and the New Reproductive Regime*, Feminist Media Studies (Urbana: University of Illinois Press, 2019).

20. Breanne Fahs, Mary L. Dudy, and Sarah Stage, eds., *The Moral Panics of Sexuality* (London: Palgrave Macmillan, 2013), https://doi.org/10.1057/9781137353177.

21. Monica J. Casper and Laura M. Carpenter, "Sex, Drugs, and Politics: The HPV Vaccine for Cervical Cancer," *Sociology of Health & Illness* 30, no. 6 (September 2008): 886–99, https://doi.org/10.1111/j.1467-9566.2008.01100.x; Breanne Fahs, "Daddy's Little Girls: On the Perils of Chastity Clubs, Purity Balls, and Ritualized Abstinence," *Frontiers: A Journal of Women's Studies* 31, no. 3 (2010): 116–42; Fixmer-Oraiz, *Homeland Maternity*; Jessica Valenti, *The Purity Myth: How America's Obsession with Virginity Is Hurting Young Women* (Berkeley, CA: Seal Press, 2009).

22. Imara Jones, "A Coordinated Attack on Trans Youth," July 7, 2021, in *The Anti-trans Hate Machine: A Plot against Equality*, podcast, 38:58, https://shows.acast .com/the-anti-trans-hate-machine/episodes/acoordinatedattackontransyouth; Imara Jones, "Money, Power and a Radical Vision," September 16, 2021, in *The Anti-trans Hate Machine: A Plot against Equality*, podcast, 35:29, https://shows.acast.com/the -anti-trans-hate-machine/episodes/money-powerandaradicalvision.

23. Heath Fogg Davis, *Beyond Trans: Does Gender Matter?* (New York: NYU Press, 2017).

24. "Gendered Racial Projects: Anti-trans, Anti-CRT, and Anti-abortion Legislation," The Gender Policy Report, July 14, 2022, para. 1, https://genderpolicyreport.umn .edu/gendered-racial-projects-anti-trans-anti-crt-and-anti-abortion-legislation/.

25. Schuyler Mitchell, "The Right's Creeping Pro-Natalist Rhetoric on Abortion and Trans Health Care," *The Intercept*, May 17, 2022, https://theintercept.com/2022 /05/17/abortion-trans-health-care-pro-natalism-authoritarianism/.

26. Barcelos, "Gendered Racial Projects"; Mitchell, "Right's Creeping Pro-Natalist Rhetoric."

27. Graeme Reid, "Breaking the Buzzword: Fighting the 'Gender Ideology' Myth," Human Rights Watch, December 10, 2018, para. 10, https://www.hrw.org/news/2018 /12/10/breaking-buzzword-fighting-gender-ideology-myth.

28. Denkovski, Bernarding, and Lunz, *Power over Rights*, vol. 1.

29. Janice M. Irvine, *Talk about Sex: The Battles over Sex Education in the United*

States (Oakland: University of California Press, 2002), 54; Richard M. Weaver, *The Ethics of Rhetoric*, repr. ed. (Brattleboro, VT: Echo Point Books & Media, 2015).

30. Mary Anne Case, "Trans Formations in the Vatican's War on 'Gender Ideology,'" *Signs: Journal of Women in Culture and Society* 44, no. 3 (March 2019): 639–64, https://doi.org/10.1086/701498; Denkovski, Bernarding, and Lunz, *Power over Rights*, vol. 1.

31. Denkovski, Bernarding, and Lunz, *Power over Rights*, vol. 1, 9–10.

32. Judith Butler, "Anti-gender Ideology and Mahmood's Critique of the Secular Age," *Journal of the American Academy of Religion* 87, no. 4 (December 12, 2019): 967, https://doi.org/10.1093/jaarel/lfz083.

33. Denkovski, Bernarding, and Lunz, *Power over Rights*, vol. 1; Reid, "Breaking the Buzzword"; Alyosxa Tudor, "Terfism Is White Distraction: On BLM, Decolonising the Curriculum, Anti-gender Attacks and Feminist Transphobia," *Engenderings* (blog), June 19, 2020, https://blogs.lse.ac.uk/gender/2020/06/19/terfism-is-white-distraction -on-blm-decolonising-the-curriculum-anti-gender-attacks-and-feminist-transphobia/.

34. Denkovski, Bernarding, and Lunz, *Power over Rights*, vol. 1; Weronika Grzebalska, Eszter Kováts, and Andrea Pető, "Gender as Symbolic Glue: How 'Gender' Became an Umbrella Term for the Rejection of the (Neo)Liberal Order," Political Critique, January 13, 2017, para. 6, http://politicalcritique.org/long-read/2017/gender-as -symbolic-glue-how-gender-became-an-umbrella-term-for-the-rejection-of-the -neoliberal-order/.

35. Roman Kuhar and David Paternotte, "The Anti-gender Movement in Comparative Perspective," in *Anti-gender Campaigns in Europe: Mobilizing against Equality*, eds. Roman Kuhar and David Paternotte (Lanham, MD: Rowman & Littlefield, 2017), 259.

36. Mark Gevisser, *The Pink Line: Journeys across the World's Queer Frontiers* (New York: Farrar, Straus and Giroux, 2020).

37. Denkovski, Bernarding, and Lunz, *Power over Rights*, vol. 1, 16.

38. Jones, "Money, Power and a Radical Vision."

39. Ariadne, *Challenging the Closing Space for Civil Society* (London: Ariadne, 2016), https://www.ariadne-network.eu/wp-content/uploads/2015/03/Ariadne _ClosingSpaceReport-Final-Version.pdf; Conny Roggeband and Andrea Krizsán, *Democratic Backsliding and the Backlash against Women's Rights: Understanding the Current Challenges for Feminist Politics* (New York: UN Women, June 2020), https:// www.unwomen.org/en/digital-library/publications/2020/06/discussion-paper -democratic-backsliding-and-the-backlash-against-womens-rights.

40. Denkovski, Bernarding, and Lunz, *Power over Rights*, vol. 1.

41. Denkovski, Bernarding, and Lunz, *Power over Rights*, vol. 1; Elżbieta Korolczuk, "Gender Ideology as Pandemic: Anti-gender Campaigns in a Time of Crisis," The New School Transregional Center for Democratic Studies, June 29, 2020, para. 7, https:// blogs.newschool.edu/tcds/2020/06/29/gender-ideology-as-pandemic-anti-gender -campaigns-in-a-time-of-crisis/.

42. Hedwig Lieback, "The Success and Dangers of Faux-Feminism and Homo-

Notes to Pages 44–46   189

nationalism," *She Thought It* (blog), September 5, 2019, https://shethoughtit.ilcml.com
/essay/the-success-and-dangers-of-faux-feminism-and-homonationalism/; Sara R.
Farris, *In the Name of Women's Rights: The Rise of Femonationalism* (Durham, NC:
Duke University Press, 2017).

43. Global Philanthropy Project, *Meet the Moment: A Call for Progressive Philan-
thropic Response to the Anti-gender Movement* (Oakland, CA: Global Philanthropy
Project, 2020), https://globalphilanthropyproject.org/wp-content/uploads/2021/02
/Meet-the-Moment-2020-English.pdf; Kuhar and Paternotte, "Anti-gender Movement,"
253–72.

44. Imara Jones, "Detransition Pseudo-Science and Misleading Examples," March
31, 2023, in *The Anti-trans Hate Machine: A Plot against Equality*, podcast, 48:55,
https://shows.acast.com/the-anti-trans-hate-machine/episodes/detransition-pseudo
-science-and-misleading-examples.

45. The Heritage Foundation, "The Inequality of the Equality Act: Concerns from
the Left," January 28, 2019, YouTube video, 1:09:43, https://www.youtube.com/watch?v
=HMj9MOuRswc; The Heritage Foundation, "The Medical Harms of Hormonal and
Surgical Interventions for Gender Dysphoric Children," March 28, 2019, YouTube
video, 1:06:57, https://www.youtube.com/watch?v=bnP_WoeNuwA.

46. Jones, "Detransition Pseudo-Science."

47. Denise Caignon, "About," 4thWaveNow, March 17, 2015, https://4thwavenow
.com/about/.

48. Imara Jones, "Seduction of Rapid Onset Gender Dysphoria," March 31, 2023,
in *The Anti-trans Hate Machine: A Plot against Equality*, podcast, 44:03, https://shows
.acast.com/the-anti-trans-hate-machine/episodes/seduction-of-rapid-onset-gender
-dysphoria.

49. Jones, "Seduction of Rapid Onset Gender Dysphoria."

50. M. K. Anderson, "Singal and the Noise," *Protean*, April 22, 2022, https://
proteanmag.com/2022/04/22/singal-and-the-noise/; Elizabeth Bibi, "Human Rights
Campaign Calls Out New York Times for Publishing Transphobic Column One Day
After an Open Letter Condemning Its Anti-transgender Coverage," Human Rights
Campaign, February 16, 2023, https://www.hrc.org/press-releases/human-rights
-campaign-calls-out-new-york-times-for-publishing-transphobic-column-one-day
-after-an-open-letter-condemning-its-anti-transgender-coverage; GLAAD, "Medical
Association Statements in Support of Health Care for Transgender People and Youth,"
GLAAD, June 21, 2023, https://glaad.org/medical-association-statements-supporting
-trans-youth-healthcare-and-against-discriminatory/.

51. Anderson, "Singal and the Noise"; Jones, "Seduction of Rapid Onset Gender
Dysphoria."

52. Denkovski, Bernarding, and Lunz, *Power over Rights*, vol. 1; Korolczuk, "Gender
Ideology as Pandemic"; Rebecca Sanders et al., *Power over Rights: Understanding and
Countering the Transnational Anti-gender Movement* vol. 2, Case Studies (Berlin:
Centre for Feminist Foreign Policy, March 2021), https://static1.squarespace.com

/static/57cd7cd9d482e9784e4ccc34/t/60cb90dc89619a5c8234aadf/1623953630210
/PowerOverRights2_web.pdf.

53. Denkovski, Bernarding, and Lunz, *Power over Rights*, vol. 1; Lucille Griffon et al., *The Fierce and the Furious: Feminist Insights into the Anti Gender Narratives and Movement* (EuroMed Rights, November 2019), https://kvinnatillkvinna.org/wp -content/uploads/2020/04/The_fierce_and_the_furious.pdf; Sanders et al., *Power over Rights*, vol. 2.

54. Denkovski, Bernarding, and Lunz, *Power over Rights*, vol. 1; Griffon et al., *Fierce and Furious*; Sanders et al., *Power over Rights*, vol. 2.

55. Denkovski, Bernarding, and Lunz, *Power over Rights*, vol. 1, 34.

56. Sanders et al., *Power over Rights*, vol. 2.

57. Zack Ford, "Fake Medical Organization Publishes Lie-Ridden Manifesto Attacking Transgender Kids," Think Progress, August 19, 2016, https://archive .thinkprogress.org/american-college-pediatricians-transgender-kids-falsehoods -384716df13c5/.

58. Erica L. Green, Katie Benner, and Robert Pear, "'Transgender' Could Be Defined out of Existence under Trump Administration," *New York Times*, October 21, 2018, sec. U.S., para. 4, https://www.nytimes.com/2018/10/21/us/politics/transgender -trump-administration-sex-definition.html.

59. Green, Benner, and Pear, "'Transgender' Could Be Defined out of Existence," para. 5.

60. Michelle Cretella, "Gender Dysphoria in Children," American College of Pediatricians, November 2018, para. 1, https://acpeds.org/position-statements/gender -dysphoria-in-children.

61. Claire Ainsworth, "Sex Redefined: The Idea of 2 Sexes Is Overly Simplistic," *Scientific American*, October 2019, https://www.scientificamerican.com/article/sex -redefined-the-idea-of-2-sexes-is-overly-simplistic1/; Laura Helmuth and Curtis Brainard, "Why Anti-trans Laws Are Anti-science," *Scientific American*, June 30, 2021, https://www.scientificamerican.com/article/why-anti-trans-laws-are-anti-science/; Simón(e) D. Sun, "Stop Using Phony Science to Justify Transphobia," *Scientific American*, June 13, 2019, https://blogs.scientificamerican.com/voices/stop-using-phony -science-to-justify-transphobia/.

62. Hesse, "Ketanji Brown Jackson Did Define 'Woman'"; Liberty Hangout, "College Students Have No Morals," November 21, 2019, YouTube video, 20:03, https:// www.youtube.com/watch?v=2xSv4veEgbk; Pamela Paul, "The Far Right and Far Left Agree on One Thing: Women Don't Count," *New York Times*, July 3, 2022, sec. Opinion, https://www.nytimes.com/2022/07/03/opinion/the-far-right-and-far-left -agree-on-one-thing-women-dont-count.html; Sun, "Stop Using Phony Science."

63. Sun, "Stop Using Phony Science."

64. Dorothy Roberts, *Fatal Invention: How Science, Politics, and Big Business Re-Create Race in the Twenty-First Century*, 2nd ed. (New York: The New Press, 2012).

65. Lisa Littman, "Rapid-Onset Gender Dysphoria in Adolescents and Young

Adults: A Study of Parental Reports," *PLOS ONE* 13 (August 16, 2018): e0202330, https://doi.org/10.1371/journal.pone.0202330.

66. Zinnia Jones, "Meet the Unbiased, Reliable, Not-at-All-Transphobic Parents from the 'Rapid Onset Gender Dysphoria' Study," *Gender Analysis* (blog), August 31, 2018, https://genderanalysis.net/2018/08/meet-the-unbiased-reliable-not-at-all -transphobic-parents-from-the-rapid-onset-gender-dysphoria-study/; Arjee Javellana Restar, "Methodological Critique of Littman's (2018) Parental-Respondents Accounts of 'Rapid-Onset Gender Dysphoria,'" *Archives of Sexual Behavior* 49, no. 1 (2020): 61–66, https://doi.org/10.1007/s10508-019-1453-2; Julia Serano, "Everything You Need to Know About Rapid Onset Gender Dysphoria," Medium, December 1, 2021, https:// juliaserano.medium.com/everything-you-need-to-know-about-rapid-onset-gender -dysphoria-1940b8afdeba.

67. Arjee Javellana Restar, "Methodological Critique of Littman's (2018) Parental-Respondents Accounts of 'Rapid-Onset Gender Dysphoria,'" *Archives of Sexual Behavior* 49, no. 1 (2020): 61–66, https://doi.org/10.1007/s10508-019-1453-2; Greta R. Bauer, Margaret L. Lawson, and Daniel L. Metzger, "Do Clinical Data from Transgender Adolescents Support the Phenomenon of 'Rapid Onset Gender Dysphoria'?," *The Journal of Pediatrics* 243 (April 1, 2022): 224–227.e2, https://doi.org/10.1016/j.jpeds.2021.11.020.

68. Alexandre Baril and Florence Ashley, "Why 'Rapid-Onset Gender Dysphoria' Is Bad Science," *The Conversation*, March 22, 2018, http://theconversation.com/why -rapid-onset-gender-dysphoria-is-bad-science-92742.

69. Baril and Ashley, "'Rapid-Onset Gender Dysphoria' Is Bad Science."

70. Jones, "Detransition Pseudo-Science."

71. Denkovski, Bernarding, and Lunz, *Power over Rights*, vol. 1.

72. Irvine, *Talk about Sex*.

73. Taylor Lorenz, "Meet the Woman behind Libs of TikTok, Secretly Fueling the Right's Outrage Machine," *Washington Post*, April 19, 2022, para. 1, https://www .washingtonpost.com/technology/2022/04/19/libs-of-tiktok-right-wing-media/.

74. Sara Ahmed, *The Cultural Politics of Emotion* (New York: Routledge, 2004).

75. Bella DiMarco, "Legislative Tracker: Parent-Rights Bills in the States," FutureEd, June 6, 2022, https://www.future-ed.org/legislative-tracker-parent-rights-bills-in-the -states/.

76. Hsu, "Irreducible Damage," 63.

77. Abigail Shrier, "Abigail Shrier on Freedom in an Age of Fear," Substack newsletter, *Common Sense* (blog), December 21, 2021, https://bariweiss.substack.com/p /abigail-shrier-on-freedom-in-an-age.

78. Glenn Greenwald, "The Ongoing Death of Free Speech: Prominent ACLU Lawyer Cheers Suppression of a New Book," Substack newsletter, *Glenn Greenwald* (blog), November 15, 2020, https://greenwald.substack.com/p/the-ongoing-death-of -free-speech; Bari Weiss, "Courage in the Face of Book Burners," in *Honestly with Bari Weiss*, podcast, 55:36, accessed June 16, 2022, https://podcasts.apple.com/us/podcast /courage-in-the-face-of-book-burners/id1570872415?i=1000534743397.

79. Hsu, "Irreducible Damage," 62.

80. Paul, "Far Right and Far Left Agree," paras. 11, 17.

81. Janice G. Raymond, *The Transsexual Empire: The Making of the She-Male* (New York: Teachers College Press, 1994); Kathleen Stock, *Material Girls: Why Reality Matters for Feminism* (London: Fleet, 2021).

82. Koyama, "Whose Feminism Is It Anyway?"; Schuller, *Trouble with White Women*; Tudor, "Terfism Is White Distraction."

83. "The Aftermath of Dobbs: Putting the Movement for Reproductive Justice in Conversation with the Fight for Trans Justice," Events, Berkeley Law, accessed May 31, 2024, https://www.law.berkeley.edu/research/center-on-race-sexuality-culture/events/.

84. Hsu, "Irreducible Damage," 63.

85. United Kingdom, House of Lords Parliamentary Debates, vol. 810, "Ministerial and Other Maternity Allowances Bill," February 22, 2021, https://hansard.parliament .uk/lords/2021-02-22/debates/EF8A7974-0A9C-4F17-B9DC-B7D26E52D52F/Minis terialAndOtherMaternityAllowancesBill.

86. United Kingdom, House of Lords Parliamentary Debates, vol. 810, "Ministerial and Other Maternity Allowances Bill," February 22, 2021, https://hansard.parliament .uk/lords/2021-02-22/debates/EF8A7974-0A9C-4F17-B9DC-B7D26E52D52F/Minis terialAndOtherMaternityAllowancesBill.

87. Bryan Lowry, "'Birthing People.' Bush Hits Her Critics for Missing Story of Children Nearly Dying," *The Kansas City Star*, May 7, 2021, https://www.kansascity .com/news/politics-government/article251224129.html.

88. Green, "Culture War," para. 14.

89. Karleen D. Gribble et al., "Effective Communication about Pregnancy, Birth, Lactation, Breastfeeding and Newborn Care: The Importance of Sexed Language," *Frontiers in Global Women's Health* 3 (February 7, 2022): 1, https://doi.org/10.3389 /fgwh.2022.818856.

90. Paul, "Far Right and Far Left Agree."

91. Leah Ceccarelli, "Rhetorical Criticism and the Rhetoric of Science," *Western Journal of Communication* 65, no. 3 (2001): 314–29; Philip C. Wander, "The Rhetoric of Science," *Western Speech Communication* 40, no. 4 (December 30, 1976): 226–35, https://doi.org/10.1080/10570317609373907.

92. Wander, "Rhetoric of Science," 233.

93. Thomas S. Kuhn, *The Structure of Scientific Revolutions*, 3rd ed. (Chicago: University of Chicago Press, 1996).

94. Kuhn, *The Structure of Scientific Revolutions*.

95. Cordelia Fine, *Testosterone Rex: Myths of Sex, Science, and Society*, repr. ed. (New York: W. W. Norton & Company, 2018).

96. Molly J. Dingel and Joey Sprague, "Research and Reporting on the Development of Sex in Fetuses: Gendered from the Start," *Public Understanding of Science* 19, no. 2 (March 1, 2010): 185, https://doi.org/10.1177/0963662508096782.

97. Liza Brusman, "Sex Isn't Binary, and We Should Stop Acting like It Is," Massive Science, June 14, 2019, https://massivesci.com/articles/sex-gender-intersex-transgender -identity-discrimination-title-ix/; Dingel and Sprague, "Research and Reporting."

98. Dingel and Sprague, "Research and Reporting"; Cordelia Fine, *Delusions of Gender: How Our Minds, Society, and Neurosexism Create Difference*, repr. ed. (New York: W. W. Norton & Company, 2011).

99. Ainsworth, "Sex Redefined"; Brusman, "Sex Isn't Binary"; Kim Elsesser, "The Myth of Biological Sex," *Forbes*, June 15, 2020, sec. Careers, https://www.forbes.com/sites/kimelsesser/2020/06/15/the-myth-of-biological-sex/; Anne Fausto-Sterling, "Why Sex Is Not Binary," *New York Times*, October 25, 2018, sec. Opinion, https://www.nytimes.com/2018/10/25/opinion/sex-biology-binary.html; Cade Hildreth, "Gender Spectrum: A Scientist Explains Why Gender Isn't Binary," *Cade Hildreth* (blog), February 5, 2022, https://cadehildreth.com/gender-spectrum/; Sun, "Stop Using Phony Science."

100. Gribble et al., "Effective Communication about Pregnancy," 1.

101. Gribble et al., "Effective Communication about Pregnancy," 1.

102. Gribble et al., "Effective Communication about Pregnancy," 2.

103. "Open Letter to MANA," *Woman-Centered Midwifery* (blog), August 20, 2015, https://womancenteredmidwifery.wordpress.com/take-action/.

104. Morgan Carpenter, "The 'Normalization' of Intersex Bodies and 'Othering' of Intersex Identities in Australia," *Journal of Bioethical Inquiry* 15, no. 4 (December 2018): 487–95, https://doi.org/10.1007/s11673-018-9855-8.

105. Carpenter, "'Normalization' of Intersex Bodies."

106. Lugones, "Coloniality of Gender"; Scott Lauria Morgensen, *Spaces between Us: Queer Settler Colonialism and Indigenous Decolonization* (Minneapolis: University of Minnesota Press, 2011); Freya Schiwy, "Decolonization and the Question of Subjectivity," *Cultural Studies* 21, no. 2–3 (March 1, 2007): 271–94, https://doi.org/10.1080/09502380601162555.

107. Deborah Miranda, "Extermination of the Joyas: Gendercide in Spanish California," *GLQ: A Journal of Lesbian and Gay Studies* 16, no. 1–2 (January 27, 2010): 258, https://doi.org/10.1215/10642684-2009-022; Morgensen, *Spaces between Us*, 44.

108. Sara Dahlen, "Do We Need the Word 'Woman' in Healthcare?," *Postgraduate Medical Journal* 97, no. 1150 (August 1, 2021): 483, https://doi.org/10.1136/postgradmedj-2021-140193.

109. Dahlen, "Do We Need the Word 'Woman' in Healthcare?," 487.

110. Dahlen, "Do We Need the Word 'Woman' in Healthcare?," 484.

111. Anne Curzan, *Fixing English: Prescriptivism and Language History*, repr. ed. (Cambridge, UK: Cambridge University Press, 2016); Nayantara Dutta, "The Subtle Ways Language Shapes Us," BBC Culture, October 6, 2020, https://www.bbc.com/culture/article/20201006-are-some-languages-more-sexist-than-others.

112. Miriam Berger, "A Guide to How Gender-Neutral Language Is Developing around the World," *Washington Post*, December 15, 2019, https://www.washingtonpost.com/world/2019/12/15/guide-how-gender-neutral-language-is-developing-around-world/.

113. Berger, "Guide to How Gender-Neutral Language Is Developing."

114. Gribble et al., "Effective Communication about Pregnancy," 3.

115. Gribble et al., "Effective Communication about Pregnancy," 3.

116. Helen Green and Ash Riddington, *Gender Inclusive Language in Perinatal Services: Mission Statement and Rationale* (Brighton and Sussex University Hospitals, 2020), https://www.liverpool.ac.uk/media/livacuk/schoolofmedicine/leo/documents/Gender-inclusive-language-in-perinatal-services,(2).pdf.

117. Sue Stableford and Wendy Mettger, "Plain Language: A Strategic Response to the Health Literacy Challenge," *Journal of Public Health Policy* 28, no. 1 (April 1, 2007): 71–93, https://doi.org/10.1057/palgrave.jphp.3200102.

118. Gribble et al., "Effective Communication about Pregnancy," 2.

119. Butler, "Anti-gender Ideology," 955–67; Denkovski, Bernarding, and Lunz, *Power over Rights*, vol. 1.

120. Gribble et al., "Effective Communication about Pregnancy," 6.

121. Butler, "Anti-gender Ideology"; Sanders et al., *Power over Rights*, vol. 2.

122. Gribble et al., "Effective Communication about Pregnancy," 2.

123. Littman, "Rapid-Onset Gender Dysphoria," 44.

124. Gribble et al., "Effective Communication about Pregnancy," 6.

125. Bryan Lowry, "'Birthing People.' Bush Hits Her Critics for Missing Story of Children Nearly Dying," *Kansas City Star*, May 7, 2021, https://www.kansascity.com/news/politics-government/article251224129.html.

126. Lowry, "Birthing People," para. 13.

127. Schuller, *Trouble with White Women*.

128. Rebecca Jo Plant, *Mom: The Transformation of Motherhood in Modern America*, repr. ed. (Chicago: University of Chicago Press, 2012); Adrienne Rich, *Of Woman Born: Motherhood as Experience and Institution* (New York: W. W. Norton & Company, 1995).

129. Plant, *Mom*, 56.

130. Nancy Mace (@NancyMace), "'Birthing people' - you mean women or moms? The left is so woke they're stripping from women the one thing that only we can do. Leave it to libs to botch highlighting an important issue ppl in both parties can agree on by catering to the fringes . . .," Twitter, May 6, 2021, 1:31 p.m., https://twitter.com/NancyMace/status/1390373617838481408.

131. Abigail Shrier, "Gender Activists Are Trying to Cancel My Book. Why Is Silicon Valley Helping Them?," *Quillette*, November 7, 2020, https://quillette.com/2020/11/07/gender-activists-are-trying-to-cancel-my-book-why-is-silicon-valley-helping-them/.

132. Beverly Hallberg and Abigail Shrier, "Abigail Shrier on Her New Book: Irreversible Damage: The Transgender Craze Seducing Our Daughters," She Thinks, September 4, 2020, https://www.iwf.org/2020/09/04/abigail-shrier-on-her-new-book-irreversible-damage-the-transgender-craze-seducing-our-daughters/.

133. V. Jo Hsu, "The 'War on the Word "Women"' Is a Dangerous Distraction," TransGriot, July 5, 2022, https://transgriot.com/recent-news/the-war-on-the-word-women-is-a-dangerous-distraction/.

134. Gribble et al., "Effective Communication about Pregnancy," 5.

135. Personal communication, 2021.

136. Doyle, "What's So Scary?"

137. Doyle, "What's So Scary?"

138. Natalie Fixmer-Oraiz and Shui-yin Sharon Yam, "Queer(ing) Reproductive Justice," in *Oxford Research Encyclopedia of Communication*, ed. Matthew Powers (Oxford University Press, 2021), https://doi.org/10.1093/acrefore/9780190228613 .013.1195; National LGBTQ Task Force, "Queering Reproductive Justice: A Toolkit," National LGBTQ Task Force, March 13, 2017, https://www.thetaskforce.org/resources /queering-reproductive-justice-a-toolkit/; Miriam Zoila Pérez, "Queering Reproductive Justice," Rewire.News, May 31, 2007, https://rewire.news/article/2007/05/31 /queering-reproductive-justice/; Kimala Price, "Queering Reproductive Justice in the Trump Era: A Note on Political Intersectionality," *Politics & Gender* 14, no. 4 (December 2018): 581–601, https://doi.org/10.1017/S1743923X18000776; Loretta Ross and Rickie Solinger, *Reproductive Justice: An Introduction* (Oakland: University of California Press, 2017).

139. Chase Strangio, "Arrested for Walking While Trans: An Interview with Monica Jones," American Civil Liberties Union, April 2, 2014, https://www.aclu .org/blog/criminal-law-reform/arrested-walking-while-trans-interview-monica -jones.

140. Powell, "Vanishing Word."

141. Elizabeth M. Inman et al., "Reports of Negative Interactions with Healthcare Providers among Transgender, Nonbinary, and Gender-Expansive People Assigned Female at Birth in the United States: Results from an Online, Cross-Sectional Survey," *International Journal of Environmental Research and Public Health* 20, no. 11 (May 31, 2023): 6007, https://doi.org/10.3390/ijerph20116007.

142. Powell, "Vanishing Word," para. 14.

143. Powell, "Vanishing Word."

144. Powell, "Vanishing Word," paras. 16–17.

145. Megan McArdle, "Can the Women's Movement Be as Effective without the Word 'Women'?," *Washington Post*, May 5, 2022, para. 3, https://www.washingtonpost .com/opinions/2022/05/05/pregnant-people-womens-rights-roe/.

146. Pollitt, "Who Has Abortions?"

147. Green, "Culture War."; Olivia McCargar et al., "POV: Who Is Forgotten in Our Discussion of Abortion," *BU Today*, September 11, 2021, https://www.bu.edu/articles /2021/pov-nonbinary-people-and-trans-men-need-abortion-care-too/; Lauren Rankin, "Not Everyone Who Has an Abortion Is a Woman - How to Frame the Abortion Rights Issue," Truthout, July 31, 2013, https://truthout.org/articles/not-everyone-who-has-an -abortion-is-a-woman-how-to-frame-the-abortion-rights-issue/; Readers and Pollitt, "Does Talking about 'Women' Exclude Transgender People?"

148. "Aftermath of Dobbs."

149. "Aftermath of Dobbs."

150. Readers and Pollitt, "Does Talking about 'Women' Exclude Transgender People?"

151. Green, "Culture War."

152. Green, "Culture War," para. 24.

153. Doyle, "What's So Scary?"

154. Dána-Ain Davis, *Reproductive Injustice* (New York: NYU Press, 2019).

155. Cori Bush (@CoriBush), "I testified in front of Congress about nearly losing both of my children during childbirth because doctors didn't believe my pain. Republicans got more upset about me using gender-inclusive language in my testimony than my babies nearly dying. Racism and transphobia in America," Twitter, May 6, 2021, 5:33 p.m., https://twitter.com/CoriBush/status/1390434462400397317.

156. American College of Nurse-Midwives, *Position Statement: Transgender/Transsexual/Gender Variant Health Care* (Silver Spring, MD: American College of Nurse-Midwives, 2012), http://www.midwife.org/ACNM/files/ACNMLibraryData/UPLOADFILENAME/000000000278/Transgender%20Gender%20Variant%20Position%20Statement%20December%202012.pdf.

157. E. Coleman et al., "Standards of Care for the Health of Transgender and Gender Diverse People, Version 8," *International Journal of Transgender Health* 23, no. sup1 (August 19, 2022): S1–259, https://doi.org/10.1080/26895269.2022.2100644.

158. "Gender Inclusivity & Human Rights," Association of Ontario Midwives, 2015, https://www.ontariomidwives.ca/gender-inclusivity.

159. Sally Pezaro et al., "Gender-Inclusive Language in Midwifery and Perinatal Services: A Guide and Argument for Justice," *Birth: Issues in Perinatal Care* (forthcoming), accessed June 17, 2024, https://doi.org/10.1111/birt.12844.

160. "Position Statement on Gender Inclusive Language," Midwives Alliance of North America, June 30, 2016, https://mana.org/healthcare-policy/position-statement-on-gender-inclusive-language.

161. "Position Statement on Gender Inclusive Language," para. 8.

162. Green and Riddington, *Gender Inclusive Language*, 11, 23.

163. A. J. Silver, *Supporting Queer Birth* (Philadelphia: Jessica Kingsley Publishers, 2022).

164. Silver, *Supporting Queer Birth*, 70.

165. Green and Riddington, *Gender Inclusive Language*.

166. Silver, *Supporting Queer Birth*.

167. Green and Riddington, *Gender Inclusive Language*, 14.

168. Green and Riddington, *Gender Inclusive Language*, 15.

169. "Reproductive Justice," SisterSong, para. 2, accessed June 17, 2024, https://www.sistersong.net/reproductive-justice.

170. Madison Feller, " 'We Have to Rethink Everything': Why the Abortion Advocacy Group NARAL Is Changing Its Name," *Elle*, September 20, 2023, https://www.elle.com/culture/career-politics/a45206633/naral-name-change-reproductive-freedom-for-all-interview/.

171. Trans Journalists Association, "TJA Best Practices for Trans-Inclusive Language in Abortion," May 5, 2022, https://acrobat.adobe.com/id/urn:aaid:sc:US:5aa3495b-6112-4986-ad65-59ed0cdf1ce8.

172. Miriam Zoila Pérez, Trystan Reese, Mac Brydum, and Emma Robinson, "They/Them/Theirs" (panel discussion, Born into This, Austin, TX, 2019).

173. Alexis Hoffkling, Juno Obedin-Maliver, and Jae Sevelius, "From Erasure to Opportunity: A Qualitative Study of the Experiences of Transgender Men around Pregnancy and Recommendations for Providers," *BMC Pregnancy and Childbirth* 17, no. 2 (November 8, 2017): 332, https://doi.org/10.1186/s12884-017-1491-5; Trevor Mac-Donald, "Transphobia in the Midwifery Community," Huffington Post, September 15, 2015, https://www.huffingtonpost.com/trevor-macdonald/transphobia-in-the-midwif_b_8131520.html.

174. MacDonald, "Transphobia in the Midwifery Community," para. 13.

175. Koyama, "Whose Feminism Is It Anyway?"; Schuller, *Trouble with White Women*.

176. Audre Lorde, "Age, Race, Class, and Sex: Women Redefining Difference," in *Sister Outsider: Essays and Speeches* (Berkeley, CA: Crossing Press, 1984), 114–23, https://doi.org/10.4324/9780429038556-22.

177. Elephant Circle, "Position Statement on Gender Inclusive Language."

178. Doyle, "What's So Scary?"; Ashley Noel Mack, "The Self-Made Mom: Neoliberalism and Masochistic Motherhood in Home-Birth Videos on YouTube," *Women's Studies in Communication* 39, no. 1 (January 2, 2016): 47–68, https://doi.org/10.1080/07491409.2015.1129519.

179. MacDonald, "Transphobia in the Midwifery Community."

180. Joshua Gamson, "Kindred Spirits?," *Reproductive Biomedicine & Society Online* 7 (June 27, 2018): 1–3, https://doi.org/10.1016/j.rbms.2018.04.002; Laura Nixon, "The Right to (Trans) Parent: A Reproductive Justice Approach to Reproductive Rights, Fertility, and Family-Building Issues Facing Transgender People," *William & Mary Journal of Women and the Law* 20, no. 1 (2013): 73–103.

181. Aph Ko and Syl Ko, *Aphro-Ism: Essays on Pop Culture, Feminism, and Black Veganism from Two Sisters* (New York: Lantern Publishing & Media, 2017), 32.

Chapter 2: Against Gender Essentialism

1. Natalie Fixmer-Oraiz and Shui-yin Sharon Yam, "Queer(ing) Reproductive Justice," in *Oxford Research Encyclopedia of Communication*, ed. Matthew Powers (Oxford University Press, 2021), https://doi.org/10.1093/acrefore/9780190228613.013.1195.

2. Joshua D. Safer et al., "Barriers to Health Care for Transgender Individuals," *Current Opinion in Endocrinology, Diabetes, and Obesity* 23, no. 2 (April 1, 2016): 168–71, https://doi.org/10.1097/MED.0000000000000227; Stef M. Shuster, *Trans Medicine* (New York: NYU Press, 2021).

3. Katie L. Acosta, "Queering Family Scholarship: Theorizing from the Borderlands," *Journal of Family Theory & Review* 10, no. 2 (2018): 406–18, https://doi.org/10.1111/jftr.12263; Natalie Fixmer-Oraiz and Grover Wehman-Brown, "Called into the World by All of Us: An Interview with Masculine Birth Ritual Podcast Creator and Host Grover Wehman-Brown," *QED: A Journal in GLBTQ Worldmaking* 7, no. 2 (2020): 94–105, https://doi.org/10.14321/qed.7.2.0094; Ashley Noel Mack, "The Self-Made Mom:

Neoliberalism and Masochistic Motherhood in Home-Birth Videos on YouTube," *Women's Studies in Communication* 39, no. 1 (January 2, 2016): 47–68, https://doi.org/10.1080/07491409.2015.1129519.

4. Shui-Yin Sharon Yam, "Complicating Acts of Advocacy: Tactics in the Birthing Room," *Reflections: A Journal of Community Engaged Writing and Rhetoric* 20, no. 2 (2020): 198–218.

5. Robbie Davis-Floyd, *Ways of Knowing about Birth: Mothers, Midwives, Medicine, and Birth Activism* (Long Grove, IL: Waveland Press, 2018); Natalie Fixmer-Oraiz, "Contemplating Homeland Maternity," *Women's Studies in Communication* 38, no. 2 (April 3, 2015): 129–34, https://doi.org/10.1080/07491409.2015.1034630.

6. Marika Seigel, *The Rhetoric of Pregnancy* (Chicago: University of Chicago Press, 2013); Mary Lay Schuster, "A Different Place to Birth: A Material Rhetoric Analysis of Baby Haven, a Free-Standing Birth Center," *Women's Studies in Communication* 29, no. 1 (April 1, 2006): 1–38, https://doi.org/10.1080/07491409.2006.10757626.

7. Monica Reese Basile, "Reproductive Justice and Childbirth Reform: Doulas as Agents of Social Change" (PhD thesis, University of Iowa, 2012), https://ir.uiowa.edu/etd/2819; JaDee Carathers, "Radical Doulas Make 'Caring a Political Act': Full-Spectrum Birthwork as Reproductive Justice Activism" (PhD diss., Portland State University, 2019), https://pdxscholar.library.pdx.edu/open_access_etds/5496/; Shui-yin Sharon Yam, "Visualizing Birth Stories from the Margin: Toward a Reproductive Justice Model of Rhetorical Analysis," *Rhetoric Society Quarterly* 50, no. 1 (January 1, 2020): 19–34, https://doi.org/10.1080/02773945.2019.1682182.

8. Loretta Ross and Rickie Solinger, *Reproductive Justice: An Introduction* (Oakland: University of California Press, 2017), 9.

9. Miriam Zoila Pérez, *The Radical Doula Guide: A Political Primer* (self-pub., 2012), 12, https://radicaldoula.com/the-radical-doula-guide/.

10. Basile, "Reproductive Justice and Childbirth Reform."

11. Carathers, "Radical Doulas."

12. Robbie Davis-Floyd, "The Technocratic, Humanistic, and Holistic Paradigms of Childbirth," *International Journal of Gynaecology and Obstetrics: The Official Organ of the International Federation of Gynaecology and Obstetrics* 75 Suppl. 1 (November 2001): S5–23.

13. Davis-Floyd, *Ways of Knowing about Birth*.

14. Seigel, *Rhetoric of Pregnancy*; Emily Winderman, "Times for Birth: Chronic and Kairotic Mediated Temporalities in TLC's A Baby Story," *Feminist Media Studies* 17, no. 3 (May 4, 2017): 347–61, https://doi.org/10.1080/14680777.2016.1192556.

15. Davis-Floyd, *Ways of Knowing about Birth*; Dána-Ain Davis, *Reproductive Injustice* (New York: NYU Press, 2019); Khiara M. Bridges, *Reproducing Race: An Ethnography of Pregnancy as a Site of Racialization* (Berkeley: University of California Press, 2011); Pérez, *Radical Doula Guide*; Cassandra Pintro, "How Chanel Porchia-Albert, Doula and Mother of Six, Is Advocating for Black Maternal Health," *Vogue*, June 18, 2021, https://www.vogue.com/article/ancient-song-doula-services; Cristen Pascucci, "Birth Monopoly," Birth Monopoly, 2024, https://birthmonopoly.com/.

16. Yam, "Visualizing Birth Stories from the Margin."

17. Alana Apfel, *Birth Work as Care Work: Stories from Activist Birth Communities* (Oakland, CA: PM Press, 2016), 11.

18. Apfel, *Birth Work as Care Work*, 99.

19. Michael K. Middleton, Samantha Senda-Cook, and Danielle Endres, "Articulating Rhetorical Field Methods: Challenges and Tensions," *Western Journal of Communication* 75, no. 4 (July 1, 2011): 387, https://doi.org/10.1080/10570314.2011.586969; Danielle Endres et al., "In Situ Rhetoric: Intersections between Qualitative Inquiry, Fieldwork, and Rhetoric," *Cultural Studies ↔ Critical Methodologies* 16, no. 6 (December 1, 2016): 514, https://doi.org/10.1177/1532708616655820.

20. Yam, "Visualizing Birth Stories from the Margin," 20.

21. "Cornerstone Birthwork Training," Cornerstone Birthwork Training, 2021, https://www.cornerstonedoulatrainings.com; "Sacred House of Eden - What Is a Birthworker?," Sacred House of Eden, 2019, https://sacredhouseofeden.com/new-page-2.

22. Davis-Floyd, *Ways of Knowing about Birth*; Paula A. Michaels, *Lamaze: An International History* (Oxford: Oxford University Press, 2014); Christine H. Morton, *Birth Ambassadors: Doulas and the Re-Emergence of Woman-Supported Birth in America* (Amarillo, TX: Praeclarus Press, 2014); Margarete Sandelowski, *Pain, Pleasure, and American Childbirth: From the Twilight Sleep to the Read Method, 1914–1960* (Santa Barbara, CA: ABC-CLIO, 1984).

23. Morton, *Birth Ambassadors*, 62.

24. Davis-Floyd, *Ways of Knowing about Birth*, 4.

25. Davis-Floyd, "Technocratic, Humanistic, and Holistic Paradigms of Childbirth," 62.

26. C. Riley Snorton, *Black on Both Sides: A Racial History of Trans Identity*, 3rd ed. (Minneapolis: University of Minnesota Press, 2017); Brianna Theobald, *Reproduction on the Reservation: Pregnancy, Childbirth, and Colonialism in the Long Twentieth Century* (Chapel Hill: University of North Carolina Press, 2019).

27. Sandelowski, *Pain, Pleasure, and American Childbirth*.

28. Morton, *Birth Ambassadors*.

29. Morton, *Birth Ambassadors*.

30. Morton, *Birth Ambassadors*.

31. Sandelowski, *Pain, Pleasure, and American Childbirth*, 136.

32. Morton, *Birth Ambassadors*.

33. Morton, *Birth Ambassadors*.

34. Ina May Gaskin, *Spiritual Midwifery* (Summertown, TN: Book Publishing Company, 2002), 147, 137.

35. Mack, "The Self-Made Mom," 62.

36. Morton, *Birth Ambassadors*, 74; Deborah A. Sullivan and Rose Weitz, *Labor Pains: Modern Midwives and Home Birth* (New Haven, CT: Yale University Press, 1988).

37. Morton, *Birth Ambassadors*.

38. Morton, *Birth Ambassadors*.

39. Dana Raphael, *The Tender Gift: Breastfeeding* (Englewood Cliffs, NJ: Prentice-Hall, 1973).

40. Morton, *Birth Ambassadors*, 76.

41. M. H. Klaus and J. H. Kennell, "The Doula: An Essential Ingredient of Childbirth Rediscovered," *Acta Paediatrica* 86, no. 10 (October 1997): 1034–36, https://doi.org/10.1111/j.1651-2227.1997.tb14800.x; Phyllis H. Klaus and John Kennell, *Mothering the Mother: How a Doula Can Help You Have a Shorter, Easier, Healthier Birth* (Reading, MA: Da Capo Press, 1993).

42. Katy B. Kozhimannil et al., "Doula Care Supports Near-Universal Breastfeeding Initiation among Diverse, Low-Income Women," *Journal of Midwifery & Women's Health* 58, no. 4 (July 2013): 378–82, https://doi.org/10.1111/jmwh.12065; Katy B. Kozhimannil et al., "Disrupting the Pathways of Social Determinants of Health: Doula Support during Pregnancy and Childbirth," *The Journal of the American Board of Family Medicine* 29, no. 3 (May 1, 2016): 308–17, https://doi.org/10.3122/jabfm.2016.03.150300.

43. Morton, *Birth Ambassadors*, 94.

44. Davis-Floyd, "Technocratic, Humanistic, and Holistic Paradigms of Childbirth," sec. 10.

45. Davis, *Reproductive Injustice*.

46. Lorraine M. Garcia, "A Concept Analysis of Obstetric Violence in the United States of America," *Nursing Forum* 55, no. 4 (2020): 654–63, https://doi.org/10.1111/nuf.12482; Elizabeth O'Brien and Miriam Rich, "Obstetric Violence in Historical Perspective," *The Lancet* 399, no. 10342 (June 2022): 2183–85, https://doi.org/10.1016/S0140-6736(22)01022-4.

47. Katy B. Kozhimannil et al., "Potential Benefits of Increased Access to Doula Support during Childbirth," *The American Journal of Managed Care* 20, no. 8 (August 1, 2014): e340–52.

48. Amy Gilliland, "A Grounded Theory Model to Effective Labor Support by Doulas" (PhD diss., University of Wisconsin-Madison, 2010), 12.

49. Davis-Floyd, "Technocratic, Humanistic, and Holistic Paradigms of Childbirth," 12.

50. Morton, *Birth Ambassadors*, 141.

51. Morton, *Birth Ambassadors*, 114.

52. Morton, *Birth Ambassadors*, 119.

53. Morton, *Birth Ambassadors*, 119.

54. Midwives Alliance of North America, "Overview of the MANA Core Competencies Revisions," Midwives Alliance of North America, September 13, 2015, para. 1, https://mana.org/blog/Overview-MANA-Core-Competencies-Revisions.

55. Midwives Alliance of North America, "Overview of MANA Core Competencies," para. 4.

56. "Open Letter to MANA," *Woman-Centered Midwifery* (blog), August 20, 2015, para. 9, https://womancenteredmidwifery.wordpress.com/take-action/.

Notes to Pages 88–91   *201*

57. "About," *Woman-Centered Midwifery* (blog), June 13, 2015, para. 1, https://womancenteredmidwifery.wordpress.com/about/.

58. "Open Letter to MANA."

59. Emi Koyama, "Whose Feminism Is It Anyway? The Unspoken Racism of the Trans Inclusion Debate," *The Sociological Review* 68, no. 4 (July 1, 2020): 742, https://doi.org/10.1177/0038026120934685.

60. "Response to the Open Letter to MANA," Birth for Every Body, 2015, http://www.birthforeverybody.org/response-to-open-letter.

61. "Response to Open Letter to MANA," para. 1.

62. Davis, *Reproductive Injustice*; Bixby Center for Global Reproductive Health, "LGBTQ Patients Face Discrimination and Erasure When Seeking Reproductive Health Care," accessed July 19, 2021, https://bixbycenter.ucsf.edu/news/lgbtq-patients-face-discrimination-and-erasure-when-seeking-reproductive-health-care.

63. Pérez, *Radical Doula Guide*, 3.

64. Yam, "Complicating Acts of Advocacy," 199.

65. Trevor MacDonald, *Where's the Mother? Stories from a Transgender Dad* (Winnipeg: Trans Canada Press, 2016).

66. "Supporting Care, Choice and Justice: Our Mission," Birthing Advocacy Doula Trainings, 2020, https://www.badoulatrainings.org.

67. Pérez, *Radical Doula Guide*, 31.

68. Pérez, *Radical Doula Guide*, 31.

69. Tara Brooke and Gina Giordano, *Born into This: A Creative Guide to Reproductive Health* (self-pub., 2020), 6.

70. Brooke and Giordano, *Born into This*, 8, 14.

71. Jo Yurcaba, "More than 1 in 8 LGBTQ People Live in States Where Doctors Can Refuse to Treat Them," *NBC News*, July 28, 2022, https://www.nbcnews.com/nbc-out/out-health-and-wellness/1-8-lgbtq-people-live-states-doctors-can-refuse-treat-rcna39161.

72. Miriam Zoila Pérez, Trystan Reese, Mac Brydum, and Emma Robinson, "They/Them/Theirs" (panel discussion, Born into This, Austin, TX, 2019).

73. Yam, "Visualizing Birth Stories from the Margin."

74. Davis, *Reproductive Injustice*; Jennifer C. Nash, *Birthing Black Mothers* (Durham: Duke University Press Books, 2021).

Chapter 3: Reimagining Family and Kin

1. Gabby Rivera, "About," Gabby Rivera, accessed June 19, 2023, https://gabbyrivera.com/about/.

2. Rodriguez-Bouchier describes the popularity of this episode as follows: "Today we are bringing back an old favorite episode. This is one of my favorite conversations that I've had on the podcast, and it's been the most listened to of all of the episodes of the Intersectional Fertility podcast."

3. Josie Rodriguez-Bouchier, "Episode 7: Gabby Rivera: 'Solo, Queer Babymaking

Is a Trip,'" June 8, 2021, in *The Intersectional Fertility Podcast*, podcast, 48:27, https://www.intersectionalfertility.com/podcast-episodes/episode-7-gabby-rivera-solo-queer-babymaking-is-a-trip.

4. Aja Y. Martinez, *Counterstory: The Rhetoric and Writing of Critical Race Theory*, Studies in Writing and Rhetoric (Champaign, IL: Conference on College Composition and Communication / National Council of Teachers of English, 2020).

5. We use the phrase "queer family" broadly to signal any range of nonnormative kinship structures, including single-parent families, families with one or more LGBTQ+-identified parent(s), and families that manage to survive or even thrive outside of whiteness, wealth, and/or nuclearity through alternative or extended family formations.

6. In this archive, we include parents as well as those pregnant and trying/planning to conceive.

7. Loretta Ross and Rickie Solinger, *Reproductive Justice: An Introduction* (Oakland: University of California Press, 2017).

8. Martinez, *Counterstory*; Shui-yin Sharon Yam, *Inconvenient Strangers: Transnational Subjects and the Politics of Citizenship* (Columbus: Ohio State University Press, 2019).

9. Yam, *Inconvenient Strangers*; Martinez, *Counterstory*.

10. Derek P. Siegel, "Policing Motherhood, Controlling Families: Race, Reproductive Governance, and Trans Women's Parenting Rights," *Gender & Society* 38, no. 1 (February 1, 2024): 60–88, https://doi.org/10.1177/08912432231213867.

11. Jason Barker, *A Deal with the Universe*, documentary (Peccadillo Pictures, 2018), https://www.peccapics.com/product/adealwiththeuniverse/; Jeanie Finlay, *Seahorse: The Dad Who Gave Birth*, documentary (British Broadcasting Corporation, 2020), https://seahorsefilm.com/; Cyn Lubow, *A Womb of Their Own*, DVD (Serious Play Films, 2016).

12. Fox Fisher, Ugla Stefanía Kristjönudóttir Jónsdóttir, and Lewis Hancox, *Raising My Baby Gender Neutral: Max & River*, documentary (My Genderation, 2018), https://www.youtube.com/watch?v=D9qemC2Mn7I; Steven Hobson, *Pregnant Dad: Giving Birth as a Transgender Man*, documentary (BBC Three, 2017), https://www.youtube.com/watch?v=KOTap-sQhu8; Phil Rossi, *My Trans Life, Season 2 Episode 7: Trans Couple Pause Transition to Become Parents*, documentary (Barcroft Media, 2017), https://www.youtube.com/watch?v=HS_6g6UZINI.

13. Thomas Beatie, *Labor of Love: The Story of One Man's Extraordinary Pregnancy* (Berkeley: Seal Press, 2008); Karleen Pendleton Jiménez, *How to Get a Girl Pregnant* (Toronto: Tightrope Books, 2011); A. K. Summers, *Pregnant Butch: Nine Long Months Spent in Drag* (Berkeley: Soft Skull Press, 2014); Trevor MacDonald, *Where's the Mother? Stories from a Transgender Dad* (Winnipeg: Trans Canada Press, 2016); Krys Malcolm Belc, *The Natural Mother of the Child: A Memoir of Nonbinary Parenthood* (Berkeley, CA: Counterpoint Press, 2021).

14. Laurel Gourrier and Danielle Jackson, *Birth Stories in Color*, podcast, https://www.birthstoriesincolor.com/; Imara Jones, *TransLash Podcast*, podcast, https://trans

lash.org/podcast/; Hillary Frank, *The Longest Shortest Time*, podcast, https://longest shortesttime.com/; Katherine Goldstein, *The Double Shift*, podcast, https://www.the doubleshift.com/.

15. Rodriguez-Bouchier, *The Intersectional Fertility Podcast*, podcast, https://www .intersectionalfertility.com/podcast; Wehman-Brown, Grover, *Masculine Birth Ritual*, podcast, https://www.masculinebirthritual.com/.

16. Aren Aizura, "Aren Aizura on Chestfeeding," Mutha Magazine, January 30, 2019, http://www.muthamagazine.com/2019/01/aren-azuria-chestfeeding/; "Andrew Rich," Romper, accessed August 25, 2023, https://www.romper.com/profile/andrew -rich-65363584; Grover Wehman-Brown, "Bearing Life With and Alongside: On Masculinity, Pregnancy, and Medical Trauma," *Autostraddle*, November 19, 2018, https://www.autostraddle.com/bearing-life-with-and-alongside-on-masculinity -pregnancy-and-medical-trauma-438219/; Syrus Marcus Ware, "Confessions of a Black Pregnant Dad," in *Birthing Justice: Black Women, Pregnancy, and Childbirth*, ed. Julia Chinyere Oparah and Alicia D. Bonaparte (New York: Routledge, 2016), 63–71.

17. Miles Feroli, "Feeling Transparent: Trans Parenthood and the American Family System" (PhD diss., University of Kentucky, 2022), https://doi.org/10.13023/etd.2022 .327; Trevor Kirczenow MacDonald et al., "Disrupting the Norms: Reproduction, Gender Identity, Gender Dysphoria, and Intersectionality," *International Journal of Transgender Health* 22, no. 1–2 (April 3, 2021): 18–29, https://doi.org/10.1080/26895269 .2020.1848692; Trevor MacDonald et al., "Transmasculine Individuals' Experiences with Lactation, Chestfeeding, and Gender Identity: A Qualitative Study," *BMC Pregnancy and Childbirth* 16, no. 1 (May 16, 2016): 106, https://doi.org/10.1186/s12884-016 -0907-y.

18. Siegel, "Policing Motherhood, Controlling Families."

19. Alessandra J. Ainsworth, Megan Allyse, and Zaraq Khan, "Fertility Preservation for Transgender Individuals: A Review," *Mayo Clinic Proceedings* 95, no. 4 (April 1, 2020): 784–92, https://doi.org/10.1016/j.mayocp.2019.10.040; Philip J. Cheng et al., "Fertility Concerns of the Transgender Patient," *Translational Andrology and Urology* 8, no. 3 (June 2019): 209–18, https://doi.org/10.21037/tau.2019.05.09; Stef M. Shuster, *Trans Medicine: The Emergence and Practice of Treating Gender* (New York: New York University Press, 2021).

20. Shuster, *Trans Medicine*.

21. Ainsworth, Allyse, and Khan, "Fertility Preservation for Transgender Individuals"; Chloë De Roo et al., "Fertility Options in Transgender People," *International Review of Psychiatry* 28, no. 1 (January 2, 2016): 112–19, https://doi.org/10.3109/09540261 .2015.1084275.

22. Brianna Richardson, Sheri Price, and Marsha Campbell-Yeo, "Redefining Perinatal Experience: A Philosophical Exploration of a Hypothetical Case of Gender Diversity in Labour and Birth," *Journal of Clinical Nursing* 28, no. 3–4 (February 2019): 703–10, https://doi.org/10.1111/jocn.14521.

23. See, for example, Alexis D. Light et al., "Transgender Men Who Experienced Pregnancy after Female-to-Male Gender Transitioning," *Obstetrics & Gynecology* 124,

no. 6 (December 2014): 1120–27, https://doi.org/10.1097/AOG.0000000000000540. This is one of the earliest studies to debunk the myth that hormonal transition necessarily results in sterility.

24. Caroline Medina, *Protecting and Advancing Health Care for Transgender Adult Communities* (Center for American Progress, August 25, 2021), https://www.american progress.org/wp-content/uploads/sites/2/2021/08/Factsheet_Protecting-and-Advancing -Health-Care-for-Transgender-Adult.pdf.

25. Beatie, *Labor of Love*, 204.

26. Beatie, *Labor of Love*, 205–6.

27. Carla S. Alvarado et al., "Polling Spotlight: Understanding the Experiences of LGBTQ+ Birthing People," Center For Health Justice, June 27, 2022, https://www .aamchealthjustice.org/news/polling/lgbtq-birth; Mari Greenfield and Zoe Darwin, "Trans and Non-Binary Pregnancy, Traumatic Birth, and Perinatal Mental Health: A Scoping Review," *International Journal of Transgender Health* 22, no. 1–2 (April 3, 2021): 203–16, https://doi.org/10.1080/26895269.2020.1841057; Medina, *Protecting and Advancing Health Care for Transgender Adult Communities*; Wehman-Brown, "Bearing Life With and Alongside."

28. Luisa Kcomt et al., "Healthcare Avoidance Due to Anticipated Discrimination among Transgender People: A Call to Create Trans-Affirmative Environments," *SSM - Population Health* 11 (August 1, 2020): 100608, https://doi.org/10.1016/j.ssmph.2020 .100608.

29. Alvarado et al., "Polling Spotlight."

30. Shui-yin Sharon Yam and Natalie Fixmer-Oraiz, "Against Gender Essentialism: Reproductive Justice Doulas and Gender Inclusivity in Pregnancy and Birth Discourse," *Women's Studies in Communication* 46, no. 1 (January 2, 2023): 1–22, https:// doi.org/10.1080/07491409.2022.2147616.

31. Grover Wehman-Brown, "He Was with These Wonderful Queers: An Interview with J Carroll on Nonbinary Single Parenting," January 14, 2019, in *Masculine Birth Ritual*, podcast, 55:22, https://www.masculinebirthritual.com/post/e8-he-was-with -these-wonderful-queers-an-interview-with-j-carroll-on-nonbinary-single-parenting.

32. Grover Wehman-Brown, "I Would Like It If You Would Listen: An Interview with Birthparent Charlie King Miller," May 2, 2019, in *Masculine Birth Ritual*, podcast, 55:51. https://www.masculinebirthritual.com/post/_e-13.

33. Olivia J. Fischer, "Non-Binary Reproduction: Stories of Conception, Pregnancy, and Birth," *International Journal of Transgender Health* 22, no. 1–2 (April 3, 2021): 77–88, https://doi.org/10.1080/26895269.2020.1838392; Yam and Fixmer-Oraiz, "Against Gender Essentialism."

34. Claire Learmonth et al., "Barriers to Insurance Coverage for Transgender Patients," *American Journal of Obstetrics and Gynecology* 219, no. 3 (September 1, 2018): 272.e1-272.e4, https://doi.org/10.1016/j.ajog.2018.04.046.

35. Dána-Ain Davis, *Reproductive Injustice: Racism, Pregnancy, and Premature Birth* (New York: NYU Press, 2019); Ryan S. Huang, Andrea R. Spence, and Haim A. Abenhaim, "Racial Disparities in National Maternal Mortality Trends in the United

States from 2000 to 2019: A Population-Based Study on 80 Million Live Births," *Archives of Gynecology and Obstetrics*, March 18, 2023, https://doi.org/10.1007/s00404 -023-06999-6; Rolanda L. Lister, "Black Maternal Mortality-The Elephant in the Room," *World Journal of Gynecology & Womens Health* 3, no. 1 (November 22, 2019), https://doi.org/10.33552/WJGWH.2019.03.000555.

36. Pasquale Patrizio et al., "The Changing World of IVF: The Pros and Cons of New Business Models Offering Assisted Reproductive Technologies," *Journal of Assisted Reproduction and Genetics* 39, no. 2 (February 2022): 305–13, https://doi.org /10.1007/s10815-022-02399-y.

37. Natalie Fixmer-Oraiz, *Homeland Maternity: U.S. Security Culture and the New Reproductive Regime* (Champaign: University of Illinois Press, 2019); Eithne Luibhéid, *Entry Denied: Controlling Sexuality at the Border* (Minneapolis: University of Minnesota Press, 2002); Dorothy E. Roberts, *Torn Apart: How the Child Welfare System Destroys Black Families—and How Abolition Can Build a Safer World* (New York: Basic Books, 2022).

38. Dorothy Roberts, *Killing the Black Body: Race, Reproduction, and the Meaning of Liberty* (New York: Pantheon Books, 1997); Rickie Solinger, *Pregnancy and Power: A Short History of Reproductive Politics in America* (New York: New York University Press, 2005).

39. Andrea Smith, *Conquest: Sexual Violence and American Indian Genocide* (Boston, MA: South End Press, 2005).

40. Luibhéid, *Entry Denied*.

41. Roberts, *Torn Apart*.

42. National Center for Lesbian Rights, *Legal Recognition of LGBT Families* (San Francisco, CA: National Center for Lesbian Rights, 2019), https://www.nclrights.org /wp-content/uploads/2013/07/Legal_Recognition_of_LGBT_Families.pdf.

43. Julie Moreau, "Changes to State Parenting Laws Help Fill Gaps for Same-Sex Couples," NBC News, August 1, 2020, https://www.nbcnews.com/feature/nbc-out /changes-state-parenting-laws-help-fill-gaps-same-sex-couples-n1235517; Sandra Patton-Imani, *Queering Family Trees: Race, Reproductive Justice, and Lesbian Motherhood* (New York: New York University Press, 2020).

44. Belc, *Natural Mother*, 217.

45. Human Rights Campaign Staff, "For the First Time Ever, Human Rights Campaign Officially Declares 'State of Emergency' for LGBTQ+ Americans; Issues National Warning and Guidebook to Ensure Safety for LGBTQ+ Residents and Travelers," Human Rights Campaign, June 6, 2023, https://www.hrc.org/press-releases/for-the -first-time-ever-human-rights-campaign-officially-declares-state-of-emergency-for -lgbtq-americans-issues-national-warning-and-guidebook-to-ensure-safety-for-lgbtq -residents-and-travelers.

46. Robin E. Jensen, "Sexual Polysemy: The Discursive Ground of Talk about Sex and Education in U.S. History," *Communication, Culture and Critique* 1, no. 4 (December 1, 2008): 396–415, https://doi.org/10.1111/j.1753-9137.2008.00032.x.

47. Kelly Jakes, "'Natural' Virtuosos: Paradoxical Polysemy and the Rhetoric of the

Fisk Jubilee Singers," *Quarterly Journal of Speech* 108, no. 3 (July 3, 2022): 271–91, https://doi.org/10.1080/00335630.2022.2088840.

48. Lloyd F. Bitzer, "The Rhetorical Situation," *Philosophy & Rhetoric* 1, no. 1 (1968): 1–14.

49. Put simply, a counterpublic refers to groups of social actors that work to oppose dominant practices or ideologies through public discourse. There is a wealth of scholarship on publics and counterpublics in the field of communication studies. See, for example, Robert Asen and Daniel C. Brouwer, eds., *Counterpublics and the State* (Albany: State University of New York Press, 2001); Karma R. Chávez, "Counter-Public Enclaves and Understanding the Function of Rhetoric in Social Movement Coalition-Building," *Communication Quarterly* 59, no. 1 (January 31, 2011): 1–18, https://doi.org/10.1080/01463373.2010.541333; Karma R. Chávez, *Queer Migration Politics: Activist Rhetoric and Coalitional Possibilities*, Feminist Media Studies Series (Champaign: University of Illinois Press, 2013); Jiyeon Kang, *Igniting the Internet: Youth and Activism in Postauthoritarian South Korea* (Honolulu: University of Hawai'i Press, 2016); Phaedra C. Pezzullo, "Resisting 'National Breast Cancer Awareness Month': The Rhetoric of Counterpublics and Their Cultural Performances," *Quarterly Journal of Speech* 89 (2003): 345–65; Michael Warner, *Publics and Counterpublics* (Boston: Zone Books, 2005).

50. Christina R. Foust, Amy Pason, and Kate Zittlow Rogness, eds., *What Democracy Looks Like: The Rhetoric of Social Movements and Counterpublics* (Tuscaloosa: University Alabama Press, 2017).

51. Yam, *Inconvenient Strangers*; Martinez, *Counterstory*.

52. Loretta Ross, Lynn Roberts, and Erika Derkas, eds., *Radical Reproductive Justice: Foundation, Theory, Practice, Critique* (New York: Feminist Press at CUNY, 2017), 22; see also Kimala Price, "What Is Reproductive Justice? How Women of Color Activists Are Redefining the Pro-Choice Paradigm," *Meridians: Feminism, Race, Transnationalism* 10, no. 2 (2010): 42–65; Ross and Solinger, *Reproductive Justice*.

53. Solinger, *Pregnancy and Power*, 10.

54. Adriana Cavarero, *Relating Narratives: Storytelling and Selfhood* (London: Routledge, 2000).

55. Michael Jackson, quoted in Yam, *Inconvenient Strangers*, 40.

56. Yam, *Inconvenient Strangers*, 30, 26.

57. Yam, *Inconvenient Strangers*, 17.

58. Fred Moten and Stefano Harney, *The Undercommons: Fugitive Planning and Black Study* (Wivenhoe, UK: Minor Compositions, 2013), 141.

59. Elaine Castillo, *How to Read Now: Essays* (New York: Viking, 2022).

60. Martinez, *Counterstory*, 3.

61. Martinez, *Counterstory*, 26.

62. Martinez, *Counterstory*, 17.

63. Judith Butler, "Is Kinship Always Already Heterosexual?," *Differences: A Journal of Feminist Cultural Studies* 13, no. 1 (2002): 14–44; Jasbir K. Puar, *Terrorist Assemblages: Homonationalism in Queer Times* (Durham: Duke University Press, 2007).

Notes to Pages 129–135

64. Beatie, *Labor of Love*, 304.

65. Beatie, *Labor of Love*, 6.

66. Beatie, *Labor of Love*, 304.

67. Beatie, *Labor of Love*, 257.

68. Charles Bramesco, "Seahorse Review—Moving Study of Man Who Gave Birth," *The Guardian*, April 27, 2019, sec. Film, https://www.theguardian.com/film/2019/apr/27/seahorse-review-freddy-mcconnell-trans-man-gave-birth; Darleen Ortega, "Two Films Not to Miss," *Portland Observer*, May 22, 2019, https://www.portland observer.com/post/two-films-not-to-miss.

69. "Seahorse: The Dad Who Gave Birth—Rotten Tomatoes Review," Rotten Tomatoes, accessed July 20, 2023, https://www.rottentomatoes.com/m/seahorse_the _dad_who_gave_birth_2019.

70. Simon Hattenstone, "The Dad Who Gave Birth: 'Being Pregnant Doesn't Change Me Being a Trans Man,'" *The Guardian*, April 20, 2019, sec. Society, https:// www.theguardian.com/society/2019/apr/20/the-dad-who-gave-birth-pregnant-trans -freddy-mcconnell.

71. Quoted in Finlay, *Seahorse*.

72. See, for example, Serene J. Khader, "Intersectionality and the Ethics of Trans-national Commercial Surrogacy," *International Journal of Feminist Approaches to Bioethics* 6, no. 1 (2013): 68–90, https://doi.org/10.2979/intjfemappbio.6.1.68; Laura Mamo and Eli Alston-Stepnitz, "Queer Intimacies and Structural Inequalities: New Directions in Stratified Reproduction," *Journal of Family Issues* 36, no. 4 (March 2015): 519–40, https://doi.org/10.1177/0192513X14563796; Dorothy E. Roberts, "Race, Gender, and Genetic Technologies: A New Reproductive Dystopia?," *Signs: Journal of Women in Culture and Society* 34, no. 4 (June 2009): 783–804, https://doi.org/10.1086/597132; Natali Valdez and Daisy Deomampo, "Centering Race and Racism in Reproduction," *Medical Anthropology* 38, no. 7 (October 3, 2019): 551–59, https://doi.org/10.1080 /01459740.2019.1643855.

73. Quoted in Finlay, *Seahorse*.

74. Bramesco, "Seahorse Review."

75. Ortega, "Two Films Not to Miss."

76. "The Longest Shortest Time: About," The Longest Shortest Time, accessed July 20, 2023, https://longestshortesttime.com/about.

77. "About Katherine Goldstein, the Double Shift," The Double Shift, May 20, 2022, https://www.thedoubleshift.com/about/.

78. "Longest Shortest Time"; "Double Shift."

79. Katherine Goldstein, "Don't Call Me 'Mom,' Call Me Ted," December 2, 2019, in *The Double Shift*, podcast, 35:49, https://thedoubleshift.substack.com/p/dont-call-me -mom-call-me-ted-043.

80. Hillary Frank, "The Accidental Gay Parents," June 24, 2015, in *The Longest Shortest Time*, podcast, https://longestshortesttime.com/podcast-60-accidental-gay -parents.

81. Frank, "Accidental Gay Parents."

82. Josie Rodriguez-Bouchier, "The Phoenix, Fertile Essence, and Queer Liberation," April 10, 2021, in *The Intersectional Fertility Podcast*, podcast, 27:22, https://www.intersectionalfertility.com/podcast-episodes/the-pheonix-fertile-essence-and-queer-liberation?rq=phoenix.

83. Grover Wehman-Brown, "Introduction to Masculine Birth Ritual," September 1, 2018, in *Masculine Birth Ritual*, podcast, 12:47, https://masculinebirthritual.libsyn.com/episode-1-introduction-to-masculine-birth-ritual.

84. Natalie Fixmer-Oraiz and Grover Wehman-Brown, "Called into the World by All of Us: An Interview with Masculine Birth Ritual Podcast Creator and Host Grover Wehman-Brown," *QED: A Journal in GLBTQ Worldmaking* 7, no. 2 (2020): 96.

85. Rodriguez-Bouchier, "Phoenix, Fertile Essence, and Queer Liberation."

86. Rodriguez-Bouchier, "Phoenix, Fertile Essence, and Queer Liberation."

87. Grover Wehman-Brown, "Welcoming Whatever Being Came: An Interview with Jacoby Ballard," August 8, 2019, in *Masculine Birth Ritual*, podcast, 51:03, https://masculinebirthritual.libsyn.com/e-16-welcoming-whatever-being-came.

88. Wehman-Brown, "Welcoming Whatever Being Came."

89. Belc, *Natural Mother*, 192.

90. Quoted in Lubow, *Womb of Their Own*.

91. Grover Wehman-Brown, "Possibility Models of Parenthood," October 1, 2018, in *Masculine Birth Ritual*, podcast, 1:01:58, https://masculinebirthritual.libsyn.com/e3-possibility-models-for-parenthood.

92. Wehman-Brown, "He Was with These Wonderful Queers."

93. V. Fixmer-Oraiz, personal communication, February 2, 2024. While the experiences of nonbirthing TGNC parents are not the focal point of this study, we felt it necessary to mark and honor the act of refusal. Here are V's words in full: "I am grateful to have a partner who was enthusiastic about being pregnant! I have always been fascinated with my body's ability to carry a pregnancy, from a scientific or biological perspective. And as I grew into adulthood and my queer/trans self, I became increasingly aware of not only the suffocatingly heteronormative spaces that pregnancy occupies, but the physical changes to my body that I felt would take a toll on my mental health. Not only the changes during pregnancy, but the lasting impacts that growing and nursing a child can have. While this could be read as selfish and too occupied with body image, I do not regret my decision, and I will never know what harms I have avoided, but I do know that I can show up every day as a parent confident in who I am and the body I occupy."

94. Grover Wehman-Brown, "It's Not Gender Weird, It's Just Weird: An Interview with Rae Goodman-Lucker," February 26, 2019, in *Masculine Birth Ritual*, podcast, 35:23, https://www.masculinebirthritual.com/post/e11-it-s-not-gender-weird-it-s-just-weird-an-interview-with-rae-goodman-lucker.

95. Rodriguez-Bouchier, "Solo, Queer Babymaking Is a Trip."

96. Summers, *Pregnant Butch*, 115.

97. Lubow, *Womb of Their Own*.

98. Belc, *Natural Mother*.

99. Wehman-Brown, "Possibility Models of Parenthood."

100. Alexis Shotwell, *Against Purity: Living Ethically in Compromised Times* (Minneapolis: University of Minnesota Press, 2016).

101. Josie Rodriguez-Bouchier, "Sara Ceiba Flores: Queerception," July 20, 2021, in *The Intersectional Fertility Podcast*, podcast, 1:01:05, https://www.intersectionalfertility.com/podcast-episodes/episode-10-sara-ceiba-flores.

102. Summers, *Pregnant Butch*, 3.

103. Wehman-Brown, "Welcoming Whatever Being Came."

104. Rodriguez-Bouchier, "Queerception."

105. Fisher, Jónsdóttir, and Hancox, *Raising My Baby Gender Neutral*.

106. Wehman-Brown, "Welcoming Whatever Being Came."

107. Wehman-Brown, "Welcoming Whatever Being Came."

108. Imara Jones, "Trans Motherhood," May 5, 2021, in *TransLash*, podcast, 40:35, https://translash.org/podcast-trans-motherhood/.

109. Belc, *Natural Mother*, 220.

110. Grover Wehman-Brown, "This Blessing Got Kind of Everywhere," October 31, 2018, in *Masculine Birth Ritual*, podcast, 50:38, https://www.masculinebirthritual.com/post/e5-this-blessing-got-kind-of-everywhere.

111. Wehman-Brown, "Possibility Models of Parenthood."

112. Rodriguez-Bouchier, "Queerception."

113. Wehman-Brown, "Welcoming Whatever Being Came."

Conclusion

1. Sarah Rotz, "'They Took Our Beads, It Was a Fair Trade, Get over It': Settler Colonial Logics, Racial Hierarchies and Material Dominance in Canadian Agriculture," *Geoforum* 82 (June 2017): 158–69, https://doi.org/10.1016/j.geoforum.2017.04.010; Rachel Forday, "Colonialism and Animal Welfare with Mel Trueblood-Stimpson," October 19, 2022, in *Out of the Woofworks*, podcast, 32:42, https://dogatheart.co.uk/woofworks-17/.

2. Paisley Currah, *Sex Is as Sex Does: Governing Transgender Identity* (New York: New York University Press, 2022).

INDEX

ableism, 159

abortion care: legislation on, 8, 127; for TGNC people, 100–101

abortion rights activists: application of gender-neutral language, 71–72; disagreements on gender-neutral language, 36, 65–66

abstinence and purity discourse, 8, 42, 43

ACP (American College of Pediatricians), 46, 48

additive approach to language, 53, 60, 69–75, 173–74

adoption, 127, 147–48, 161

advocacy: in practice, 108–10; as rhetorical strategy, 98–101

affective drift, 51

African Americans. *See* Black people

agency, 87, 131

Aizura, Aren, 121

Alliance Defending Freedom, 42, 46

alternative medicine movement, 88

American Center for Law and Justice, 42

American College of Nurse-Midwives, 68

American College of Pediatricians (ACP), 46, 48

anti-gender movement: overview, 42–44; allies and actors associated with, 46–47; and gender ideology concept, 44–45; invocation of competing rights, 50–52, 59, 92; mobilization of public fear and anger, 50; pseudoscientific and naturalistic/essentialist claims, 36, 47–50, 91–92; resistance to gender-neutral language (*See* gender-neutral language, opposition to); as transnational phenomenon, 45–46

anti-miscegenation laws, 7

anti-trans legislation, 5, 35, 42, 43, 50–51, 54, 128

Apfel, Alana, 78, 81

Arendt, Hannah, 131, 132

Asian American masculinity, 137

assimilatory rhetorical strategies, 135–36, 137–39, 140–43, 146, 156

assisted reproduction, 122, 126, 140, 142, 145

Association of Ontario Midwives, 68

Atlantic, The (magazine), 36, 47, 145

audience, and dual address, 129–30. *See also* storytelling

BADT (Birthing Advocacy Doula Trainings), 97–98, 99, 100

Ballard, Jacoby, 152–53, 157, 159, 162

Barcelos, Chris, 43

Bay Area Doula Project, 106

Beatie, Thomas, *Labor of Love: The Story of One Man's Extraordinary Pregnancy*, 120–21, 123, 137–39

Belc, Krys Malcolm, *The Natural Mother of the Child: A Memoir of Nonbinary Parenthood*, 121, 128, 153, 155–56, 161

Beverly (doula), 94–95

Bey, Marquis, 12, 16, 17, 21, 26

biases, and self-reflexivity, 104–7, 112–13

binary gender system. *See* sex/gender binary

biological essentialism. *See* sex/gender binary

BIPOC people (Black, Indigenous, and people of color): birthworker support for (*See* doulas, RJ); disagreements on gender-neutral language, 25–26; inclusive understanding of kin, 160,

BIPOC people (*cont.*)
162; and intersectional birthworker
training, 95–96, 98, 100; and liberation
discourse, 160; marginalizing medical
practices against, 86, 89, 95, 114, 123,
126; and poverty, 22–23, 89, 126; racialized stereotypes, 137. *See also* race;
specific groups
birth certificate requirements, 127
birth control, access to, 8
birth discourse. *See* pregnancy and birth
discourse
Birth for Every Body, 93
Birthing Advocacy Doula Trainings
(BADT), 97–98, 99, 100
Birth: Issues in Perinatal Care (journal),
68
Birth Partner, The (Simkin), 87–88
Birth Stories in Color (podcast), 121
birthworkers: disagreements on gender-
neutral language, 2, 57, 90–96; growing
numbers of queer, trans, and nonbinary, 78–79; historical overview, 85–89;
as term, 84. *See also entries at doula*;
pregnancy and birth discourse; reproductive health care providers and
settings
Blackness, and transness, 20–21
Black people: and liberation discourse,
160; marginalizing medical practices
against, 67, 89, 95, 114, 126; and poverty,
22–23; and reproductive justice movement, 6, 7, 14; reproductive violence
against, 7, 22, 126; in sex/gender binary
system, 17–19, 20–21, 27–28, 61–62, 92
Black trans feminism, 12, 13, 26, 28
bodyfeeding/breastfeeding/chestfeeding,
70, 103, 111, 146, 147, 173
Bold Futures, 7
bonding, and biogenetic kin, 139
Born into This (conference), 101–2
*Born into This: A Creative Guide through
Reproductive Health* (Brooke and
Giordano), 102–3, 104
Boston marriages, 11
Bramesco, Charles, 144
breastfeeding/chestfeeding/bodyfeeding,
70, 103, 111, 146, 147, 173
Bridges, Khiara, 7, 13, 36, 52, 66, 80

Brighton and Sussex University Hospitals
NHS Trust (BSUH), 59, 69–70, 73, 74
Brooke, Tara, 95, 98, 101, 103; *Born into
This: A Creative Guide through Repro-
ductive Health* (with Giordano), 102–3,
104
Brown, Jenna, 172
Brown, Rita Mae, 11
Brydum, Mac, 102, 154, 161
Buchanan, Pat, 41
Bush, Cori, 2, 35, 54, 61, 62, 67, 92
Butler, Judith, 14, 21, 44

Caignon, Denise, 47
Canadian Association of Midwives, 68
Care We Dream Of, The (Sharman), 172
Carey, Tamika, 40
Carlson, Tucker, 50
Carney, Timothy, 61
Carpenter, Morgan, 57
Carroll, J, 124, 154
Catholic Church, 46
censorship, 5, 42, 43, 50–51, 128
Chaney (midwifery student), 111
Chávez, Karma, 40
chestfeeding/breastfeeding/bodyfeeding,
70, 103, 111, 146, 147, 173
chest size/appearance, 122
Childbirth and Family Education, 88
Chinese people, 7, 18
coalitional potential, 132, 144
Collins, Patricia Hill, 12
colonialism: and decolonial scholarship,
4, 16, 20, 26–27; genocide and gendercide, 3–4, 57, 126; and repurposing
social justice discourse, 60; sex/gender
binary in racialized framework of,
17–21, 27–28, 57, 61–62, 170–71
colorblind discourse, 26
Combahee River Collective, 11
comfort levels, in supporting nonnormative birthing people, 95, 100,
103–6
competing rights, invocation of, 50–52,
59, 92
Cornerstone Doula Trainings, 97–98, 100,
103–4
Council for National Policy, 42
counterpublics, 129

212   *Index*

counterstory: affirming one another's reproductive experiences/decisions/desires with, 151–55; challenging ableism with, 159; challenging family/kin definitions with, 156, 160–62; challenging gender binary with, 146, 153–54, 155–56, 158; challenging linguistic norms with, 156–58; challenging parenting norms with, 158–59; challenging structural violence with, 147–48; defined, 130; as rhetorical strategy, 29, 132–35, 149–50; TGNC parenting media inspired by, 150–51

Crenshaw, Kimberlé, 11–12

criminalization, 22, 71

critical race theory (CRT), 43, 51, 133, 134

critical rhetoric, 29–30, 40–41

Crofoot, Danie, 111

culture wars, as concept, 41–42. *See also* anti-gender movement

Dahlen, Sara, 58

Davis, Angela, 12

Davis, Dána-Ain, 7, 80

Davis, Heath Fogg, 15

Davis-Floyd, Robbie, 80, 85, 90

DCT (Doula of Color Training), 95, 97–98, 99–100, 105

deadnaming, 110, 123

Deal with the Universe, A (documentary film), 120

decolonial scholarship, 4, 16, 20, 26–27

deliberative empathy: defined, 130; engagement with, 139, 141–44, 146–47, 148–49; as rhetorical strategy, 131–32, 134–35

denial of medical care, 106, 123

depravity discourse, 40, 44

disabled people: and ableism, 159; doula support for, benefits of, 88; RJ doula organization collaborations with, 100; sterilization of, 126

discomfort, engaging with, 95, 100, 103–6

Dobbs v. Jackson Women's Health Organization, 35, 127

domestic violence, 137, 147–48

dominance, defined, 131

DONA (Doulas of North America), 83, 88–89, 94–96

Double Shift, The (podcast), 121, 145, 146–47

doula, as term, 84, 88, 90, 100

Doula of Color Training (DCT), 95, 97–98, 99–100, 105

doulas, mainstream: deference to medical authority, 89, 95; professional organizations, 88–89; training rhetoric, 87–88, 93–96

doulas, RJ: advocacy, as rhetorical strategy, 98–101; advocacy, in practice, 108–10; liminal position of, 79, 80–81, 97; and mainstream birthworker training, 87–88, 93–96; and medicalized childbirth, historical overview, 85–87; mission of, overview, 79–80, 96–97; organizations for, overview, 97–98; radical inclusion and nonjudgmental care, as rhetorical strategy, 101–4; radical inclusion and nonjudgmental care, in practice, 110–12, 124–25; self-reflexivity, as rhetorical strategy, 104–7; self-reflexivity, in practice, 112–13

Doulas of North America (DONA), 83, 88–89, 94–96

Doyle, Jude, 63–64

Driskill, Qwo-Li, 20

DTI (Doula Training International), 97–99, 100, 103

dual address, defined, 129–30

dysphoria, gender, 49–50, 51, 142–43, 152, 154

economic inequality, 22–23, 89, 95, 126, 140

Economist, The (newspaper), 36, 51

educational curricula: for birthworkers, mainstream, 87–88, 93–96; for birthworkers, in RJ framework, 97–107; censorship campaigns, 5, 42, 43, 50–51, 128; lack of comprehensive, 59

egg freezing and gamete storage, 22, 122

Elephant Circle, 68–69, 73, 74, 92–93

emotional support, 79, 86, 87, 108

empathy. *See* deliberative empathy

Enck-Wanzer, Darrel, 40

Endres, Danielle, 82

Erickson-Schroth, Laura, *Trans Bodies, Trans Selves* (ed.), 172

Index 213

eugenics, 8, 126
Evidenced Based Birth (podcast), 81

family formation, cisheteronormative: and assimilatory rhetorical strategies, 135–36, 137–39, 140–43, 146, 156; legal architecture of, 42, 126–28; and natural order discourse, 44, 48; "threats" to, 42, 44; in white nationalist agenda, 21–24, 42–43, 62–63, 126–27
family formation, queer: and assimilatory rhetorical strategies, 135–36, 137–39, 140–43, 146, 156; rhetorical strategies to advocate for (*See* counterstory; deliberative empathy; doulas, RJ); sociopolitical barriers against, 122–28, 148–49. *See also* kinship; pregnancy and birth discourse
family policing, 127
Family Research Council, 42, 46
family separation, 126–27
Farris, Sara R., 46
fatherhood, 139
femininity and womanhood: delinking reproduction from, 146–47, 153–54; fluidity and instability of, 155–56; and pregnancy term, 156–57; racialized, 20–21, 27
feminist activism and scholarship: alliance with LGBTQ+ movement, 11; disagreements on gender-neutral language, 2, 14, 25–26, 36, 64–66; and intersectionality, 11–12, 15, 64, 65–66; queer studies, 15–17; trans-exclusionary and gender-critical, 14, 16, 42, 46, 52
femonationalist language, 46
Feroli, Miles, 121
fertility: preservation options for TGNC people, 122–23; and white nationalist agenda, 22, 23, 62–63
fetal personhood movement, 71
Flores, Lisa, 40
Flores, Sara Ceiba, 156, 157–58, 161–62
Forward Together, 7
foster care system, 127, 147–48
4thWaveNow, 47, 49
Frank, Hillary, 145
free speech, invocations of, 51

full-spectrum doulas, defined, 80
Furies Collective, 11

gamete donors, 142, 145
gamete storage and egg freezing, 22, 122
Gandy, Imani, 7
Gaskin, Ina May, 85, 101; *Spiritual Midwifery*, 87, 88, 98
gender-affirming health care, 35, 38, 46–47, 49–50, 62–63, 68, 128. *See also* doulas, RJ
gender binarism. *See* sex/gender binary
gendercide, 3–4, 57
gender dysphoria, 49–50, 51, 142–43, 152, 154
gender-expansive parenting, 158–59
gender ideology, as concept, 44–45
gender-neutral language, defense of: and additive approach to language, 53, 60, 69–75; institutional guidelines and statements, 59–60, 68–70, 90–91, 93. *See also* counterstory; deliberative empathy; doulas, RJ
gender-neutral language, opposition to: conflation of sex and gender, 56–58; division over intersectional alliances, 64–67; gendered biological essentialism, 61–64, 91–92; misunderstood as replacement of woman-centered language, 25–26, 36, 52, 54, 64–65, 66, 70, 92; repurposing social justice discourse, 58–61; rhetorical tactics, overview, 53–56
gender-nonconforming people. *See* trans and gender-nonconforming people (TGNC)
gender respectability politics, 27–28
genocide, 126
germination, as term, 157
gestational surrogacy, 140
Giordano, Gina, 98, 101; *Born into This: A Creative Guide through Reproductive Health* (with Brooke), 102–3, 104
Goodman-Lucker, Rae, 155
Gossett, Che, 20
great replacement theory, 43
Green, Emma, 66
Green, Helen, 69–70

214   *Index*

Gribble, Karleen D. (et al.), "Effective Communication about Pregnancy, Birth, Lactation, Breastfeeding and Newborn Care: The Importance of Sexed Language," 55, 56–67
groomer label, 50
Guardian, The (newspaper), 55, 144
Gumbs, Alexis Pauline, 7
Gwen (doula and midwife), 108, 111, 112

Haaland v. Brackeen, 127
Halberstam, Jack, 21
Halley, Janet, 15–16
Hawley, Josh, 36
Hayman, Helene, 54
Hayward, Eva, 20
health care providers and settings. *See* reproductive health care providers and settings
Heritage Foundation, 42, 46
heteronormativity. *See* sex/gender binary
Hill, The (newspaper), 55
home births: *vs.* medicalized childbirth, 85–86, 124–25; unmedicated, 87
hormonal transition, and fertility, 122–23
How to Get a Girl Pregnant (Jiménez), 120–21
Hsu, V. Jo, 18, 20, 40, 51, 53, 63
humanistic turn in childbirth, 88
Human Rights Campaign, 128
Human Rights Watch, 44
Hunt, Philip, 54
Hunter, James Davison, 41

ICE (US Immigration and Customs Enforcement), 8, 23
Illegal Immigration Reform and Immigrant Responsibility Act (IIRIRA), 24
immigrants and immigration: restrictions, 7, 23–24, 126; sterilization of, 8, 23
inclusion. *See* gender-neutral language, defense of; gender-neutral language, opposition to; radical inclusion and nonjudgmental care
Indian Child Welfare Act (1978), 127
Indigenous people: forced removal of children from, 126, 127; gendercide

of, 3–4, 57; marginalizing medical practices against, 126; reproductive violence against, 7, 8, 19, 126; in sex/gender binary system, 17–20
Indigenous studies, 19, 57
individualized *vs.* standardized care, 85
insurance, medical, 125
intake forms and records system, health care, 111, 112, 125
interdisciplinary scholarship, 13
inter-est, as concept, 132
International Confederation of Midwives, 90
interracial marriage, 126, 127
Intersectional Fertility Podcast, The, 116–17, 121, 149, 151, 155, 156, 157–58
intersectionality: application of, 12–13, 15; in birthworker care, 91 (*See also* doulas, RJ); and oppression, 73–74; and resistance to gender-neutral language, 25–26, 64–67; theory of, 11–12
intersex people, 57, 93
intersubjectivity, 131, 132
Ipas, 12

Jackson, Ketanji Brown, 2, 35
Jackson, Michael, 131
Jeffreys, Sheila, 16
Jenner, Caitlyn, 16
Jensen, Robin, 129
Jiménez, Karleen Pendleton, *How to Get a Girl Pregnant*, 120–21
Joe Rogan Experience (podcast), 37, 50
Johnson, Marsha P., 160
Jones, Imara, 47, 160
Joy Uprising (podcast), 116

Kali, Kristin Liam, *Queer Conception*, 172
Keegan, Cáel, 15, 16
king yaa, 172
kinship: biological understanding of, 23–24; inclusive understanding of, 94, 160–62
Kitchen Table: Women of Color Press, 11
Ko, Aph, 76–77
Koyama, Emi, 27, 92
Kuhn, Thomas, 55
Kukla, Elliot, 161

Index   215

Labor of Love: The Story of One Man's Extraordinary Pregnancy (Beatie), 120–21, 123, 137–39

Lamaze, Fernand, 86

Lamaze-trained nurses, 88

language: additive approach to, 53, 60, 69–75, 173–74; creativity and dexterity with, 156–58, 173; expansiveness of, 66–67, 79; polysemy of, 129

Latinx people, 26, 126

legislation and legal system: abortion, 8, 127; anti-trans, 5, 35, 42, 43, 50–51, 54, 128; birth certificate requirements, 127; immigration, 23–24; marriage, 42, 126, 127; and parental rights, 127, 148–49

Leo, Brooklyn, 28

LGBTQ+ people: alliance with feminist movement, 11; ideological alliance with RJ, 6, 10, 12–13, 170–71; and intersectional birthworker training, 100; marginalizing medical practices against, 89, 100, 106, 123–24; parental rights for, 127; same-sex marriage legislation, 42, 127. *See also* trans and gender-nonconforming people (TGNC)

liberation discourse, 160

Libs of TikTok (Twitter account), 50

listening openly, 112

Littman, Lisa, 49, 61

Longest Shortest Time, The (podcast), 121, 145, 147–49

Lorde, Audre, 74

Loving v. Virginia, 127

Lowe, Lisa, 18

Lubow, Cyn, 153

Lugones, María, 17, 26

MacDonald, Trevor, 73–74; *Where's the Mother? Stories from a Transgender Dad*, 99, 121

Mace, Nancy, 62

Mack, Ashley Noel, 87

MANA (Midwives Alliance of North America), 2, 57, 68, 90–93

marriage legislation, 42, 126, 127

Martinez, Aja, 117, 130, 133, 134

Masculine Birth Ritual (podcast), 121, 124, 150–51, 152–53, 154, 155

masculinity, 137, 153, 155

Max (non-binary parent), 158

McArdle, Megan, 65

McConnell, Freddy, 140–45

McKerrow, Raymie, 29, 40

medical insurance, 125

Melling, Louise, 54, 66

Méndez, Xhercis, 26, 27–28

mental health, protecting, 154–55

mental health conditions, people with, 126

mentorship and scholarship programs, for birthworker training, 98, 100

Merino, Stevie, 27, 63, 95–96, 99–100, 105, 109–10

methodology, 29–30, 40–41, 81–83, 119–21

Middleton, Michael K., 82

midwives: disagreements on gender-neutral language, 90–93; European, 86; *vs.* medicalized childbirth, 85–86. *See also* birthworkers; *entries at doula*

Midwives Alliance of North America (MANA), 2, 57, 68, 90–93

Mignolo, Walter, 41

Miller, Charlie King, 124

Ministerial and Other Maternity Allowances Bill (UK), 54

Miranda (doula and midwife), 108–9

misgendering, 89, 109, 110, 123, 158

misogyny and sexism, 15, 143

Monica (doula and midwife), 110, 111, 112

Morgensen, Scott, 18

mortality rates, racial disparities, 126

Morton, Christine, 85, 89, 90, 94

Moten, Fred, 132

motherhood: denial of Black, 18; idealized, 42–43; in sex/gender binary framework, 48, 62–63, 87–88, 94, 128

Murray, Pauli, 11

My Trans Life: Trans Couple Pause Transition to Become Parents (short video), 120

NARAL Pro-Choice America, 71

Narayan, Uma, 29

narratives. *See* storytelling

Nash, Jennifer, 12

natalism, 138, 140

nation: and cisheteronormative family ideal, 21–24, 42–43, 62–63, 126–27; and culture war discourse, 41–42. *See also* colonialism

National Center for Lesbian Rights, 127

National LGBTQ Task Force, 12

National Network of Abortion Funds, 71

National Organization for Women (NOW), 11

Native people. *See* Indigenous people

natural childbirth movement, 86

Natural Mother of the Child, The: A Memoir of Nonbinary Parenthood (Belc), 121, 128, 153, 155–56, 161

natural order discourse, 44, 48

New Statesman (magazine), 36

New York Times (newspaper), 36, 47, 52, 55, 64–65

nonbinary people. *See* trans and gender-nonconforming people (TGNC)

nonjudgmental care. *See* radical inclusion and nonjudgmental care

NOW (National Organization for Women), 11

nurses: Lamaze-trained, 88; obstetric, 85, 86–87. *See also entries at doulas*; reproductive health care providers and settings

Obergefell v. Hodges, 127

obstetricians and obstetrics. *See* reproductive health care providers and settings

obstetric violence, 67, 89, 98, 123–24

Olivia Records, 11

opportunistic synergy, 46

oppression, as intersectional, 73–74

Ortega, Darleen, 144

Our Bodies, Ourselves, 87

Out (magazine), 12

Page Act (US, 1875), 7

parental rights: in anti-gender discourse, 50–51; for same-sex couples, 127, 148–49

parenting, gender-expansive, 158–59

parenting names, 94, 173

participatory critical rhetoric, 29–30

Pascucci, Cristen, 80

patriarchy, in mainstream medical in-

stitutions, 86–87, 101. *See also* family formation, cisheteronormative; white supremacy

Patterson, GPat, 40

Paul, Pamela, 52

Pavan v. Smith, 127

pelvic delivery, as phrase, 111, 173

Pérez, Miriam Zoila, 7, 73, 80, 102, 111–12; *The Radical Doula Guide*, 96, 101

Perez, Polly, 88

Planned Parenthood Action Fund, 71

Pollitt, Katha, 65

polysemy of language, 129

population control strategies, 7–8

Porchia-Albert, Chanel, 80

Portland Observer (newspaper), 144

poverty and economic inequality, 22–23, 89, 95, 126, 140

predator label, 50

pregnancy, as term, 156–58, 173

pregnancy and birth discourse: delinking gender from, 146–47, 153–54; gender essentialism in, 87–88, 90, 91–92, 101; humanistic turn, 88; and linguistic creativity, 156–58, 173; medicalization of, 85–87; scholarship on, 79–80; women defined in relation to reproductive capacity, 48, 62–63. *See also* doulas, RJ; family formation, cisheteronormative; family formation, queer; gender-neutral language, defense of; gender-neutral language, opposition to

Pregnancy Justice, 25, 71

Pregnant Butch: Nine Long Months Spent in Drag (Summers), 120–21, 155, 158

Pregnant Dad: Giving Birth as a Transgender Man (short video), 120

Prince, Virginia, 16

privilege. *See* white privilege

pronatalist ideologies, 138, 140

pronouns, preferred, 103, 109, 110, 111, 113, 124

Prosser, Jay, 15–16

pseudoscience, 46–47, 49–50

psychoprophylaxis, 86

Puar, Jasbir, 12

public discourse. *See* anti-gender movement; sex/gender binary

purity and abstinence discourse, 8, 42, 43

Index   217

Queer Conception (Kali), 172
Queer Doula Network, 78
Queering Reproductive Justice (National LGBTQ Task Force), 12
queer people. *See* LGBTQ+ people; trans and gender-nonconforming people (TGNC)
queer studies, 15–17
queer theory, 60–61

race: and anti-gender discourse, 43, 49, 51; and barriers to nonnormative family formation, 126–27, 142, 145; and colonial gender system, 17–21, 57, 126, 170–71; and colonial gender system, perpetuation of, 26–28, 61–62, 92; interracial marriage, 126, 127; and stratified reproduction phenomenon, 21–24. *See also* intersectionality; *specific groups*
Radical Doula (blog), 96
Radical Doula Guide, The (Pérez), 96, 101
Radicalesbians, 11
radical inclusion and nonjudgmental care: in practice, 110–12, 124–25; as rhetorical strategy, 101–4
Raising My Baby Gender Neutral: Max and River (short video), 120, 158
Raphael, Dana, 88
rapid onset gender dysphoria (ROGD), 49–50, 51
Raymond, Janice, 16, 52
records system and intake forms, health care, 111, 112, 125
Reese, Trystan, 100, 102, 147–49, 172
refusal of medical care, 106, 123
Reid, Graeme, 44
religion: and culture wars, 41; and natural order discourse, 44, 48
reproduction discourse. *See* pregnancy and birth discourse
reproductive desire, 138, 140, 155
Reproductive Freedom for All, 71
reproductive health, defined, 9
reproductive health care providers and settings: authority of, birthworker deference to, 89, 95, 98; call to action for, 171–74; defense of gender-neutral language, 59–60, 68–75 (*See also*

doulas, RJ); marginalizing practices, 122–24, 125–26; and patriarchal authority, 86–87, 101; resistance to gender-neutral language, 54, 57–58, 65; technocratic model of, 80, 85–87; and trend toward at-home birthing care, 124–25. *See also* birthworkers; pregnancy and birth discourse
reproductive justice (RJ): as framework and movement, 6–9; personal narratives and storytelling in, 29; reframing, to include TGNC people, 4, 9, 10–14, 26–27, 170–71. *See also* doulas, RJ
reproductive technologies, 22, 122, 126, 140, 142
Republican motherhood, 62
respectability politics, 27–28
Restar, Arjee Javellana, 49
reunification provisions, immigrant, 23–24
rhetorical analysis, critical approach to, 29–30, 40–41
rhetorical audiences, 129
rhetorical criticism, 129–30
rhetorical field methods, 82
rhetorical strategies. *See* assimilatory rhetorical strategies; counterstory; deliberative empathy; doulas, RJ
Rich, Andrew, 121
right-wing discourse: and anti-gender movement, 45, 46, 48, 50; and culture wars concept, 41–42
Rivera, Gabby, 116–17, 155; *America*, 116; *Juliet Takes a Breath*, 116
Rivera, Sylvia, 160
RJ. *See* reproductive justice
Roberts, Dorothy, 7, 22–23, 127
Robinson, Emma, 101–2
Rodriguez-Bouchier, Josie, 117, 149, 151
Roe v. Wade, 5, 8
Rogan, Joe, 37, 50
ROGD (rapid onset gender dysphoria), 49–50, 51
Ross, Loretta, 7, 14, 116, 118

same-sex marriage, 42, 127
Sanchez, Corrine, 25
Sandelowski, Margarete, 86
Schneider, Bethany, 19

scholarship and mentorship programs, for birthworker training, 98, 100

Schuster, Mary Lay, 79

science, in anti-gender discourse, 48–50, 55

science writing, as rhetorical, 55–56

Seahorse: The Dad Who Gave Birth (documentary film), 120, 139–45

Seigel, Marika, 79, 102

self-reflexivity: in practice, 112–13; as rhetorical strategy, 104–7

Senda-Cook, Samantha, 82

Serano, Julia, 15, 16

sex/gender binary: *vs.* additive approach to language, 74; in anti-gender discourse, 36, 48–49, 61–62, 91–92; calls to dismantle, 26–28; and conflation of sex and gender, 56–58; delinking reproduction from, 146–47, 153–54; as framework, 14–15; and gendered expectations of reproduction and birthwork, 48, 62–64, 87–88, 90, 103; *vs.* gender fluidity, 155–56; *vs.* linguistic creativity, 158; in mainstream birthworker discourse, 87–88, 90, 91–92, 101; problematized by trans* studies, 15–17; in racialized colonial framework, 17–21, 27–28, 57, 61–62, 170–71; and sexism, 15, 143; in Western health care contexts, 125

sexism and misogyny, 15, 143

sexual purity discourse, 8, 42, 43

Sharman, Zena, *The Care We Dream Of*, 172

Shrier, Abigail, 37, 51, 61, 62–63

Simkin, Penny, *The Birth Partner*, 87–88

Simone (doula), 103, 104

Simpson, Monica, 12–13

Sims, James Marion, 20

SisterSong, 12–13, 25, 71

slavery, and marriage, 126

Smithers, Gregory, 19

Snorton, C. Riley, 20–21

social contagion theory, 47, 49, 61

social justice: and birthwork, 96, 99; repurposing discourse of, in anti-gender movement, 58–61. *See also* reproductive justice (RJ); trans justice

social-welfare systems, 22–23

socioeconomic inequality, 22–23, 89, 95, 126, 140

soft advocacy, 97

Solinger, Rickie, 7, 116, 118, 130–31

Spanish colonizers, 3–4

SPARK Reproductive Justice NOW, 7

spectacularization, 107

Spencer, Leland, 40

sperm donors, 142, 145

Spillers, Hortense, 20

Spiritual Midwifery (Gaskin), 87, 88, 98

standardized *vs.* individualized care, 85

STAR House (for Street Transvestite Action Revolutionaries), 160

sterilization: abuse, 8, 22, 23, 126; and hormonal transition, 122–23

Stock, Kathleen, 52

storytelling: archive of TGNC, 119–21; as rhetorical strategy, 128–31. *See also* counterstory; deliberative empathy

Strangio, Chase, 13, 52, 64, 66

stratified reproduction, as phenomenon, 21–24

Street Transvestite Action Revolutionaries, 11, 160

substance use disorders, people with, 95, 100

Summers, A. K., *Pregnant Butch: Nine Long Months Spent in Drag*, 120–21, 155, 158

Supreme Court decisions, US, 127

surrogate pregnancies, 140

survivors of sexual violence, 100

Sydney Morning Herald (newspaper), 55

technocratic model of health care, 80, 85–87

Ted (birth dad), 146–47

teen mom trope, 43

TGNC. *See* trans and gender-nonconforming people

third-gender Indigenous people, 3–4

Thomas, Clarence, 127

Thomas, Greg, 20

Tilsner, Nickie, 103–4

Time (magazine), 145

Times, The (newspaper), 36

Timmaraju, Mini, 71

Title IX, 48

TJA (Trans Journalists Association), 72

trans and gender-nonconforming people (TGNC): and anti-trans legislation, 5, 35, 42, 43, 50–51, 54, 128; birthworker support for (*See* doulas, RJ); fertility preservation options, 122–23; in mainstream birthworker discourse, 91–96, 101; marginalizing medical practices against, 100, 123–24, 125–26. *See also* anti-gender movement; family formation, queer; LGBTQ+ people

Trans Bodies, Trans Selves (Erickson-Schroth, ed.), 172

Transgender Trend, 49

Trans Journalists Association (TJA), 72

trans justice, ideological alliance with RJ, 13, 170–71

TransLash (podcast), 121, 160

transnationality, 45–46

transness: and Blackness, 20–21; and feminism, 16, 17

trans* of color scholarship, 2, 3, 4, 27–28

trans* studies, 15–17

trans youth, 46–47, 49–50, 62–63

Trujillo-Pagán, Nicole, 26

Truth, Sojourner, 12, 27

Tudor, Alyosxa, 18

Two Spirit Indigenous people, 19, 20

Tyson, Khye, 27, 28, 134, 172

unmedicated births, 87, 88

US Immigration and Customs Enforcement (ICE), 8, 23

Vicki (doula), 94

violence: colonial genocide and gendercide, 3–4, 57, 126; domestic, 137, 147–48; obstetric, 67, 89, 98, 123–24; survivors of sexual, 100; as tool of oppressive regimes, 7, 23, 126

Wade, LaSaia, 160

Wade, Sabia, 98, 99, 111

Walks, Michelle, 121

Wallace, Michele, 16

Wander, Philip, 55

Ware, Syrus Marcus, "Confessions of a Black Pregnant Dad," 121

Washington Post (newspaper), 65

Wehman-Brown, Grover, 7, 116, 121, 150–51, 159

welfare queen trope, 43

Where's the Mother? Stories from a Transgender Dad (MacDonald), 99, 121

white privilege: and respectability politics, 27–28; and self-reflexivity, 107; and singular focus in advocacy efforts, 10

white savior discourse, 104

white supremacy: and anti-gender discourse, 43, 44–45; and cisheteronormative family ideal, 21–24, 42–43, 62–63, 126, 145; and colonialism, 17–21, 57, 62, 126, 171; and hegemony of white-led medical institutions, 86–87; and stratified reproduction, 21–24; and stratified reproduction phenomenon, 21–24

white women: and colonial civilization discourse, 37; national interest in reproduction of, 22, 42–43, 62–63; victimization trope, 137

WHO (World Health Organization), 9, 90–91

Willard, Frances, 11

Wingard, Jennifer, 24

woman-centered language: gender-neutral language misunderstood as replacement of, 25–26, 36, 52, 54, 64–65, 66, 70, 92; in mainstream birthworker discourse, 87–88, 91–93, 101; as misleading and inaccurate, 68–69

Woman-Centered Midwifery, 91–93

womanhood. *See* femininity and womanhood

Woman's Hour (radio program), 55

Womb of Their Own, A (documentary film), 120

women's health movement, 87

women's rights movement: invisibility of LGBTQ+ people in, 11; trans inclusivity framed as mutually exclusive to, 52, 64–65

women's studies, 15, 16–17

World Health Organization (WHO), 9, 90–91

World Professional Association for Transgender Health (WPATH), 68

Wynter, Sylvia, 20

Yam, Shui-yin Sharon, 6, 97, 130, 131
Youth Trans Critical Professionals, 49

Zavella, Patricia, 7

Explore other books from HOPKINS PRESS

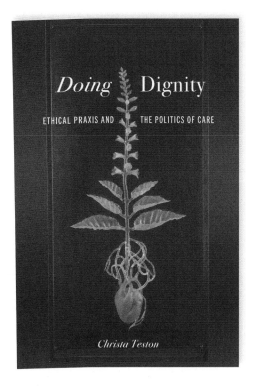

"Teston offers a practical and honest and, most importantly, heartfelt look at what it means to value dignity in an unyielding world."

—Keisha Ray,
author of *Black Health*

"Eminently readable, clearly and compellingly argued. It's one of the best academic books I've read in a long time."

—Jenell Johnson,
author of *American Lobotomy*

JOHNS HOPKINS UNIVERSITY PRESS | PRESS.JHU.EDU |